THE DESERT ROUTE
TO
INDIA

THE DESERT ROUTE TO INDIA

BEING

THE JOURNALS OF FOUR TRAVELLERS BY THE GREAT DESERT CARAVAN ROUTE

BETWEEN ALEPPO AND BASRA
1745-1751

Edited by
DOUGLAS CARRUTHERS

GYAN

Published by

GYAN

Gyan Publishing House
5, Ansari Road
Daryaganj, New Delhi-110002
Phone: 011-47034999, 9811692060
E-mail: books@gyanbooks.com

Distribution Network
gyanbooks.com
India, USA, Canada, UK, Australia, France

ISBN : 978-81-212-3313-2 (PB)
First Published, 1929

2nd Impression 2020

Printed at: Gyan Press, Delhi.

The Desert Route to India
Edited: Douglas Carruthers

WORKS ISSUED BY

The Hakluyt Society

THE DESERT ROUTE
TO
INDIA

SECOND SERIES
No. LXIII

ISSUED FOR 1928

COUNCIL
OF
THE HAKLUYT SOCIETY
1928

SIR WILLIAM FOSTER, C.I.E., *President.*

SIR CHARLES PRESTWOOD LUCAS, K.C.B., K.C.M.G., *Vice-President.*

ADMIRAL OF THE FLEET THE RIGHT HON. SIR EDWARD HOBART SEYMOUR, G.C.B., O.M., G.C.V.O., LL.D., *Vice-President.*

LIEUT.-COLONEL SIR RICHARD CARNAC TEMPLE, BART., C.B., C.I.E., F.B.A., F.S.A., *Vice-President.*

JOHN F. BADDELEY, ESQ.

MAJOR-GEN. SIR PERCY Z. COX, G.C.M.G., G.C.I.E., K.C.S.I.

DOUGLAS W. FRESHFIELD, ESQ., D.C.L.

G. M. GATHORNE-HARDY, ESQ.

EDWARD HEAWOOD, ESQ., *Treasurer.*

ARTHUR R. HINKS, ESQ., C.B.E., F.R.S.

SIR EVERARD IM THURN, K.C.M.G., K.B.E., C.B.

T. A. JOYCE, ESQ., O.B.E.

SIR FREDERIC G. KENYON, G.B.E., K.C.B., F.B.A., LITT.D.

E. W. O'F. LYNAM, ESQ., M.R.I.A.

ALFRED P. MAUDSLAY, ESQ., D.SC.

PROFESSOR EDGAR PRESTAGE, D.LITT.

THE RIGHT HON. JAMES PARKER SMITH.

BRIG.-GEN. SIR PERCY M. SYKES, K.C.I.E., C.B., C.M.G.

SIR REGINALD TOWER, K.C.M.G., C.V.O.

SIR JOHN A. J. DE VILLIERS.

SIR ARNOLD T. WILSON, K.C.I.E., C.S.I., C.M.G., D.S.O.

F. P. SPRENT, ESQ., *Hon. Secretary.*

THE CITY OF ALEPPO.

THE DESERT ROUTE
TO
INDIA

Being

THE JOURNALS OF FOUR TRAVELLERS

BY THE

GREAT DESERT CARAVAN ROUTE

BETWEEN *ALEPPO* AND *BASRA*

1745–1751

Edited by

DOUGLAS CARRUTHERS

LONDON

PRINTED FOR THE HAKLUYT SOCIETY

1929

CONTENTS

LIST OF PLATES

ERRATA

For Della *read* della on p. xxi, *n.* 1, ll. 1 and 4; p. xxxi, l. 14; p. 84, *n.* 1, l. 25; p. 139 *n.* l. 9 from bottom; and p. 161, *n.* 1, l. 6.

p. 134, l. 5, *for* 1755 *read* 1758.

p. 170, *n.* 2, for *Wadi abul m'ris* read *Shaib Abà el Mris*; and l. 3 from bottom *read* p. 203 *for* p. 20.

p. 171, reference for footnote 3 should be after Imaum; and *n.* 3 *after* 'Imaum' *read* [Imam].

INTRODUCTION

In view of the ever growing desire for fast communication between East and West—Europe and the Orient—the achievements and experiences of the earlier travellers demand even greater attention. For the most modern lines of communication with the Orient are harking back to the most ancient. Even as the growth of sea-borne trade destroyed the old caravan-traffic, so the air-lines of the present day are in many cases superseding the ocean routes, and are actually reverting to those well worn tracks so familiar to the pioneers of Eastern commerce. A very particular example of this is the short cut to India by way of the Syrian Desert—the land-bridge between the Mediterranean and the Persian Gulf. It may come as a surprise to many—even with our greatly increased knowledge of this region resulting from the war, and the reshuffling of power in the Middle East—that, in the latter half of the eighteenth century, quite a number of Englishmen, chiefly East India Company officials going to or returning from India, used the 'Overland' route, known as the 'Great Desert Caravan Route,' as a short cut from the Mediterranean ports to the Indian seas, preferring the tedious desert journey, from Aleppo to Baghdad or Basra, to the long sea passage round the Cape, or the more hazardous way of the Red Sea and Egypt. The 'Great Desert Route' led the traveller direct from Aleppo to Basra; the 'Little Desert Route' described the itinerary which cut the desert journey short by making for Baghdad, and thence down the river to Basra.

Of the three great routes which have been the main thoroughfares between Europe and Asia—namely, the Red Sea, the Euphrates Valley and the Caspian—the Euphrates is the most ancient and most direct. From remotest antiquity it had been the main channel by which the riches of the East flowed to the West. It was one of the Golden Roads of the Ancient World, and its story is a theme which runs through all history. To possess this Indo-Syrian trade route has been the desire of all great Powers, for the region it traverses is the pivot of European domination in Asia.

The history of the Euphrates Valley route in relation to Europe began with the Phoenicians—the first great traffickers between East and West—their success in commerce being based very largely on their trade connections across the Syrian desert with the Persian Gulf. Egypt and the great empires of south-western Asia absorbed all Eastern commerce for a long period, and when they ceased to be in a position to demand it, 'the wealth of Ormus and of Ind' still found its way up the Gulf and across to the Mediterranean, whence it was distributed to the marts of Greece and Rome. Trade continued to flourish from the sixth to the twelfth centuries, the Arab irruption interfering with it to no very great extent. As yet the wealth of spices, pearls, and perfumes, jewels and jade had come through Oriental hands to the marts of the Levant and the Black Sea. No Western eye had yet seen that Eldorado, nor had Europe even dreamt of the vast trade awaiting development beyond her Eastern horizon, until the commercial republics of the Mediterranean—Venice and Genoa—following in the footsteps of the Phoenicians, built up an immense Eastern commerce, both by the Persian Gulf and the Red Sea. The main cause of the prosperity of the merchant cities of Italy was their trade with the East: whilst Venice held it, she remained the centre of civilisation and the mistress of the Mediterranean; when she lost it, 'grass grew in the fair and pleasant streets of Venice.' Then the Mongol avalanche burst into the Euphrates Valley, and Europe lost touch with Asia, for the land route was severed. On the heels of the Mongols came the Turks; the Ottoman Empire, laying its foundations on the bridge between Europe, Asia and Africa, completely strangled all Indo-European intercourse. It is true that the commercial states of the Mediterranean—Genoa and Venice—still carried on a certain amount of trade, but the direct land routes were either interrupted or closed; trade was spasmodic and confined to the Red Sea and Caspian routes, but even this eventually shared the common fate which had already overwhelmed all European marts of Eastern commerce. Great necessity arose for a new approach to the Orient.

The end of the fifteenth century saw the re-awakening of Europe to the importance of Asia. Not only was the demand for Eastern commodities as insistent as before, but men learnt that 'the trade of the Indies was the trade of the world.' The rapidly rising sea-powers of the West looked for a sea-route to the Orient. The great quest began with the exploits of Dias and Columbus, and led on to the voyages of Frobisher, Drake and Davis; this occupied a hundred romantic years of sailing uncharted seas and discovering unimagined lands. The first discoveries fired the enthusiasm of the whole western world; the craving for power and gain in Asia became the ruling passion. Out of this grew the first trading companies, such as 'The Merchant Adventurers,' the 'Muscovy,' the 'Turkey' or the 'Levant,' and eventually the 'East India Company.' Nothing shows more strongly the desire that the West had, at that period, for intercourse with Asia, than the fact that much of the sixteenth century was taken up with innumerable and serious attempts to reach India and Cathay by way of the North-West passage, along the Arctic shores of Siberia, and by the Caspian route. The great adventures of Dias, Covilhao, Columbus, Cabot, Vasco da Gama, Magellan, Jenkinson, Frobisher, and many others, were all undertaken with the same object; all had the same prize in view—the untapped wealth of the Orient. The Portuguese were the first to re-open the road to the East, and to reap the reward. They even attempted to monopolise their success by obtaining a Papal Bull which allowed them complete control of the ocean highways. Their one line of communication was by sea; the old land routes sank to the lowest ebb of their career, for it was the policy of Portugal to hinder all trade but her own. She went to great pains to cut off all overland traffic which still went by the Gulf or the Red Sea to the Mediterranean. Considering the power of the Ottoman Empire at that moment, and the fact that the inland sea was dominated by the Corsairs, it is not strange that they were successful. But the quest had produced daring explorers, and had increased the knowledge of the world to such an extent that the Portuguese were unable to keep their secret long. The Dutch and the English were also striving for their place in the Oriental sun, and for their share of its trade. Great was the consternation of the Portuguese when the English first appeared on the Persian Gulf, having come *overland* from Aleppo! The captain of the fortress of Ormuz had special instructions to guard against this new danger, for the Gulf was 'the gateway by which they are chiefly likely to enter[1].' It was at this moment, late in the sixteenth century, that the land route from the Levant to the Persian Gulf began to be used by Western travellers and adventurers, and many of them left us records of their journeys. It continued to be used, more or less without interruption, until the end of the eighteenth century, when ocean traffic superseded the tedious land journeys, and eventually the cutting of the Suez Canal again shortened the sea route, and once for all nullified the Euphrates Valley scheme. Then the 'Great Desert Caravan Route' disappeared alike from memory and from the map. It has never been followed since, nor is it likely to be used again, for although the need for a short cut to the East is more imperative than ever, the short cut, when made, will be on an even more direct line than that of Aleppo to Basra. Already the modern routes are harking back on to the lines of the oldest caravan tracks. In earliest times merchant-caravans doubtless moved direct from Egypt due eastwards to the head of the Persian Gulf, passing through Petra and Jauf. Later on, when this route became impracticable, the line swung northwards, perhaps by Damascus and across to the Euphrates at Hit, and certainly by way of Palmyra, skirting the inhospitable desert. The opposite process is now taking place. The desiccation of Arabia and even hostile tribes matter not to modern science (desiccation is indeed a blessing to mechanical transport). Regular motor-transport

[1] In a letter from Philip II of Spain to the Viceroy of India (1585), quoted in *The Travels of Pedro Teixeira*, Hakluyt Soc. Publ. II, No. IX, p. xxviii.

exists between Damascus and Baghdad, and it may not be long before a railway runs on the line that the Petra caravaneers knew so well. Whilst, over all—careless of desert dust and Arab feud—aircraft hum on the direct crow-fly to the Persian seaboard.

To go back three hundred years. As British influence at the 'Porte' increased, it bore fruit in the establishment of the Levant Company, which gave the first impulse to the revival of the old Euphrates route; but at that particular moment the Spanish fleet and the Barbary Corsairs still rendered this route difficult. The Levant Company failed in its real object—that of opening up direct overland trade with the Orient—but forced us to seek a sea path, thereby indirectly helping to establish the East India Company, which eventually altered the whole history of European domination in Asia. As British power grew and Portuguese and Dutch declined, the old land route gradually revived, until, in 1750, the Aleppo-Basra track—the famous Indo-Syrian caravan route of the earliest days—came back into use as the quickest route to India, and enjoyed a brief period of comparative prosperity. It is the itineraries of four of the travellers who used this old caravan route in the middle of the eighteenth century that we here publish.

The region traversed by the 'Great Desert Caravan Route' is one of immense historical interest, for its story goes back to the very dawn of man. Ur itself was noted as a landmark by one of the eighteenth-century travellers (yet its treasures are only now being brought to light). The site of ancient Babylon lay just across the river, while the deserts west of the Euphrates throbbed to the sound of passing *ghazzus* when Babylonian and Assyrian raided westwards to Damascus, Phoenicia and Judea. In later years Moslem hosts concentrated at those desert watering places so well known to our caravaneers, before falling on the Persian rulers of Iraq. Sassanian, Lakhmid, and early Muhammadan ruins lie all along it. Ghassanide princes were familiar with those now desolate camping grounds in the Palmyrene region, and the caravans eventually came to rest outside the walls of Aleppo itself, the hub of the Middle East, and main corridor between Orient and Occident.

It is a region which has always baffled the administrative powers of, and always avoided assimilation by, every great race which has attempted domination in Western Asia. It has therefore been a debatable land, forming the fringe of various successive empires. Hittite, Egyptian, Babylonian, Assyrian, Persian, Greek, Roman, Byzantine and Arab have come in turn, drawn their red lines of empire along or around it, and retired. Even the Mongol cyclone swept across its northern half. The Turks kept it for a time, but already our region is divided again between the Mandatory Powers of Great Britain and France. The dominating factor in its story is the desert sea which flanks it, with its desert men—restless and predatory, always ready to hurl themselves into the fertile lands between the Rivers. They have come at periodic intervals for the last 5000 years, and they come still, and the story is always the same. They come, they conquer, they vanish, unable to establish any form of government, and unable to resist the slightest contamination with the luxury of a sedentary life.

The first Western travellers to use the Aleppo-Basra caravan route of whom we have record were Portuguese. Although the policy of Portugal was to destroy overland traffic so as to increase her own sea-borne trade, yet her possessions in India and on the Gulf forced her to use the Euphrates Valley route. The short cut to India came to be recognised as such; it began to be used by merchant-travellers and Portuguese officials, and more especially for the transmission of important despatches. Antonio Tenreiro (1523) was the first[1] European to cross the desert from Aleppo to Basra and to leave a record of his journey; he was also the first to make the return journey, for in 1528 he rode post haste by the same route carrying important despatches from the

[1] Possibly Covilhao, on his return journey from Ormuz to Cairo, in 1487, may have used this route wholly or in part. See Whiteway's *Rise of Portuguese Power in India*, p. 54.

Governor of Ormuz to Lisbon[1]. The next traveller was a Venetian, Caesar Frederick, who in 1563 went through Aleppo to Bir (Birejik, then as now the place of embarkation), and down the Euphrates to Falluja, thence to Baghdad, Basra, Ormuz and India (Hakluyt's *Voyages* (MacLehose Ed.), vol. v, pp. 365 et seq.). It is strange that we have not been left more records by Venetian travellers, for there were still at this date many merchants of Venice established at Aleppo, Baghdad, and on the Persian Gulf. Bernardino forty years later met a Basra-bound caravan containing no less than *nine* Venetians. In 1565 we know of another party of Portuguese, led by Antonio Teixeira, making the return journey from Basra to *Babylonia* by the Euphrates, and thence by riding-animals to the 'Great Sea'; but we have no further details of their journey[2]. In the same year a certain Mestre Afonso attempted the overland route, but as Basra was beleaguered by the Arabs he had to go from Ormuz through Tabriz and Mosul to Aleppo[3].

In 1573 Dr Leonhart Rauwolff set out on his three years' wanderings in the East, in the course of which he took the river route from Bir to Falluja. Landing at Tripoli, he went up to Aleppo, where he was greatly struck with the trade of this emporium of Western Asia. 'Great caravans of pack-horses and asses, but more camels, arrive there daily from all foreign countries, viz. from Natolia, Armenia, Egypt and India, etc....' And again, 'the trading here was very great, so that they did not only deal from hence into Armenia, Egypt and Constantinople,...but also much into Persia and India.' At Aleppo he found a Dutchman, in whose company

[1] Tenreiro's original *Itinerario* was published in 1560; 2nd ed. 1565. It is included in the 1725 edition of Mendez Pinto's *Peregrinacio*, and in the reprint of 1829. His outgoing journey is just mentioned, and a somewhat garbled account of his return journey appears in Couto's *Da Asia*, Dec. IV, Liv. V, Cap. VII, pp. 371–8. Also noted by Barros, Dec. IV, Liv. I, Cap. VIII, p. 53. See also Whiteway, *op. cit.* p. 55.

[2] Couto, *op. cit.*, Dec. VIII, Cap. V, pp. 43–6. See also Hakluyt Soc. Publ. II, No. IX, p. xxi note.

[3] *Annaes Maritimos e Coloniæs*, 1840–6, No. 5, 4th Series, p. 214, and following numbers; catalogued in British Museum under 'Associacão Maritima,' etc. See also Whiteway, *op. cit.* p. 55.

he travelled on into Mesopotamia. He contemplated going 'by land with caravans which go from hence and Damascus very strong to Bagdet through great sands and desarts in fifty days, more or less...,' but he eventually went by river (Ray's *Travels*, vol. II, pp. 61 and 88). In 1579 a Venetian jeweller, Gasparo Balbi, took the same route on his way to Baghdad and Basra, giving an excellent account of the river journey[1]. These East-bound travellers used the Euphrates 'to avoid the great weariness of the Desert journey.' We have to wait until 1581 for the first itineraries of West-bound travellers, who were forced to traverse the desert[2]. Caesar Frederick, returning in 1581 from his eighteen years' wanderings in the Indies, describes the desert route between Mesopotamia and Aleppo. 'From Babylon to Alepo is 40 dayes journey, of the which they make 36 dayes over the Wildernes, in which 36 dayes they neither see house, trees, nor people that inhabite but onely a plaine, and no signe of any way in the world. The Pilots go before, and the Carovan followeth after....I say in 36 dayes we passe over the wildernesse. For when we depart from Babilon two dayes wee passe by villages inhabited until we have passed the river Euphrates. And then within two dayes of Alepo we have villages inhabited' (Purchas, MacLehose Ed., vol. v, p. 446). Frederick probably crossed the Euphrates at Falluja, and joined the old caravan route somewhere west of Hit.

At this same date the first Englishman appeared on the scene, and henceforward the story of the overland route is largely occupied with the exploits of the first agents and emissaries of the Levant Company establishment at Aleppo. These were the men who laid the foundations of British prestige in the East. In 1580 John Newberry passed through Tripoli and Aleppo, and made the journey down the Euphrates to the Gulf. In 1583 he again made the same journey in

[1] Gasparo Balbi, *Viaggio dell' Indie Orientali*, Venice, 1590; also Purchas, vol. x, chap. v.

[2] In some cases travellers made use of the river as far as Baghdad. Teixeira mentions that 'cafilas' of boats took thirty-five to fifty days on the up-river journey from Basra to Baghdad when the river was in flood; at low water about double that time.

company with the famous Ralph Fitch—'England's pioneer in India'—John Eldred and 'other honest merchants,' the party bearing letters from Queen Elizabeth to the Emperor of China and the Mogul Emperor. In 1584[1] Eldred returned, crossing the desert from Hit to Aleppo; Fitch did not return until 1590–1, and then took the northern track *via* Mosul, Urfa, and Birejik. In 1599 Sir Anthony Shirley made the journey down the Euphrates; while John Mildenhall, a merchant of London, sent to further trade interests at the Court of the Great Mogul, passed the same way the following year[2]. He was accompanied by John Cartwright, who wrote an account of their wanderings, viz. *The Preacher's Travels*, etc., London, 1611[3].

With the opening of the seventeenth century some famous travellers appeared, and we have the first detailed itineraries of the desert route. Pedro Teixeira, on his return from India to Italy in 1604–5, passed by way of Basra, Baghdad, Ana and Aleppo. His narrative is one of the fullest and most interesting of all those that have been left us by the overland travellers[4]. Gaspar de Bernardino crossed the desert from Meshed Ali to Aleppo in 1606–7, but his account does not tell us much of geographical interest[5]. Apart from the imposing ruins of the Sassanian capital, Ctesiphon, the great arch of which he described as being large enough for a

[1] In 1584 a Dutchman, Bernard Burcherts, a comrade of Linschoten, returned from Goa to Europe by way of Ormuz, Basra, Babylon and Aleppo. He described his journey in letters to Linschoten, who repeats only the barest outline of a narrative which might have been most entertaining. See *Voyage of Linschoten to the East Indies*, Hakluyt Soc. Publ. I, No. LXXI, p. 175.

[2] For Newberry, Fitch and Eldred, see Hakluyt's *Voyages*, vols. V and VI; Purchas, vol. VIII, p. 451, and vol. X, chap. VI, and Foster's *Early Travels in India*. A good summary of Fitch's wanderings appears in *Travels of Teixeira*, Hakluyt Soc. Publ. II, No. IX, pp. xxv–xxvii; also Horton Ryley's *Ralph Fitch* (1899). For Shirley, Mildenhall and Cartwright, see Purchas, vol. VIII, pp. 382 and 482 and Foster, *op. cit.*

[3] Cartwright was later appointed chaplain to the ill-fated *Weymouth* Expedition, which attempted the North-West Passage in 1602. Its failure was attributed to 'the faint-hearted exhortations of Preacher Cartwright'! See Hunter's *History of British India*, Vol. I, p. 268.

[4] Hakluyt Soc. Publ. II, No. IX. Also B. Tellez, *Travels in Ethiopia* (1710).

[5] *Itinerario da India* (1611). I have consulted a reprint of 1854 (Lisbon).

sailing-ship to pass under, the most wonderful thing he saw in all his travels was a group of four springs within a stone's throw of each other, one of which was boiling hot, another cold and sulphurous, the third threw up bitumen and the fourth was saline! This was somewhere to the east of Taiyibe. Perhaps the most interesting observation he makes is concerning the use of homing pigeons during the desert journey. The caravan-bashi released one every two days to inform his friends at Baghdad of their welfare. When blackmailed by the Arabs, he was thus enabled to put the 'Basha of Babylonia' on the tracks of the robbers, who were in turn spoiled of their ill-gotten gains!

Carrier, or rather Homing, Pigeons (for the last two centuries anyway the 'Carrier' has been a 'fancy' variety, in no way related to the Homing pigeons) were trained and used by the European merchants at Aleppo as a means of obtaining news of the arrival of their merchandise at the port of Iskanderun[1] (Alexandretta). The practice, of course, dates from the earliest times and was especially highly developed in Turkey. According to Linschoten, regular communication was kept up between Basra, Babylon, Aleppo and Constantinople. He credits them with flights of 1000 miles (to-day 500 miles is a long one) but this was accomplished by a highly organised system of relays, the birds passing from tower to tower, 50 miles apart. Della Valle made an effort to introduce the Baghdad race into Italy, the Baghdad pigeons being superior to all others in Asia or Egypt. Teonge says the birds were bred at Aleppo, and taken down in cages on horseback to the coast. They were released with a small note made fast to their wings, close to their body, with silk. On their return to Aleppo they were 'caught in a coffer, trapped and taken and examined.' They made the journey, a distance of sixty miles, over the Amanus mountains—an average height of three thousand feet—in two and a half to three hours, or, according to other authorities, in exactly four hours, the letters being antedated by four hours

[1] 'Basra' and 'Iskanderun' are known breeds of homing pigeons according to Darwin's grouping of the varieties.

(Hakl. Soc. Publ. I, No. LXXXVII, p. 32). Present-day fanciers estimate that their racing pigeons fly at 40–50 miles per hour.

We learn from the Journal of 'Captaine Nicholas Downton' (Purchas, IV, p. 217) that a certain Richard Steele arrived in Surat in 1614, having 'come by land from Aleppo,' but we do not know his route. Steele again made the overland journey on his return from the Gulf in 1615–16 (see Purchas, MacLehose Ed. vol. IV, p. 279). Pietro della Valle, who travelled much in Turkey, Persia, and India between 1615 and 1625, passed twice across the desert, going from Aleppo to Baghdad in 1616, and from Basra to Aleppo in 1625[1]. The Portuguese were also using the desert route, for Consul Lanoy of Aleppo reports, in Aug. 1622, to the Ambassador at the Porte, that 'four Portugal fathers have arrived here from Goa, sent with letters of importance to their King' (see *Hist. MSS. Comm. Reports on MSS. of Allan George Finch*, vol. I, p. 228). And, indeed, we have records of Portuguese emissaries travelling between Goa and Lisbon up till 1663, for the remaining hard-pressed outposts of Portugal in Asia had need of the fastest possible communication with Europe. Of such a nature was the secret mission of the Jesuit father Manuel Godinho. In 1663 Godinho came up the Gulf to Basra; here, waiting neither for boat to carry him up stream to Baghdad, nor for caravan protection during the desert crossing, he pushed on with small and insufficient escorts by way of Meshed Ali, Baghdad, Ana, Taiyibe and Aleppo to the Mediterranean seaboard. Godinho probably viewed Palmyra from a distance, unless his reference to a magnificent edifice built of finest marble, with Corinthian pillars, is an exaggerated conception of Qusur el Ikhwan[2].

[1] *Viaggi di Pietro Della Valle*, etc. (Bologna, 1677); Parte prima, Lettera 17 da Baghdad; Parte terza, Lettera 11 da Aleppo. An edition in French (1664) has portraits. The map reproduced in the Hakluyt Soc. Publ. I, No. LXXXIV, *Travels of Della Valle in India*, showing the desert route, is taken from one of Du Val's compilations; see No. 46900 (5) in Brit. Mus. Cat. of Printed Maps. For an account in English of the return journey, see *Travels into East India and Arabia Deserta* (London, 1665).

[2] Godinho's account appeared first in 1665, *Relação do novo caminho...*

One other traveller of note used the desert route early in the seventeenth century, namely Tavernier, the Parisian jewel merchant, who went by the desert from Baghdad to Aleppo in 1632 and from Aleppo direct to Basra in 1638[1]. After this there was a pause in the use of the overland route. If we are to judge by the records left us, scarcely any European crossed the desert, but we do know that the route must still have offered the shortest means of communication with Europe for such religious establishments of Western origin as existed in the Orient. It is disappointing, for instance, that we have not been left such records by the particularly strong settlement of Carmelites which existed at Basra from 1623 to 1733[2]. Any light thrown on that period would have been of unusual interest.

When, in the middle of the eighteenth century, travellers again appeared on the scene, they were almost all of British nationality, and most of them were in the service of the East India Company. For all attempts to find an alternative route to the East by way of the Arctic seas round Siberia, or by the N.W. passage round America, had failed. The idea of opening a backdoor into India and Cathay by way of Russia and Central Asia had been given up. The sea route was long and dangerous. The short cut by the Mediterranean and the Persian Gulf alone presented itself as a possible medium for speedy contact with India. This brings us to our four travellers —William Beawes, who went by the desert route from Aleppo to Basra in 1745; Gayland Roberts, who traversed the same route in the opposite direction in 1748; Bartholomew Plaisted, who returned to England from India in 1750 by the 'Great Desert' to Aleppo; and John Carmichael, who journeyed that way to India in 1751.

These four travellers, whose journeys are here described,

vindo da India para Portugal; a second edition was published, also in Lisbon, in 1842. There is no translation of the work, and the only *résumé* of it in English which I can find is in Murray's *Asia*, vol. I, chap. VIII. Godinho is referred to by Birdwood, see *Report*, etc., p. 182.

[1] *Les Six Voyages de Jean-Baptiste Tavernier*, Paris, 1682.

[2] Sir Hermann Gollancz, *Chronicle of Events between the years* 1623 *and* 1733 *relating to the Settlement of the Order of Carmelites in Mesopotamia (Bussora)*.

are typical of a certain age—a great age in the annals of British rule in India. The middle of the eighteenth century was epochmaking in that the early struggles of the East India Company culminated in complete triumph—a trading venture grew into an empire. Beawes was the first representative of this new Power which had established itself in India to use and record the short-cut home; the first, indeed, of a series of British travellers who habitually used the overland route as a short cut to, and from, the newly acquired, and now prospering, possessions in the East. 1745—the year of Beawes' journey—was also a landmark in the chronicles of the desert route, for it came back into favour after being more or less out of use for nearly a century. The intervening 109 years between Tavernier and Beawes was a period of great unrest. Portuguese, Dutch and English were struggling for the mastery of the trade of the Indies—in other words, for complete supremacy and empire. The wars of 1652 and 1665 between the English and the Dutch were nothing more than commercial wars brought about by their commercial rivalry in the East. During the latter part of the seventeenth century the Gulf was the scene of keen competition and even sharp encounters between the two nations, which may in some measure have accounted for travellers avoiding the land route, and for our lack of records over this period. Added to this was a great recrudescence of piracy, which reached such alarming proportions that the East India Company suffered severely from their depredations. In fact, during the whole of this period, the affairs of the East India Company were in a very unsatisfactory condition. It was not until 1708 that the rival companies were incorporated in 'the United Company of the Merchants of England trading to the East Indies.' The end of the seventeenth century saw the turn of the tide. By 1750 the Dutch had lost their commercial status in the Gulf, and the English appeared in numbers. Although we have little or no record of the desert route being used by European travellers during this period, the Levant Company was not to blame. During the later years of the seventeenth century the Company may be said to have been at the height of its prosperity. It was certainly the palmy days of the Factory at Aleppo. The amusing and enlightening diary of Henry Teonge, chaplain on board H.M. Ship *Assistance*, who visited Aleppo in 1676, gives a vivid picture of those times. Teonge preached there one Sunday morning to a congregation of fifty Englishmen—'a brave show for that wild place.' The send-off feast, to which the whole 'nation' was invited, covered a table 24 yards in length—'sixty and odd Franks sat down, besides many that would rather stand or walk about'—and on departure he was escorted out of the city by 'at least 200 English, French, Dutch, and Venetians.' The Factory had its Sports Club in the vicinity of the city, and its Hunt, at which the 'field' was 'seldom less than fifty English.' It is indeed difficult for us to gauge the place that Aleppo held in Western minds in those days. From the reign of Elizabeth onwards to the end of the eighteenth century Aleppo ranked second to Constantinople. She was the Eastern Metropolis of overland trade with the Orient. Aleppo was then the gate to the East even as Port Said is nowadays. Standing, as she did, at the strategic point twixt Mediterranean and Euphrates Valley, her position was unique. Caravans converged on her from north, south and east, and created a vitality that remained hers until the present century. For countless centuries East and West have met in her deep bazaars and exchanged their wares, but no period in her career has been so full of interest to us as when the Levant Company did its business in the largest khan in the city, and its Factory consisted of 'his worship the Consul[1], a

[1] The Consuls at Aleppo, in those days, were *not*, as might be supposed, merely commercial agents pushing the trade interests of the Levant Co., for they also carried out in full the duties of a political representative. Lanoy, in 1661, was forwarding from Aleppo to the Ambassador at the Porte despatches crammed with the latest diplomatic developments in Persia, India, on the Gulf, and even in the Spice Islands. His letters contained reports of Portuguese decline and Dutch supremacy; and now and again optimistic rumours of Dutch defeats, which were not always authentic! The Consulate of Aleppo was the channel through which the Ambassadors at the Porte felt the pulse of Asia. In fact the Levant Co. was the medium for all diplomatic and commercial relationships between England and the Orient. The Ambassadors at the Porte were actually the

Vice-Consul, a Chaplain, Doctor and other gentlemen of the nation,' to the number of 40 to 50. A truly isolated community even for those days, but they were imbued with the spirit of the moment—the alluring prospects of trade with, and the apparent inexhaustible wealth of, the Orient—and stoically endured their exile. Yet the members of the community also came in for a fair proportion of relaxation and amusement, as Teonge shows. They occupied themselves with 'duck-hunting, fishing, shooting, handball, cricket, etc.'; they had their coursing meetings, they hunted and hawked. Bell describes how the English nation led the European community in the matter of field sports. He says that the main recreation of the Factory from 15 September until March was coursing with 'Grayhounds.' 'Their course is often after the pusse [hare]...sometimes they hunt the wild boar. They generally have ten brace of greyhounds in the field at once, and seldom less than 50 English. Many Turks at certain times attend their sports, some French and Dutch'; their 'grayhounds' are like 'monggrell grayhounds in England [*lurchers*—Ed.], corse shapt, and their feete more longe and large and will endure besides beinge rapid and swifter a larger Corse'—a good description of the Saluki gazelle hound (*Indian Antiquary*, Vol. 37, 1908, p. 163). The scope offered to the Factory for seeing the region around Aleppo was limited to their hunting grounds in Sabkha Jebbul. None went further afield; although Aleppo was full of English from 1632 to 1745 we learn nothing from *them* of the 'Great Desert Caravan Route.' The brilliant exception to this apparent lack of initiative was the expedition of Timothy Lanoy (son of the Consul Benjamin Lanoy), Aaron Goodyear, and other Englishmen—'eminent merchants of this worthy Factory' at Aleppo—who, in July 1678, rediscovered Tadmor (Palmyra), and again, in 1691, made a more thorough examination of its ruins, accompanied by the Rev. William Halifax[1]. This was the one shining light in the

servants and representatives of the Levant Co.; they were paid by the Company, although they received their credentials from the King, and were expected to carry on any diplomatic negotiations that were necessary.

[1] See footnotes on pp. 17, 86, 87.

otherwise dark period of our story—the vacant years between Tavernier and Beawes. This period synchronises with a time of greater unrest than usual in Persia, on the Gulf and along the Iraq-Arabian borderlands.

Many may have been the causes which combined to account for the paucity of travellers passing by the land route between 1640 and 1745, but principally we may blame the commercial rivalries which resulted in wars between the English and the Dutch. Dutch power was in the ascendancy on the Gulf in the last decades of the seventeenth century. The East India Company did not even found its permanent Factory at Basra till 1730–40[1]. Another incident which may well have affected the use of the desert route was the Shammar invasion of the Euphrates Valley in about 1640—one of those periodic eruptions of nomadic peoples from desert Arabia, 'eternal motherland of vigorous migrants,' which are typical of her history, and have profoundly influenced her neighbours. Iraq itself, during their period, suffered twenty-five years of Persian campaigns within its boundaries.

We know of only one[2] other Western traveller—and he a Scotchman!—in the Syrian Desert during this period. John Campbell ended his adventurous travels in India and Persia by crossing from Baghdad to Aleppo by way of Ana and Taiyibe in 1669. Campbell's narrative, as related by Richard Bell[3], is as curious and interesting a manuscript as any

[1] The East India Company's factory at Basra was founded in 1640, and although withdrawn after a few years, ships were dispatched thither from Surat for a fairly long period. Letters were also sent overland regularly both ways.

[2] Taylor (*Travels from England to India*, etc. (London, 1799), vol. 1, p. 18) refers to *Darvieux* as having made the journey to India by way of Aleppo in 1664; he means, of course, Arvieux, who travelled much in the Levant between 1653 and 1683. Arvieux was in Syria in 1664 and acted as Consul for France at Aleppo, 1679–86, but I cannot trace any indication of his having travelled east of Aleppo; while Sir Thomas Roe, with whom Arvieux is coupled as a land traveller to India, certainly did not go by the Aleppo-Basra route, but by sea.

[3] Richard Bell's manuscript is in the British Museum. An exact copy of it has been printed in the *Indian Antiquary*, 'The Travels of Richard Bell (and John Campbell) in the East Indies, Persia and Palestine, 1654–1670,' by Sir R. C. Temple, to whose notice the original was brought by

traveller ever wrote, while his traverse of the Syrian Desert, accompanied by a French padre and one guide, is perhaps the most wonderful part of an almost incredible story. He journeyed alone without the protection of a caravan, and although he carried a pouch full of precious stones, including, it would appear, a famous diamond 'engraved with the English Arms[1]' and was in the habit of firing off his pistol at anyone he did not like the look of, yet he got through safely!

The story of the caravan route subsequent to 1751, as told by Western travellers, is brief. In 1765–6 Niebuhr recorded

Sir William Foster. See *Indian Antiquary*, vols. 35, 1906; 36, 1907; 37, 1908. The journey across the Syrian Desert will be found in vol. 36, 1907, pp. 130–3. It should be noted that Campbell was the traveller, Richard Bell the author, of this part of the 'Travels'; the first mention of Bell being in August 1669, when Campbell 'in a ragged and weather beaten condition' reached the 'Consulls in Aleppo, Richard Bell then at dinner with him.'

[1] Campbell's possession of this stone, 'a Dymond as Bigg as a pidgions Egg wth ye King of Englands Armes Cutt in it,' if true, is of considerable interest. For some two years before this, in 1667, Lord Winchelsea, Ambassador at the Porte, had been making special enquiries about this particular diamond, and it would appear that instructions had been issued through Lanoy of Aleppo to other agents further East to try and recover it. Apparently others were also in pursuit of this elusive and historic diamond, for Campbell himself states that 'many Dymond Merchants from ffrance Holland and other Contreys had beene sent into India to purchas it, but money could not procure what love did' (*Indian Antiquary*, vol. 35, p. 133). It is supposed to have been one of the jewels pawned by Charles II during the Exile (Finch MSS. p. li), and doubtless fell into Tavernier's hands in Paris; it was certainly amongst the £30,000 worth of jewels he carried East in 1664. We know he sold great numbers to Shah Abbas II at Isfahan in December 1664, and that he showed the Shah this particular stone. Tavernier then went down to Bandar Abbas, and in spite of the efforts of the English agent—Flower—to buy this diamond, it passed into the hands of Van Wick, the Dutch agent. This was in April 1665. Tavernier went on to India, and in May was selling jewels to Aurangzeb, but makes no mention of Campbell, who was at that time in the service of the Great Mogul.

Campbell's dates are incorrect, but it would appear that 1666 was really the date of the escape of the young Prince from Delhi, for his share in aiding whom he says he received 'the Diamond Seal ring of his Majesty.'

It is difficult to combine the two accounts, but I am inclined to treat Campbell's story of how he came by the stone as pure fiction. On the death of Van Wick at Bander Abbas, the jewel is *said* to have been sent 'to Batavia to the Dutch General (Maatzuiker) and his Council,' but it *may* have been acquired by Flower who doubtless still had his eye on an itinerary of this same caravan route, from information gathered from a Bedawin who had made the journey more than twenty times, and from a merchant of Basra[1]. Mr Hunter took the same route in 1767[2]; while in 1771 General, afterwards Sir Eyre, Coote crossed the desert from Basra to Aleppo[3]. In 1774, one Abraham Parsons, after six years as Consul and Factor Marine at Alexandretta, set out on a 'voyage of commercial speculation' to Baghdad, the Persian Gulf and India. He started by crossing the desert from Aleppo to Taiyibe, and first saw the Euphrates at Sheikh Jabir. The caravan of 'near 800 camels' was ferried across the river at Ana and reached Baghdad on the fifty-fourth day[4]. In 1778, James Capper went overland to India; his book is a survey of the various land and sea routes to India, with their qualifications. The 'Supplement' to that volume contains some itineraries not published elsewhere[5]. In 1779, a party of officers of the Bombay Army and Civil Service passed over the northern section of the desert between Hit and Aleppo, having come up to Baghdad from India[6]. In

it. Campbell and his 'cousin' and 'kinsman' Flower were together at Isfahan in 1668 or 1669, when Campbell was actually on his return journey, and it may have been Flower who entrusted him with the stone. The next thing we know is that Campbell divided up his jewels for safety whilst crossing the Syrian Desert; he gave half to the padre accompanying him, and kept amongst others 'a great Dymond with King's arms on it.' For references see Tavernier, 1676 ed. vol. I, p. 484; Campbell in *Indian Antiquary*, vol. 35, p. 133, vol. 36, p. 131; also Finch MSS. Introduction, p. li, also pp. 439, 477, 509.

[1] Carsten Niebuhr, *Voyage en Arabie et en d'autres pays circonvoisins*, Amsterdam, 1774–80, vol. II, p. 193.

[2] Hunter is referred to by Rennell in *Philosophical Trans. Roy. Soc.* vol. XVII, pp. 38 et seq., and in his *Geog. Western Asia*. Apparently he kept a route-book, but I cannot find that his Journal has been published.

[3] 'Diary of a Journey with Sir Eyre Coote from Bussora to Aleppo in 1780 (?).' This was communicated to the *Geog. Journ.* by Sir Woodbine Parish in 1860 (see vol. XXX, p. 198), 'from the original MS.' The writer of the diary is unknown; it begins: 'Jan. 30. Set out from Xebire [Zubair] with the caravan, in company with General Coote and Mr Thompson.'

[4] *Travels in Asia and Africa. Including a Journey from Scanderoon to Aleppo, and over the Desert to Baghdad and Bassora*, etc., by the late Abraham Parsons, edited by John Paine Berjew, London, 1808.

[5] James Capper, *Observations on the Passage to India*, etc., 3rd ed. 1785.

[6] An account of this journey was published anonymously by 'A Gentleman, late an officer in the East India Company's Service'—in reality Lieut. Samuel Evers.

1781[1], Mr Irwin, of the Madras Establishment (in company with several other Englishmen), 'entrusted with despatches too important to admit of delay,' rode from Aleppo to Ana, and thence passed to Baghdad, Basra, and India. Irwin wrote a good account and published a 'Map of Syria, Mesopotamia, and Babylonia,' which he compiled for the use of the East India Company, from observations of Niebuhr, Ives, Carmichael, and his own personal travels[2]. In 1785–6, we have the disastrous journey of Mr David Hays, merchant and Consul at Aleppo, who travelled with his small daughter and Julius Griffiths, M.D. The journey was undertaken in midsummer, and Hays died *en route*. Griffiths published an account of the journey in his *Travels in Europe, Asia Minor, and Arabia*[3]. It may be worthy of note that the little Miss Hays eventually became the wife of John Barker, the famous British Consul-General at Aleppo.

In 1789, Major John Taylor, 'of the Bombay Establishment,' went out to India by the same desert route, and recorded his journey with considerable detail. Mrs Taylor went too, but she is barely mentioned in the narrative. He published two volumes, in which he incorporates itineraries by various routes, instructions to travellers, with tables of expenses, etc.; even time-tables—in miles and hours—by a choice of routes, from London to Basra, are given. He specially studied the question of a 'more speedy communication between Great Britain and her Eastern dependencies' (*Travels from England to India*, etc., 1799). In 1797, Olivier

[1] 1780 is given by Rennell as the date of Holford's journey between Aleppo, Ana and Baghdad. I cannot trace Holford's narrative. Rennell is able to record his route on the map, and he says he kept a regular Journal (see *Philosophical Trans. Roy. Soc.* abridged, vol. XVII, p. 40); in original ed. 1791, vol. LXXXI, there is a map—Tab. III. It seems that the Itinerary in the 'Supplement' to Capper's book, titled 'A Journey over the little desert of Arabia from Aleppo to Baghdad and Semmeva by the Euphrates to Bussora,' is Holford's, for he records certain place-names not mentioned elsewhere.

[2] Eyles Irwin, *A Series of Adventures*, etc. (London, 1787). Vol. II has a supplement of 'A Voyage from Venice to Latichea, and of a Route Through the Desarts of Arabia,' etc.

[3] J. Griffiths, *Travels in Europe, Asia Minor, and Arabia* (London, 1805). The diary of his journey from Aleppo to Basra also appears in Barker's *Syria and Egypt under the Last Five Sultans of Turkey*, vol. II, Appendix B.

followed over a section of the route between Taiyibe and Aleppo, having cut across from Rahba on the Euphrates[1]. In 1808, Rousseau, Consul-General for France at Aleppo, Baghdad, and elsewhere, crossed the desert from Hit to Aleppo. Coming, as he did, of a family long resident in the East, his father and grandfather having spent their lives in Persia and Mesopotamia, he had an unrivalled knowledge, and wrote an excellent journal which was not published until 1899[2].

The overland route was used for official despatches to India while Napoleon was campaigning in Egypt; in fact the direct route from Constantinople to Aleppo and Basra, or to Egypt, was of vital importance to England during that period. Even after Nelson's victory at the Nile, the French still held the Red Sea; so our Consul at Aleppo was still kept busy receiving and sending official correspondence by fast riders to the Persian Gulf. We know that in 1798 Nelson, 'aware of the designs of the French, in case of succeeding at Egypt, to attack the British East India possessions, despatched, overland to Bombay, with the intelligence of the victory, Lieut. Thomas Duval, of the *Zealous*, an officer selected by Captain Hood.' Duval rode from Aleppo to Baghdad direct in twelve days, and ten days later reached Basra by water[3].

Here ends the story of the 'Great Desert Route.' For the last hundred and twenty years we have heard nothing, and learnt nothing of it, and very little of the region it traverses. No modern or Western traveller has passed along it, and it has entirely ceased to be used even as a native caravan track. The routes of the more recent explorers, such as Ormsby, Chesney, Thielmann, Cernik, Sachau, Bischoff, Huber, Moritz, Ostrup, Musil, Fowle and Bell, have crossed it at certain points. In one section only of its 760 odd miles, namely, between Kubaisa and Ukhaidir, has it been actually

[1] G. A. Olivier, *Voyage dans L'Empire Ottoman*, etc., vol. III, chap. XXIII. For map, see Atlas, Pl. 22.

[2] Louis Jacques Rousseau, *Voyage de Bagdad à Alep*, edited by Louis Poinssot (Paris, 1899).

[3] See William James, *The Naval Hist. of Great Britain*, vol. II, p. 206, and Appendix No. 14, p. 465.

traversed, and described afresh, and that by Thielmann[1] in 1872, and Gertrude Bell[2] in 1909, although, of course, since the war, the eastern portion has become comparatively well known to Iraq frontier officials, and the maps of that region now show for the first time the desert stations of the early caravaneers in their true position. The trans-Syrian desert surveys of Holt, 1920–2, have also added very considerably to our knowledge of the western affluents of the Euphrates whose names occur repeatedly in the journals of our travellers.

The topography of the greater part of the rest of the region traversed by the 'Desert Mail' is known to us almost exclusively from the descriptions given by travellers prior to 1808. Much of the information gathered by Teixeira, Della Valle, Beawes, Carmichael, Capper, Evers, Irwin, Holford, Olivier and Taylor was incorporated in the map completed by Major James Rennell to accompany his *Treatise on the Comparative Geography of Western Asia*. Rennell was quick to appreciate their value, but it is curious to note how much of this first-hand data has been discarded by later compilers, in spite of the fact that there is nothing to take its place.

The chief interest attaching to this route lies in the fact that it was essentially a desert route. With the exception of a few poor oases—such as Rahhaliya and Shithatha lying on the fringe of the desert in the Najaf-Karbala region—the caravans successfully avoided all habitations and settled sites for the 700 odd miles between Aleppo and Basra. The caravans did not follow the valley of the Euphrates, but made a direct line across the North Syrian Desert from Aleppo to Hit, and on approaching the river valley, sheered off again into the desert —following a course parallel to, but about 20 to 30 miles distant from it. It was a route of emergency, suitable to the conditions of the moment but quite impracticable to-day. It avoided all settlements, principally in order to avoid payment of extra dues and 'baksheesh' to the little chiefs—as Plaisted puts it, 'the impositions on the road are less.' In

[1] See *Caucasus, Persia and Turkey*, London, 1875.

[2] See *Amurath to Amurath*, pp. 117–58.

these days travellers hug the Euphrates valley in all its twists and turns, never even venturing to cut across the desert zones which lie between its numerous bends; Bedawin raiders being more to be feared than the extortions of petty village chiefs. But the early merchant-travellers thought nothing of steering a direct course from Aleppo to the head of the Persian Gulf; they regarded the desert with little dread, considering it an easy country over which camels moved fast and well and found sufficient nourishment. It was probably the reports of these early travellers that set in motion the idea of navigating the Euphrates, for none would have been so alive to the possibilities of the great river as those weary voyagers who toiled across the desert for nearly 800 miles parallel to, and sometimes within sight of, its waters!

Desert conditions were then very much as they are to-day—unstable. Bedawin nomads periodically raided the sedentary riverine tribes. But there was one great difference: whereas now there is a sort of central zone, or no-man's land, between 'the desert and the sown,' in those days powerful Arab confederacies held power right up to the Euphrates and had their strongholds, such as Ana and Deir ez Zor, on the river itself. Therefore the 'desert route' for a long section of its length lay wholly within their sphere. From Najaf to Deir ez Zor 'Kings of Arabia' held dominion, dared the power of the Sultan, and behaved as they liked to travellers. These conditions prevailed from the days of Teixeira down to the middle of the seventeenth century, and it would appear that on the whole the desert roads were safer then than now.

This route must have been an important one even in the days of its decline. It is titled 'The common route of the Caravan from Aleppo to Basra' on Ives' map illustrating his *Journey from Persia to England*. Taylor speaks of the 'Grand Annual Caravan' trading between Aleppo and Basra. Rennell observes that, from the existence of fortified posts along the route, 'one may conclude that a regular system of protection was established across the Arabian Desert (to support which the profits of commerce must have been very considerable), until the discovery of the passage to India by the Cape of Good Hope. And even down to the end of the sixteenth century the Euphrates appears to have been the medium of a considerable commerce between Aleppo, Baghdad and Basra.' Linschoten records 'that every year twice there cometh a great companie of people overland which are called Caffiles or Caravanes, which come from Aleppo...'; and he attributes the prosperity of Ormuz to the fact of it being situated on the great trade route to India[1]. Barker speaks of caravans of from 2000 to 5000 camels going twice a year between Baghdad and Aleppo. Plaisted estimated that the caravan with which he travelled from Basra to Aleppo was made up, at the start, of 2000 camels in all, and about 150 'Musqueteers.' These camels did not compose a laden caravan, but were being taken to market at Aleppo. Halfway they were joined by the Baghdad caravan of 3000 camels, making up the total to 5000 camels and 1000 men; of the former about 400 laden. Della Valle, on his journey in 1615, reckoned his caravan at '1500 souls, with 40 or more tents.' Tavernier went with 600 camels and 400 men; Beawes had 2000 camels, 400 of which were laden; John Eldred went with 4000 camels 'laden with spices and other rich merchandises' from Baghdad to Aleppo. Carmichael's caravan consisted of 50 horses, 30 mules, and 1200 camels, '600 of which were laden with merchandise valuing £300,000.' It was guarded by an escort of 240 Arab soldiers. Bernardino travelled with a caravan of 2000 people, comprising 'nearly all the nations of the East'; there were 1400 camels and 800 riding-animals. Teixeira had only 150 camels, 95 donkeys and 12 horses. Individual merchants pursued this route with small caravans, of from 80 to 200 camels, and about 40 to 100 men. English travellers sometimes hired a complete outfit, including both riding and

[1] *The Voyage of John Huyghen van Linschoten to the East Indies*, Hakluyt Soc. Publ. I, No. LXX, pp. 9, 48. Marco Polo says: 'Merchants come thither [Ormuz] from India, with ships loaded with spicery and precious stones, pearls, cloths of silk and gold, elephant's teeth, and many other wares, which they sell to the merchants of Hormos, and which these in turn carry all over the world to dispose of again. In fact, 'tis a city of immense trade.'

baggage camels, as well as a small force of armed guards (see Irwin, *op. cit.* vol. II, p. 291). Taylor recommends travelling in comfort, by hiring a caravan at a cost of from £500 to £600, engaging 40 to 60 armed men, and 20 camels for water, tents, etc.[1] Roberts complained that the cost 'for bare necessaries' from Basra to Aleppo amounted to 1600 rupees. As regards the time occupied on the road between Aleppo and Basra, both the size of the caravan and the method of travelling have to be taken into account. Large caravans went slowly (7 hours per day) and took 45–70 days; small caravans did it in 25 days. Beawes took 29 days, at 11¼ hours' travelling per day. Roberts took 35 days. Plaisted was 24½ days travelling between Basra and Aleppo; this was with a fairly large caravan. Carmichael, averaging about 7 hours a day, took 318 hours or 45 days. Capper took 310 hours and Hunter 299½. Native riders could do the journey in half the time. Taylor reckoned that despatches could be sent overland in 16–18 days, while Manesty, British Resident at Basra, reported in 1799 that 'Tartars,' *i.e.* native couriers, had recently arrived from Aleppo in 13–15 days[2]. Europeans could not compete with the native; Tenreiro, who rode alone with one Arab guide at express speed, resting only 3 or 4 hours out of the 24, and only stopping to water their camels four times on the whole journey, took 22 days between Basra and Cocana (Sukhne), including a halt of 6 or 7 days, and Sukhne is counted 8 days from Aleppo, at caravan pace[3]. Beawes records meeting an Arab messenger at a point over 530 miles from Basra, who had been 10 days on the road; there would be another 220 miles on to Aleppo, which might be estimated at another 4 or 5 days. The time occupied between Aleppo and Baghdad is given as 18–20 days, large

[1] See also Major John Taylor in *Considerations on the Practicability and Advantages of a more speedy communication between Great Britain and her Eastern Dependencies*, 1795.

[2] Manesty kept up a regular service of native couriers between Basra and Aleppo by the desert route; from Aleppo the despatches went direct to Constantinople in sixteen days.

[3] Whiteway refers to this journey (*op. cit.* p. 55), 'The halt of eight days,' should, I think, be six or seven days; while 'the senseless panic' which resulted in the laming of his camel was caused by being chased by two lions!

caravans taking between 28 and 36 days[1], but the post did it in 14–15 days. Eldred, with a large laden caravan, took 40 days. In all cases the west-bound convoys were the faster, for they were chiefly composed of unladen camels being driven to Aleppo for sale, while the east-bound caravans were always laden, and therefore slower.

Aleppo's glory has departed, in fact that once great city is dying—the slow but certain death resulting from a diverted trade. Basra, on the other hand, is still alive and retains her position on the Gulf; she has perhaps a brighter prospect than hitherto, but she reflects a glory different to that which she used to reflect, for Basra has now a new mistress and one nearer at hand than Aleppo, namely the war-born Arab State of Iraq. Basra no longer stretches out her arms to the Mediterranean, no longer sends forth those merchant-caravans to Aleppo. The caravan route betwixt the two has likewise ceased to exist, but its well-furrowed track and its desert-stations have been preserved in these pages.

Sir William Foster, C.I.E., whose interest in and knowledge of these regions at that particular date are such as to inspire others, incited me to add this volume to the Hakluyt Society's Series. For many suggestions and much direct help I must thank him. For the elucidation of several obscure Arabic words I am indebted to Mr C. A. Storey, M.A., Librarian of the India Office; while I am more than grateful to Mr F. D. Harford, C.V.O., my collaborator over many years, and always a very ready helper.

[1] Irwin expected to take only sixteen days (*op. cit.* p. 292).

NOTE ON ORTHOGRAPHY

All place-names in the following narratives, and in quotations from other writers, have been left in their original forms, in spite of all inconsistencies of spelling. For their modern equivalents, where known, I have used the system authorised by the *Permanent Committee on Geographical Names* published by the Royal Geographical Society. I have, however, dispensed with marks such as – over long vowels, and the inverted ‘ representing the Arabic ع, which are difficult in small printed footnotes, and impossible on small scale maps. By following this system, one has been able to be more or less consistent, but even in this comparatively small Arabic-speaking region the difficulties are apparent, for the definite article is *Al* in Iraq and *El* a short distance away across an undefined desert boundary. In dealing with a region which includes Iraq and Syria, I have kept to *El* throughout.

§ I

NARRATIVE OF A JOURNEY FROM *ALEPPO* TO *BASRA* IN 1745

by

WILLIAM BEAWES

PREFATORY NOTE

CONCERNING the personal history of the author of the following narrative nothing has been discovered. Presumably he was on his way to India; yet no trace of him occurs in the lists of servants of the East India Company, nor is there any record of his applying to the Directors for permission to visit that country. A Captain William Beawes was in the eastern seas in 1701–2, commanding the English East India Company's ship *Albemarle*[1]; but inasmuch as he must have been at that time a man of mature age, it is scarcely possible that he would have been travelling in Mesopotamia more than forty years later. On the other hand, the identity of their names suggests that the traveller may have been the son of the sea captain. Whether he was in any way related to Wyndham Beawes, of the consular service, author of *Lex Mercatoria Rediviva*, has not been ascertained.

His narrative, which has not before been printed, is known to us only from a copy preserved among the Orme MSS. in the India Office Library. This collection comprises the materials collected by Robert Orme in the course of his historical investigations and bequeathed by him (through a friend) to the library of the East India House. The section in which the transcript of Beawes' narrative is found is described by Orme himself as consisting of copies of documents 'communicated to me with permission to be copied'; and since Major James Rennell quotes Beawes freely and certainly used his material in compiling his map of Western Asia, it is conceivable that the original was in the hands of Rennell and was lent by him to Orme. The transcript—which will be found in the volume marked 'Extracts from

[1] See Alexander Hamilton's *New Account of the East Indies*, 1727, vol. I, pp. 13, 294; also *Settlement of the Carmelites in Mesopotamia* (edited by Sir Hermann Gollancz), p. 122, which records the arrival of Beawes at Basra from Surat in September 1702. In the Latin text his name is disguised as 'Bius,' while that of his ship is transcribed as 'Alma Marre.' In the English version (*ibid*. p. 444) 'Bins' and 'Alma Murray' are given as the probable equivalents.

vols. VIII, IX and XVII'—was made by someone who was both ignorant and careless. Even ordinary words are often mis-copied, while there are apparently some omissions. These defects, however, do not seriously obscure the narrative, which contains much that is interesting and valuable, especially the account on pp. 21–24 of a visit to the celebrated mosque at Najaf.

REMARKS AND OCCURRENCES IN A JOURNEY FROM *ALEPPO* TO *BASSORA*, BY THE WAY OF THE DESERT

By *William Beawes, Esqr.*

BEING resolved upon passing from Aleppo to Bassora, and meeting with an agreeable companion, one Mr. Robert Golightly, of the same intention, we solicited advice from the Gentlemen of our factory[1] and several itinerant merchants of the country, concerning the various routes and were informed as follows.

1ST. From Aleppo with a Caravant to Mosul and thence down the Tugris to Bagdat and Bassora. This is the common route of merchants and travellers, but has these inconveniences. Firstly, the journey to Mosul is often tedious, the Caravan loitering at places on the road, either to procure the vent of merchandize, and fresh freight, or to avoid the Gordeens[2] who frequently plunder or oblige them to the expence of a guard where the passes are dangerous. Secondly, the water carriages from Mosul to Bagdat being only supported by skins swelled by the induction of air, they sometimes burst and several accidents have happened[3].

2D. From Aleppo to Bir, only four days journey, where a sort of boats are procurable and will cost each from Bir down the Euphrates to Hilla about 60 dollars, and at Hilla are found very commodious vessels for proceeding to Bassora.

N.B. If a traveller chuses to see Bagdat in his way, he must land some leagues higher than Hilla, at a place that is only half a days journey over to that city, being a very narrow pass between the two rivers[4].

This passage from Bir to Bassora is performed in about 20 days and would be the pleasantest and most commodious

[1] 'The Factory' comprised the offices and residences of the members of the staff of the 'Levant Company.'

[2] Kurds.

[3] *Kelek*, or raft laid over inflated skins.

[4] Falluja: the usual point of disembarkation, 35 miles from Baghdad.

of any, and according to what several inhabitants of those places have assured me, this way should be particularly the choice of a traveller, for ancient medals are so common it seems at Arachba[1], and some other places on the river, that in default of curious purchasers, who exceeding rarely pass that way, the women adapt them for ornaments (as elsewhere chequins) and few are without them; likewise antique stones are here daily found, and sold for little. However, both merchants and travellers are deterred from steering this course, being liable everywhere to impositions and in some places to being plundered, tho' I've known Armenians that had gone that way, without any such grievous impediments, and who gave me a different character of these people in general.

3D. Some travellers have chose to direct their course viz.

From Aleppo to Geboul[2], a small village upon the edge of the desart, one easy days journey.

From Geboul to Jaiba[3], a town in ruins, 2 days journey into the desert.

From Jaiba to Arachba[4], a town bigger than Aleppo, and standing on the river Euphrates, 1½ days journey[5].

From Arachba to Ana, upon the river-side, 3 days journey.

From Ana to Haditha, one day.

From Haditha to Juba[6], one day.

From Juba to Heyt[7], one day.

When arrived at Heyt both danger and difficulty is over, for from hence to Bagdat is not above two days and half journey, and tho' sometimes merchants with goods are disturbed by the Arabs in crossing from river to river, I never heard that European travellers were molested; and, if their

[1] Rahba: 26 miles S.E. of Deir ez Zor.

[2] Jebbul (see p. 9, note 3).

[3] Taiyibe.

[4] Rahba had of course its great days, probably greater than Karkisiya (Circesium), its neighbour across the river, but it had long since fallen from high estate, and in Beawes' day must already have been deserted; our nearest contemporary—Olivier (1797)—saw only a fortress and a ruined site.

[5] Beawes' information was at fault. The route between Taiyibe and Rahba was never used by the Caravans, and we have only one record of its being used by an individual traveller—namely Olivier in 1797.

[6] Island of Jubba.

[7] Hit.

curiosity will excuse the sight of that city, the passage from Heyt down the Euphrates to Bassora is quite secure.

4TH. With the Arabian Caravans, of which there are two from Aleppo, one to Bassora and the other to Bagdat, and often set out together, keeping company till they arrive at a place called Cobiesie[1], which is a poor village within four hours of Heyt. This latter route we preferred, and that our experience may be of some utility to future travellers, I shall here set down the necessary provisions for such a journey. And first, I think whoever by common necessity or curiosity urged a large Tartaravan (or litter) with the improvement of a double ceiling will render his passage easy; the carriage here being the principal consideration, for as to other inconveniences it is supposed that those who undertake to travel any parts of the East are informed that long stages, a slow pace, course far [*i.e.* fare], and a warm sun are to be the common trials of their patience and constitution.

2DLY. Be careful with what Arab you engage for the camels, as choice and recommendation in [this] as much concerns your welfare in the desart as the difference of commanders at sea.

3DLY. To visit the principal Shaik with a small present, as a vest of cloth or the like.

4THLY. Agree with the said Shaik, and procure from him in writing what you are to pay [for] each camel for desert dues, whereby disputes are avoided at the journeys end.

5THLY. Concerning water, it is customary for travellers to agree with their conductor for supplying throughout the journey and are [we?] paid for ourselves and two servants one and a half camel load, which they reckon six loaders or large skins, and these they oblige themselves to keep replenished as they find water in the desart; and if travellers are careful and don't regard the expence carrying a few more loaders than usual, they may drink what is wholesome the greatest part of the way, by seeing themselves the said loaders filled where the water is best and strictly in charging their own servants to be watchful of it; which we imprudently

[1] Kubaisa.

trusted to the Arabs and were served accordingly, for notwithstanding the provision we made was extraordinary I gave him, I question if two skins were ever employed for our particular use, or that we fared a whit the better for such precaution.

6THLY. Concerning the other provisions, a person setting out for Aleppo may procure variety of articles that will endure the journey, but the grand articles are rice, bread, coffee, and country butter, of which a large store should be provided, as all the Arabs that attend the loads expect to partake thereof and indeed deserve it, being always ready and desirous to afford the servants their assistance. Salt-meats are very improper for the desart, as they heat and augment thirst (which without such increase is hard to satisfie); nor does much of any food agree with this journey, but eating little and drinking often of weak sour punch is the diet to preserve health and greatly lessen the fatigue; wherefore variety of food is an useless embarrassment, and the best in my opinion that can be carried is fowls, which at night we used to eat with pullow [pilau], or made into broth and dress to eat cold the next day at noon. All fruits that can be preserved any time as also roots are excellent refreshments for the desart.

Of liquors the principal to be provided is shrub, which, made into weak punch, is not only the most refreshing draught but is equally wholesome, particularly to prevent the bad effects of the desart waters, as we very sensibly experienced; for some days before our arrival at Bassora, the shrub being finished which till then had preserved us free from any disorder. Leban[1] also with water makes a cool and pleasant mixture but is apt to offend the stomach. As to wine, brandy and other spirituous liquors a very small quantity is sufficient, the heat rendering them not desirable and unless indisposed the use of them hurtful.

7THLY. We agreed with our conductor for camels at thirty five dollars per load of 500 lb weight. And there needs no care about the size of package, the Arab being exceeding dextrous at accommodating the burthens. For a servant is

[1] Sour milk or buttermilk (Arabic *laban*).

always paid half a camel load and for ourselves that went in a double cradle (in their language called mahoffi[1]) we paid fifty dollars.

We provided one small post tent for our own accommodation and another for the servants. Our cots we made to stand a more than ordinary distance from the ground, as a security from the snakes and scorpions that are common it seems in the desart. And having presented our conductor with a vest of fine broad cloth, all was ready for a march.

1745. *Aug. 5th.* This morning about seven we left Aleppo, in expectation to join our caravan at Spheera[2] three hours off, but on the road were informed they had proceeded to Gaboul[3], and when arrived there they were gone a league farther, as accordingly we found them about four in the afternoon, having then been riding and fasting, which made this days journey very disagreeable; but a fresh westerly wind which lasted the whole day made some amends.

We found our tents pitched and all our baggage about it in good order. The evening was delightfully cool, and the night so cold that a quilt was scarce sufficient covering. About this place it seems are abundance of scorpions, and a Jew merchant in the night was wounded by one; which gave him great pain, but found relief in a few hours from the application of a squeezed garlick. We neither felt or saw any. Consider our having cots a good prevention.

[1] *Mihaffa* (Arabic) is the same as Roberts' *kajāwa* (Persian)—panniers or wooden cages slung in pairs across the camels; usually used by natives for transporting their women-folk.

[2] Sifra, Sfira: a small village 14 miles S.E. of Aleppo. Caravans coming up from Iraq halted here for customs inspection.

[3] El Jebbul: a village of salt-workers on the edge of the great saline depression Ṣabkha Jebbul, which supplied the salt industry of the neighbourhood. Teixeira had already described the 'Salt Lake' and the great value of its salt deposits. Parsons in his *Travels in Asia and Africa*, etc., describes how the depression fills up during the winter with water, fresh enough for his horse to drink, but by the end of May it is dry, and in June it is covered with a cake of salt. Maundrell, Chaplain to the Factory at Aleppo, gives a good account of 'the Valley of Salt' in the 4th edition of his *Journey from Aleppo to Jerusalem in 1697*. See also Drummond's *Travels*, p. 193; Russell's *Natural History of Aleppo*, vol. 1, pp. 55–6; Teonge's *Diary*, p. 154, and Note in Appendix. Musil gives an historical sketch of *Ǧabbûl* up to Yaqut's day in Appendix VIII of his *Palmyrena*.

6th. This morning early we mounted and for the first time tried our mahoffi; but the camel happened to be as great a stranger to this machine as ourselves, and with difficulty consented to the burthen, which neither being to-day well fixed made us conclude this manner of travelling nothing near so commodious as we had imagined; but the Arabs assured us a day or two would remedy all such inconveniences. At ten this morning we again encamped, this small journey into the desart being it seems designed to separate the caravans with any further communication with Aleppo, as otherwise there would be no end to delays; and also this day is designed to put everything in due order for a regular march in future. Our course to-day was somewhat to southward of the East, and the country the same as about Aleppò, only quite a level. A fresh westerly wind continues, whereby we find not the least inconveniency from heat, tho' otherwise it must be very hot, for we observe a single tent is but a slender defence against the sun and the ground reflects the rays with great force. We have given orders always to pitch our tents somewhat apart from and to windward of the rest of the caravans, as else at the time of cooking you are molested with smoke and also with dust from the camels continually rambling about you.

The order for diet in the caravan is coffee in the morning before mounting; then when they stop about noon for an hour coffee again and what else any[one] has ready drest; in the evening it is pleasant for anyone to observe soon after encamping there appears almost as many fires as men and all hands set to preparing the pallow or what better their stores may afford. The water here is very foul, but we brought from Aleppo (a lucky thought) some fine hebit[1], which, formed into an Hypocrites's[2] sleeve, makes an excellent

[1] A puzzling word. Can there be a connection with 'habit-shirt,' defined in the *O.E.D.* as 'a kind of chemisette with linen collar, worn by women under the outer bodice'?

[2] Hippocrates' bag or sleeve, a conical bag of cotton, linen or flannel used as a filter or strainer. Bacon's *Sylva* (1626): 'Passing it [Ippocrasse] through a wollen bagge, which they call Hippocrates sleeve.' 'Ippocrasse' was a wine (*vinum Hippocratum*) so called because filtered through Hippocrates' sleeve.

strainer. Our caravan is reckoned large, consisting of two thousand odd hundred camels[1], of which about four hundred are loaded with merchandize and near as many more with passengers and baggage, the rest mounted by the Arabs themselves or empty for want of freight, the returns from Aleppo being considerable compared to what is carried from Bassora; and what likewise renders the caravan numerous, independant of merchants, are the armed Arabs in case of necessity. The Shauks [Sheikhs] and their attendants and many poor Arabs join the caravans from Bassora with one, two or three camels, either loaded with things of small import to barter at Aleppo, or in hopes the greater cameleers may favour them with some freight back again. We have several horses and mules in the caravan which are carried for sale, being cheap in Aleppo and afford a good profit at Bassora; but they arrive there such skeletons that many months are necessary to [recover] them, especially those that have performed the journey mounted.

This afternoon, not finding here water sufficient to supply the caravan, we went on an hour farther. A pleasant westerly wind and a very cold night.

7th. Mounted this morning about six and travelled till noon, when we stopped and unloaded the camels; but I think to little purpose, for in half an hour we were again under way. At seven finished our days journey. The country quite level and fair horizon all round. The wind to-day fresh and westerly; our course S.S.E. No water. Night cold.

8th. Mounted between four and five and travelled till noon, when we rested an hour and proceeded till seven. The country and course the same. Wind westerly and heat moderate. Evening agreeable. Night cold.

I asked our conductor today by what means they directed their course; who told [me] there are beaten paths throughout the journey (which I afterwards found) wherein the guides constantly keep, and thereby hower [*i.e.* however] the caravan extraviales[2] on one side or other, they are sufficient to keep

[1] See Introduction, p. xxxiii.

[2] This appears to be a copyist's error for 'extravagates' (wanders).

them in due course. But these paths are sometimes by gales of wind covered with sand, and then the caravan is obliged to halt, and the guides spread themselves, as far as not losing sight of the body will permit, to discover a tract; or, not succeeding therein, wait till night and proceed by the stars. And one evening desiring them to shew me those they particularly observed, there was scarce an Arab but manifested such a knowledge of the heavens as I little expected, and that which they said was their chief director between Bassora and Aleppo, they pointed to, calling Judda[1], and is the north star.

We observed no order in our march, but spread over the waste in different figures; which being so large, the caravan affords a diverting prospect, especially the objects being so various, and to us strange. And one reason for their spreading I suppose may be on account of the camels, who feed as they travel, having absolutely no other provision than what they meet with in the way, which hitherto has been only a small sort of farzbush, and that in no great plenty.

9th. Set out this morning about four, lasted [*sic*] the same till about nine, when we got amongst hills quite barren and parched up, and tho' the westerly wind continues it is extremely hot; at one we pitched our tents, being come to water, which is not bad, and we shall therefore stay to enjoy it till tomorrow. Course today S.S.E. Our mahoffi terribly fatigues us, and was certainly only intended for such who have only no legs or can bestow them independant of their bodies. It is imposible to maintain a tolerable easy posture for two minutes together, and the motions moreover are so diabolical that I have frequently in a day worse qualms than a breeding woman and am sooner [sorer?] bruised by night than Sancho in his government. However, it keeps the immediate heat of the sun from us, which we should probably find at this season insupportable; tho' here also the benefit is not much greater than being baked instead of roasted, and therefore the mahoffi is but a trumpery machine, and a wheelbarrow in comparison to a princely carriage.

This evening were killed in our quarters two snakes, of

[1] El Jady (Arabic), the Pole Star.

which it seems there is no want in the desart and in some places very large ones. I enquired of Hodgee[1] Salek, our conductor, what remedy they had when bit thereby; who told me none but Allah Kerim, that God was great and protected them, not having in his time known one instance of their doing harm. The evening and night agreeable, cool.

10*th*. Today being the Jews Sabbath, they prevailed on the Caravan Bashi with (30) thirty dollars not to proceed, which seems a trifling sum to detain so large a company; but he commands and it may be supposed that nobody bid against him. This conductor in chief is always a man of extraordinary note amongst the Desert Arabs in general, and ours was called Said Mahud, and his business is to protect the caravan from being molested by any tribe we may meet in our way, for which he receives a Tanto per load. But altho' this man is principally necessary for the security of the caravan, he is not absolutely sufficient, for we have also several others of different tribes, who likewise receive a gratuity for their protection; and this expense amounts to the merchants in the whole, from Aleppo to Bassora, to about (14) fourteen dollars each load; but provisions should be excused for only a small present. As we were necessitated to defer proceeding on our journey till tomorrow, I fain would have employed the idle day in visiting a town we saw in sight, about seven miles distance, called by the Arabs Jaiba[2], which seems a large place, having a large tower in the middle. The Arabs inform us it is a place of great antiquity but now in ruins, which is all they know of the matter; and as to my going thither no one that I invited would accompany me thither, or could I prevail by any means with Hodgee Salek to supply me with a beast and some Arabs for enjoying the pleasure alone; whether because there might be dangers and any accidents be imputed to his defect of care, or that Arabs don't approve of our examining these places in the desart, I know not; but all the reasons he gave were, the undertaking was improper and that the sight would rather

[1] Haji: one who has made the pilgrimage to Mecca.

[2] Taiyibe: for fuller description see pp. 85–6, note 3.

afford a horror than pleasure, as time and other circumstances have produced a scene which only serves at present to excite a melancholy reflection of the instability of human things. The place, they say, had some inhabitants till within these four years, but now totally deserted[1], every company of Arabs in their passage despoiling them at pleasure and otherwise contributing to render their situation intolerable. At a small distance there is another town called Suckna[2], which is inhabited. At Jaiba is a spring of hot water[3]; from hence to Suckna six hours of a caravan, and from Suckna to Tadmor or Palmiza[4] fourteen hours; those famous ruins bear of us here S.W.

We got acquainted today with an inhabitant of Arachba, who informed us there are many ruins about this part of the country, but none that bespeak any magnificence or very great antiquity, for as to Tabia which I have expressed so much concern at not visiting, he assures us that little else besides the tower and ruins pertaining thereto are of stone, the rest being only earth. He says the country about the Euphrates, from whence we are not above a days journey, so abounded formerly with towns and villages that only between Dier[5] and Arachba, which is also a days journey, there were upwards of 300, whereof scarce one at present remains entire[6].

[1] Inhabited in 1691 at the time of Lanoy's and Goodyear's second visit. Niebuhr reported it destroyed in about 1730–40.

[2] Sukhne: once a town, now a poor village; it has hot springs, hence its name, and a fortress. Doubtless once one of the Roman frontier block-houses, and always a station on the caravan route from the Euphrates to central Syria.

[3] The springs are sulphurous, there is no evidence of the excellent water from which it is supposed to take its name. 'Tiebe, so called, as they say, from the goodness of the waters, the word signifying good, but we found them not so over excellent' (*Palestine Exploration Fund Quarterly*, 1890, p. 296, from the original manuscript of Dr William Halifax, 'Relation of a Voyage to Tadmor in 1691').

[4] Palmyra.

[5] Deir ez Zor: 70 miles away.

[6] His informant was correct. The section of the Euphrates Valley referred to is that where the Khabur joins it, and is a region abounding in historic names. It was actually the Eastern frontier of the Roman Empire under Diocletian. Circesium and Rahba probably vaunted considerable 'magnificence' in their great days, and the sites must have had an antiquity much older than Rome.

This watering place is called Ain il Kom or the fountain of Kom[1], and I reckon its distance from Aleppo about 80 miles. I intended to have regulated the distance by counting the camels steps for a number of minutes and measured his step, with which, and knowing the time travelled, I might have been tolerably exact; but this method is rendered useless in a caravan, because the camels feed as they go, and consequently have not that constancy in their pace as is requisite. We passed today without any great fatigue from the heat, and the evening and night was cool, the wind westerly.

11th. Mounted this morning about four, and travelled in a hilly uneven country, but pleasant enough, till ten, when got again upon a plain unbounded almost every way by anything but the horizon. Here we found such a multitude of hares as afforded us good diversion the whole day, and I believe to every one in the caravan a good supper. The manner of taking them is very expeditious, and puss has little chance of escaping, for she can turn no way without meeting a stick, which the Arabs fling so dextrously as seldom to miss their aim; but the flesh of these hares is exceeding disagreeable, which seems to proceed from their food[2]; for having frequently of a night when the camels were brought in from feeding a very offensive smell, the Arabs upon enquiry told me it was the breath of these animals and the taste of the hares correspond exactly thereto.

We passed this morning by the ruins of a castle called Gussorah Seveyge[3]; the building has been large and the figure square; at present most of the southward is standing, built of stone with turrets at equal distances, but within there appears no remains. We baited about noon about an hour and at six encamped. The day has been warmer than aggreable, tho' the wind continues westerly. Our course about E.S.E. Country level. No water. The evening and night pleasant.

[1] Ain el Qom, a famous watering, see p. 140.

[2] Hares, in Asia, are often foul feeders.

[3] This is Carmichael's *Seveyge*, *Swayeagee*, or *Sawye*—identical with Qusur el Ikhwan of other travellers, a ruined site of some importance. See further, pp. 143–44. Parsons calls it *Soor*—battlements.

12th. Set out this morning at four; baited an hour at noon, and proceeded till seven. Course and country the same. Hotter than usual. Wind westerly. No water. The evening and night pleasant.

13th. Set out this morning at three and about eleven came to a water they call Geubil Canam[1], or the sheep pool, which we found well tasted; but before we could procure any was become very muddy, and is what will always happen unless a person is sent time enough before the caravan to make the necessary provision, which our conductor ought to have done. Here our Arachba friend took his leave and shaped his course for that place about N.E. b[y] N. distance about nine hours[2]. No further today. Course and country the same. Wind westerly, and excessive hot, with some blasts almost insupportable. We have not broke our fast the whole day except with drink, which indeed has been our chief sustenance since we left Aleppo; for what with being baked and bruised in that confounded invention the mohoffi, and the tedious tiresome stages we daily undergo, our appetites at night (which is the only time of getting anything drest) are so palled that the little we then eat is merely because we think it necessary; and by what we are already experienced of the desart we may in my opinion conclude that no man who has the least regard for his ease should attempt the passage in this season unless provided with a more commodious carriage, for as to riding so many hours a day exposed to the sun, such is only tolerable to an Arab; and as to the mahoffi, Satan himself would not be able to continue a shape or posture accommodate to so perverse a movement. And therefore, upon the whole, it seems to me that, concerning the passage of the desart compared to the way of Mosul and Bagdat, the latter has much the advantage with regard to refreshments, a pleasant variety of the country and the satisfaction

[1] Jubb el Ghanam; see further, p. 146.

[2] For the position of Jubb el Ghanam we are still dependent on the rough reckonings of these early travellers, from such distant points as Ain el Qom and Abu Kemal. No modern traveller has been there. The wells are probably about 25 miles S.S.W. of Rahba, for which 9 hours is a fair estimate for a cameleer.

of being accommodated if sickness or other impediments should render proceeding uneasy; and tho' the former for security, avoiding delays and the impertinence of Turkish officers, is greatly preferable and consequently the choice of merchants, yet where interest is not concerned there appears but little reason to determine a meer passenger in favour of the desart; and was I again to choose my way in this journey, it should always be between Bagdat and Bassora by water and between Bagdat and Aleppo either with the desert caravan in a litter, or being in circumstances to afford such a present to the Bashaw as might procure me a safe passage, it should be from town to town upon the banks of Euphrates.

We have observed about this place a vast quantity of christaline tales [talcs], which I imagined would afford a plaister for stuces [stucco?] work infinitely exceeding any other material and might be brought to Aleppo, and thence transported to Scanderoon for embarkation at a small expence. In a journey mentioned in the Mesulinua Curiosa[1] by some English from Aleppo to Tadmore it is said that between Ain il Kom and Arzoffa[2] there are several quarries of this tale [talc] which they call gypsine [gypsum?] stone or rock isinglass, and say at Arzoffa there is a building entirely thereof. Whether the tale [talc] here mentioned is the same with that the adepts pretend to extract from an oil of such admirable quality I am uncertain, nor have I made the experiments I intended with this curious production, but find it to disagree with the European tale [talc] in a very essential quality, which is the resistance of fire, for this exposed to a common calinary [culinary?] heat presently falls into an impalpable powder.

[1] *Miscellanea Curiosa*, London, 1708, a small collection of exceedingly miscellaneous tracts in three volumes. Vol. III is devoted to Travels and Natural History, and contains 'A Relation of a Voyage from Aleppo to Palmyra in Syria, by the Rev. Mr William Halifax.' Also 'An extract of the Journals of two several Voyages of the English Merchants of the Factory at Aleppo to Tadmor.' For reprints of these journeys, see Titles of Works consulted. See also pp. 86–7.

[2] Risafe: 33 miles N. of Ain el Qom, the ancient Sergiopolis, and a station on the caravan route from Raqqa to Homs, fully described and illustrated in Musil's *Palmyrena*, New York, 1928.

14th. Set out this morning about four, and soon after met an Arab messenger from Bassora, with letters for the English nation at Aleppo, having been only ten days[1] upon the desart. We offered him refreshments, but he excused accepting any for the rest of his journey, having only the camel he rode on. At noon we baited an hour as usual; about seven encamped. Course S.E. Little wind from the northward. Country in the afternoon hilly, and the weather very hot, but the night cool.

15th. We are [were?] under way this morning by five and directed our course nearly East, which about ten brought us upon the banks of the Euphrates, where we expected to have been regaled with verdure and those pleasant scenes that generally such copious rivers produce; but here the bounty of nature finds no returns, bestowing a gift which other soil would gratefully manifest, and this incapable even to acknowledge, for since our leaving Aleppo we have not had such a wretched prospect. The river here (if I remember right) is near as broad as the Thames at London and the current brisk. The Arabs dwellings are scattered on each side, and opposite to us is a poor village called Jorsa[2], from whence they brought us sheep, goats, melons and some other provisions, which were welcome refreshments. But as at the same time they afforded us more of their company than was quite convenient, we hastened to leave them, they being it seems hereabout numerous, well armed, and a sort of freebooters, who upon all occasions in their favour are apt to consider that strength and right are synonimous terms. Wherefore, the necessary compliments being past between their Sheik and ours, the former treating with a fatted sheep, and the latter corresponding with a present of greater value, we departed in peace about two this afternoon; and striking into the desart for three hours pursued our usual course

[1] This was quick going. The post used to take 14–15 days from Baghdad to Aleppo, and at this rate of travel, viz. 10 days from Basra to a point near Jubb el Ghanam, the post would reach Aleppo in 13–14 days. See Introduction, p. xxxiv.

[2] Carmichael also mentions *Jurfa*, but I can find no modern equivalent. The locality is that bend of the Euphrates which so many travellers by the desert route sighted, between Abu Kemal and El Qaim. There are several villages on the left or E. bank.

till seven. Today very hot. The country hilly and strong. Scarce any wind, but night cool.

16*th*. Mounted at four; baited at noon as usual, and proceeded till six in the evening. Course about S.S.E. Little wind. Country for the most part hilly. No water. Day very hot, but the night cool.

17*th*. Mounted about five; baited about noon, and encamped in the evening at seven. Course and country the same. No water. A northerly wind. The day hot, but the night cool.

18*th*. Set out this morning at three, and about nine got to a water called Agelat Hawrin[1], where we remained the whole day, and found our situation much warmer than desirable, but the night, as usual, cool. Course, country, wind and weather the same this stage as last.

19*th*. Mounted at five, and baited at noon; proceeded till four, and arrived at a water called Ain il Ernul[2] or the Hares pool, where we encamped and are only three hours and a half from Cobiesse[3], a poor Arab village. Today we met a messenger from Bassora. Course today S. Little wind and very hot. The country the same, and night cool as usual.

20*th*. Under way this morning. Directed our course within two points of the East, which brought us about nine to Cobiesse, situated in a grove of date trees, where, however we expected to be otherwise regaled, all that occurred, except dates and a few sheep, is absolutely no refreshment whatever; even water being scarce and (unless brought from the river) not by any but the inhabitants drinkable. Here one-third of our caravan separated, being bound to Bagdat, and embarked at a place called Heit on the river Euphrates, about three hours from hence; from which place they are carried down in two or three days, according to the currents, which are governed by the season or the Tygris. The camels they

[1] Aqulat or Uglet Hauran: an important watering in the bed of the Wadi Hauran, about 15 miles from its entrance into the Euphrates. All caravans watered there; the wells are numerous and the water near the surface. See also p. 152.

[2] Ain el Arnab: see also p. 155.

[3] Kubaisa: see p. 155.

bring the goods to Heit. But this affair is badly managed, so that, with getting boats sufficient and other impediments, they are commonly five, six, and sometimes more days before the merchants with their goods are fairly embarked. But passengers who have only their baggage are easily accommodated and, as a small imposition of expence is to them of no consideration, they may immediately get boats to Hilla, and from thence may be well provided with others to Bassora; and is the way that I proposed to have taken; but the few journals we have of passing this desart, and those so contradictory, made me resolve to prefer curiosity to ease and proceed throughout by land. This afternoon we left Cobiesse, and at seven encamped; country hilly, very sandy, barren and strong. A hot day, being little wind, and the night not so pleasant as usual.

21st. Set out this morning about four, and baiting an hour at noon proceeded till five, when encamped by a stagnated water, that stunk abominably but seemed not the least offensive to the camels or their masters, who it is certain have the best stomachs and least delicacy, both one and the other, of any men or beast in the universe. When a camel is old or infirm, that he is not able to proceed, they not only butcher him for food but eat thereof, when no carrion can stink worse; as it happened in this journey that they once had some of the said flesh remaining so long as was sufficient to infect the whole caravan. The country today for the most part plain, except here and there a few breaks and elevations; and our situation this evening is not unpleasant, being a good deal of verdure about, the water and the shrubs everywhere thicker than ordinary. Near one of the pools is a small hillock upon which I found two groves [graves?] of some unhappy travellers, with some leather flasks rotted by the sun lying by them. Our course today was about S.S.E. The wind northerly, and tolerably cool.

22nd. Departed about four, and this morning several went out of the road some distance and got a supply of good water. At noon we baited as usual; and proceeding until sunset, encamped in a bottom, where the soil was so sandy and loose

MESHED ALI or NAJAF.

that the tents with difficulty could be pitched. But there was a spring called Ain il Chebeira[1], and food for the camels in great plenty, tho' if the water proved no better than the former, we suffered a warm night to little purpose. Our course today was more easterly; the wind yet more northerly; the heat moderate; and the country for the most part plain, very thick of shrubs, and not unpleasant.

23rd. We mounted this morning at five, and in a few hours came by a delightful spring of water excellent in quality and abundant, and where the pleasant verdures invited a longer stay; for we only refreshed our beasts without unloading and proceeded. Some hours after we passed within sight of a village[2] inhabited by professed robbers and from whom the caravan had no security than their sufficiency of strength to attack us. This afternoon we passed near a large fortress of ancient fabrick[3], and the Arabs pretend it was built by the Christians. Encamped at sunset. The country thick covered with shrubs and not unpleasant. The heat moderate. Course about S.S.E., and the night agreeable.

24th. Set out at four and, baiting as usual, finished our days journey about seven in the evening, travelling most of the day upon an ascent, of which in the afternoon we reached the summit, and then descending into a sandy plain encamped. Course and weather much the same.

25th. This morning departed at four, and travelling in a sandy plain till about eleven we encamped eight miles from Meched Ali[4], a town so called from the meched or mosque said to be the burying ground of Ali, a place of the highest veneration amongst the Persians and all Mahometans of their sect. And the mosque having been lately adorned at a vast

[1] Ain el Khabeira is not placed on any modern map, but Beawes' description of the locality, a bottom, with plenty of camel food, makes one suspect that he was in the depression to the S.W. of Rahhaliya and Shithatha. His march of 29 hours from Kubaisa brings him to this point precisely. It is the region where Gertrude Bell discovered ruins—the 'whole area is known as Kherâb (ruins)'—which she identified as a possible site of Yaqut's 'Ain et Tamr.'

[2] Shithatha: of evil repute, see p. 158.

[3] Obviously Ukhaidir, and possibly of Lakhmid origin, hence the Arab tradition as to its founders.

[4] Meshed Ali, or Najaf.

expense by the present King of Persia, Shack Nadir[1], we resolved not to pass without seeing of it; and therefore after taking some refreshments we joined a party of Arabs and got to the town in about [*blank*] hours; which we found situated upon a mount of sand and stones, and the country for some miles round it of the same wretched appearance, without the least sign of a vegetable to be seen; nor can anything more miserable or forlorn be conceived than this place in every respect appears. The town is small and surrounded with a low wall of unhewn stone and mortar, of which fabrick there is also at a little distance two fortresses, the one large and seemingly strong. The houses, if such they may be called, look more like heaps of rubbish than dwellings, and the inhabitants more despicable than anything mentioned. As soon as we entered the town a swarm of rabble encompassed us and with rude shouts and worse railleries and such like welcomes accompanied us to a place where coffee was and near the outward gate of the mosque, which they permitted us to view[2]. This famous building stands in a spacious court, the form being much like that of the other mosques save that the dome is differently shaped, swelling at bottom and rising to a point like a mitre; on the top are fixed two large glories [*i.e.* haloes] or suns, cutting each other at right angles. This mosque has also minoretts on each side, which are curiously wrought, and as well these as the whole fabrick are intirely covered with plates of copper thickly gilt and very neatly laid on[3], and all the doors, windows, galleries &c.,

[1] Nadir Shah, who had just gained a decisive victory over the Turks and who at that particular moment may himself have been somewhere in the vicinity. The campaigns in central Iraq were drawing to a close, Turk and Persian were entering on a series of diplomatic discussions, a principal point of which was the ownership of the Holy Cities Karbala and Najaf, the Persian Shias naturally claiming the tomb of their saint Ali. Nadir Shah had been on pilgrimage to Najaf a year or two before. Two years later he was assassinated.

[2] Beawes was lucky in the time of his visit. The Shia shrine was enjoying a brief period of Shia occupation, and no doubt its intolerant temper was calmed. Most travellers avoided Meshed Ali, as a hot-bed of fanaticism; Griffith, alone of our travellers, besides Beawes, entered it, and nearly lost his life in consequence.

[3] Niebuhr describes the famous dome; *op. cit.* pp. 210 et seq.

beautifully decorated with fret work, azure borders with inscriptions of gold ideas after the Eastern manner; making together, it is most certain, a grand appearance and must have cost an infinite sum; but yet the outside we were assured bears scarce any proportion to the beauty and riches within, where particularly the tomb of Ali is adorned with jewels of infinite value and works of immense cost. However, we were also told by some that the jewels adorning the inside of the mosque were far from being all real, for many were fictitious, not only by appointment, but also the roguery of some who have found means to make an exchange to their advantage. And what seems somewhat surprising is the conduct of the Turks with regard to this place, who, tho' at war with Persia and always abominating that sect, have nevertheless thro' fear or superstition hitherto refrained from any attempt on this unguarded deposit of riches.

The King of Persia has here a Chan, as well in reverence to the holy place as to inspect the work, which is not as yet finished[1]; the outward gate being a very mean entrance, and the wall surrounding the court is at present only rough stones and mortar, which makes a sorry appearance; but the design is that the whole shall be finally compleat, and no great space of time will be necessary thereto, unless it be to finish the pavement of the court, which, by what already appears, will be exceeding curious, and when the design is entirely effected, the most exquisite and lasting monument of devotion and grandeur the rebel monarch could possibly leave to the followers of Ali in particular and the Mahometan world in general.

From the gate of the mosque and with the same company we were carried to a house, where our conductor informed us we must remain till next morning; and tho' we signified no small discontent at his insisting thereon, it was all to no purpose. The country, he said, was full of robbers, and going from the town to the caravan without strong company endangered us to be robbed and even murdered, and that no

[1] It was Nadir Shah's policy to embellish the Tomb of Ali; see Niebuhr, *op. cit.* p. 210.

such security could be procured till next day. So, spreading a carpet upon a small terras, we passed the evening as patiently as so uncomfortable a situation could admit, being excessive hot and we had brought no refreshments of water or liquor from the caravan; but we got a supply for our future journey of mutton, fowls, very good leban with a few melons, pomgranates &c.; all which and what little else the place affords, even water, is brought from the rivers wide [side?], distant from them, they told us, about four hours.

From hence, it seems, when the medicum [medium, *i.e.* air] is clear of dust, may be seen the ruins of an ancient Couffa[1], and not far off is also the tomb of the Prophet Ezekiel[2], believed to be such by the Jews, who are at some expense in expression of their veneration for it.

The Persian Chan this evening complimented us by a messenger with enquiries concerning our welfare and tenders of service, to which we returned the necessary compliments, and desired his order for safely viewing the inside of the mosque; but his Excellency vouchsafed us no answer, nor did so impertinent a request deserve his attention.

As an instance of the Arabian hospitality to strangers remaining yet an indispensable duty amongst them, I cannot omit mentioning that from the moment we entered the house in Meched Ali till that of our departure, a venerable old Arab (who by the respect paid him appeared a principal man) accompanied us and expressed by an interpreter great concern we could not discourse together, desired we would consider him as our servant come to do us all the good offices in his power, and to these expressions were joined an invitation almost every instant to either fruit or something else before us.

26th. This morning about eight we had the pleasure to leave the most wretched place and seemingly miserable people in the universe, and got in a few hours to our caravan. Today the heat was very fatiguing, but the night so cool that

[1] Kufa: 7 miles away to the N.E.

[2] The reputed Tomb of Ezekiel is at Kifl, 17 miles to the N.N.E. See Niebuhr, *op. cit.* p. 216.

a quilt double was scarce sufficient to keep me warm. And the night before within the town was excessive hot. Towards the morning our quarters were alarmed by the approach of some straggling Arabs, which is common in the night, wherever the caravan is pitched, and tho' a very regular and careful watch is constantly observed the rogues do sometimes find their account in these visits. But fear oftener occasions these alarms than any real danger, and that of a Jew merchant on this occasion made me laugh very heartily, who, instead of betaking himself to his arms, fell into a vehement expostulation with God Almighty; for, first crying to Him very loud for His assistance, he told Him there was thieves a-coming to despoil His chosen people, and will you, says he, suffer it after so many instances of care for preservation? No, no, that can't be; we know, Lord, our merchandize is very safe under Thy protection, but hasten to help us or all is lost; and so he proceeded louder and louder whilst the alarm continued, and then with a dozen hearty curses, and brandy sufficient to compose him, the noise of his agonies ceased. And talking with this Jew afterwards, the rascal denied that any fear was concerned in his lamentations, but a meer compliance with his duty on such occasions, and adding that he himself had several times made a caravan from Bagdat to Aleppo which had not consisted of above thirty loads, which, says he, may demonstrate that my fears are not extraordinary. But to me it seems that rather the dangers of the desart are not so considerable as commonly imagined, for these people in general we know full well are far from remarkable in exposing either their persons or fortunes.

This man acquainted me that the best way for a merchant to transport his goods, supposing it don't suit him to wait at Bassora for a general caravan, is sending by the river to Bagdat, which may be done in about thirty days, and his person and baggage in ten or twelve; from whence he proceeds to Cobiesse, and then very safely to Aleppo by the same road that we came. But however easy such a transportation of merchandize may be to one of the country, I am persuaded that a stranger to the language, likewise the custom and manner of conducting such undertaking would experience insurmountable difficulties, and [as?] to procuring a person capable of acting for him, the risk of imposition would thereby become greater. Wherefore, as to myself, if I had merchandize to transport from either place to the other, they should always go by the general caravan, and would personally proceed as before mentioned.

The country from Cobiesse to this place we have found in general much pleasanter than before; a greater plenty of water, and the ground covered thicker with shrubs, of which latter there is upon some spots great variety, and from some I gathered seeds, two whereof are particularly curious and worth travellers notice, the one a kind of thistle and most beautiful plant imaginable, the other a sort of gourd resembling a small water melon[1], and smells when cut exactly the same, but the taste extremely bitter, and the Arabs say is infallible for curing the flux.

27th. We remained here all the morning, and then mounted. Our course about S.E. Little wind and hot. The country very barren. We encamped at sunset. The night very hot.

28th. Set out about four, and at noon came where upon a rising was a tower, seemingly the remains of a larger building designed for defence[2]. Here we baited and proceeded on our journey till sunset. Course today much the same. A fresh northerly breeze, and heat not very fatiguing. The country uneven, sandy and full of loose stones; and what is very particular, these stones, which lie very thick on the ground, are for some miles all of a colour, then for some miles all of another; and those I observed were one sort very black, another sort iron colour, and others of a deep orange colour, all of which are extremely ponderous and hard. In other places these stones are all white, and upon some spots

[1] The 'colocynth' gourd (*Citrullus colocynthus* Tristram), exclusively confined to the most arid deserts, and growing best in rainless years. The pulp, when dried, forms a powder—a drastic and efficient purge. Doughty says that 'little indeed and even the leaf is a most vehement purgative; they say it will leave a man half dead,' but the goat, the ass, the porcupine, will eat greedily of it.

[2] I cannot identify this, but it was probably Qasr Ruhaima.

are most of them chrystaline and sometimes gathered for cutting into ornaments. I picked up some, and amongst them one about the bigness of a pigeons egg which a jeweller in Bengal[1] assured me was harder than any pebble he had ever seen.

We saw today smoke at a distance ascending in several places, which they told us was from habitations on the river side, and this day the dome of Meched Ali was yet in sight, which appeared on the hill like a globe of fire[2].

29th. Departed at five. Course somewhat to eastward of S.E. Country and wind much the same. At noon baited as customary, and finished our days journey about sunset. Found pits of bad water today twice, and passed the night indifferently well.

30th. Mounted this morning at five, and in our way discovered an empty camel, which many of the Arabs immediately pursued with the utmost speed, being wholly the property of him who first reaches the prize. We baited at noon near some pits of very bad water, and ended our stage about six. The days course more easterly than usual. The country more level, and somewhat more better provided with food for the camels. Wind northerly and excessive hot, but the night more temperate.

31st. Set out this morning at four and baiting as usual ended our stage in the evening. Wind, weather and country near the same. Our situation here was near the ruins of a large fortress[3], and the water better tasted than any we had for many days past. And is what we have experienced at all such places in the desart, that the water is there better and in greater plenty than ordinary elsewhere; which occasions me to imagine that the fortified structures were either erected and maintained by merchants whose commerce required their passing that way to secure themselves water, as without such certainty the journey would be impracticable, or else by the Arabs of the desart in their defence against each other,

[1] For 'in' read 'of,' for the account was written at Basra.
[2] See p. 167.
[3] Probably Rahba [Rahaba].

or (which I think most likely) in order to extort from travellers an acknowledgment for being supplied; which appears yet more probable, as the pits of water now found so frequently throughout the journey are certainly of much later date than the above mentioned buildings, and sometimes a very little way from them, and it may therefore be well supposed were dug to avoid the difficulty or expence of being otherwise supplied; and which remedying the evil those fabricks lost the benefit and consequently went to decay.

Sept. 1*st*. We got under way at four, and travelling through hills of sand till ten we encamped in the midst of several [severe?] and continued roasting till noon, when we proceeded thro' the like country till five, and rested. Little wind today and excessive hot. Course much the same. About eight this evening we again loaded and travelled till midnight. No want of water.

Sept. 2*nd*. Mounted at five, and baiting at noon ended our days stage before five. Course the same. Country level, but sandy and bare. The weather very hot, and we have had the whole day a strong N.E. wind, which raised such thick clouds of fine sand as almost blinded and suffocated us. The air was so charged with dust that the guides could hardly perceive the way, and the sun was as red as scarlet; which together with the melancholy of the desart, and the fatigue both men and beasts appeared to labour under, I thought exhibited the saddest scene imaginable. We saw this afternoon at a distance a pyrimidical structure and the ruins of other buildings; which the Arabs gave us to understand was formerly a place of no small account[1].

This evening Sey'd Mahmud, the principal Shaik of the Arabs, paid us a visit, which he told us was to enquire if we had passed the journey with satisfaction, whether any of the

[1] He does not say on which hand, but caravans usually viewed to the westward the first fortified stations on the Darb Zobeida—such as the Minarat el Qurun; see p. 169. But if it were to the east of his route it might have been the same as Taylor's 'Spire marking the watering of Eyn-el-Gyan,' *i.e.* Qaim, 9 miles W. of Shinafiya. At the moment Beawes' position must have been somewhere between the two landmarks.

Arabs had presumed to offer us any offensive language, or otherwise disgust us, and particularly if our conductor had complied with his obligation, being sensible of the hospitable regard that is due to strangers, and had himself been watchful of our welfare; to which fine speech we answered that nothing had been amiss and expressed ourselves infinitely obliged for the attention and care his example had procured us from the Arabs. But the good Shaick seemed little pleased at the bare exchange of compliments, and manifested that he expected a more substantial acknowledgment; which being told us by Hodgee Saluk, we replied, as to demands we were subject to none, and if a present only was meant, that such depended on our generosity, which we should not submit to any regulation but our own will and pleasure; tho' herein we were deceived, as hereafter will appear.

I enquired upon this occasion of the Shaick (who is a noted desart traveller) concerning the different rout[e]s, who informed me that from Bassora to Aleppo there are three different, the one of which they don't touch either at Meched Ali or Cobiesse but strike more exactly across[1], which makes the journey some days shorter, he himself having performed it in 25[2] days; but in the dry season water is there scarce and at all times the common way or tract is what we came, unless any impediments to or from the desart tribes, or otherwise, obliges them to alter their course. As to the ways upon the rivers side, where towns are frequent and consequently good water and other refreshments are never wanting, this agreeable rout[e] he said was impracticable, the imposition of the Turks and other inhabitants along the banks, both to the merchant and cameleer, would be insupportable. The other route of the desart for caravans is that from Damascus to Bagdat or Bassora[3], exclusive of that which goes yearly and

[1] The track usually followed by native riders and such travellers who went with their own outfit, unattached to a caravan, such as Chesney in 1837. Niebuhr records an even more direct route; see *Voyage en Arabie*, etc., 1780, vol. II, p. 194.

[2] Plaisted spent only 24 days actual travelling.

[3] We have no record of caravans passing direct between Damascus and Baghdad. We only know of the 'Desert Post' between the two centres, which was kept up until early in the twentieth century.

precisely from Aleppo to Mecha, which is more properly the holy pilgrimage of Damascus, as these of Aleppo and other parts of the Turks are obliged to meet there and prosecute jointly the performance of the said duty.

As to the desart tribes their tracts throughout the waste and into both the other Arabias, the Happy and the Stony, are innumerable.

I enquired further after the camels, of whose abiding so long without food such strange reports are common, and was informed that they suck between two and three years and arrive at full strength at seven, continuing vigorous according to the labour they endure, but generally till thirty; and as to their enduring the want of food, they say that if for experiment only it should be tried how long they would live without sustenance, it might be found that their strength therein is superior many days to any other animal, but far short of thirty odd days as commonly believed; and as to ordinary observations amongst the Arabs, it is certain that a loaded camel having passed three days without food complains grievously; the fourth day he will trip frequently, and the fifth is not able to proceed, nor will he hold out so long without absolutely anything. But what renders these animals seemingly adapted for the desart by Providence, and may have given rise to fables concerning them, is that upon desart journeys nothing is provided for their subsistance, and moreover whatever they meet, even the dryest brush, is food for them, and having dry food, tho' of such sort, they will endure many days that want of water, and finally having water they will march a long time with very little food[1].

We proceeded again this evening till midnight, which manner of travelling we find very fatiguing, and am surprised the Arabs themselves can endure it; but they are certainly in many respects so very like their camels, that Providence seems to have equally designed them for the desart. I have observed them to walk and work all day, watch at night, and

[1] Camels can go without water for long periods, but *not* without food, nor is there any reason so to drive the 'cattle' on empty bellies, for the desert is seldom without camel food of sorts.

repeat their labour next day without any sign of fatigue, and have likewise remarked that, like unto their beasts, when food and water have been plenty their chops were never still, but can in proportion to their strength go as long without either.

We saw tonight two or three scorpions very large and black, which are the worst sort and their stings are dangerous; but this is the only time throughout the journey that any have appeared, nor have we seen a snake but once, tho' said to be common. As to the other animals we found only hares (which in some places are plenty) and lately a small creature called a Jabous[1], whose body, size, and shape is most like a ground rat, but the head rounder and eyes very large and protuberant. The tail is long and has a bush at the end; but the greatest singularity of this animal is his legs, the fore ones not exceeding two inches and those behind are above eight, which enables him to proceed forward with incredible celerity.

Sept. 3rd. We mounted this morning early, and a few hours after passed by a tribe of Arabs under their tents, which occasioned our caravan to travel close and with their arms in readiness, being, as they told us, necessary, tho' the others were professedly friends. These wanderers of the desart remain sometimes on or near one spot for a whole season, and these cultivate gourds, cucumbers and such like vegetables; and the remains of these miserable plantations we met with three or four times in our journey.

We baited about noon, and proceeded till five. Course more easterly. The country level, sandy and bare. The wind blowing strong at N.W. was equally troublesome as before mentioned, and in so much that I declare for my own part I had much rather undergo again the whole fatigue we otherwise endured in the passage than such another day; but with the setting of the sun the wind abated and we passed the evening tolerably well till about nine, when we again loaded and travelled four hours farther.

[1] *Jaculus Loftusi* is the common jerboa of the region, but the large five-toed *Alactaga* is also found in the Syrian Desert towards Palmyra.

Sept. 4th. Set out at five and in a few hours came to a village[1], where we rested some time and then proceeded. Arrived in the afternoon at another called Izbiz[2], two hours and a half from Bassora. We had all day the same N.W. wind and equally troublesome. Here the caravan remained, and the merchants are not allowed to remove their effects till all demands from the Shaiks &c. are satisfied, which commonly requires some days; and we were not suffered to carry with us to Bassora the least part of our baggage, because we refused to pay the dues for our loads as if they were merchandize, which now they insist shall be considered upon the same footing, but we resolving to maintain the contrary left our things to the servants care, and having horses sent us by the English chief at Bassora, Thos. Dorrell Esqr., we mounted and arrived there in the evening, where that gentleman was pleased to receive us with the utmost civility and a hearty welcome.

The passage from Meched Ali to this place is in all respects the worst part of all the journey; the country exceeding bare and sandy; the weather hotter and water tho' frequent very brackish, and foul in most places, which often disorder our bowels and occasion severe sickness of the stomach.

According to the foregoing journal the direct course from [Aleppo?] should be about [*blank*], and the distance I reckon as follows, viz.:

From Aleppo to Ain il Kom, about	80 miles.
From thence to where we saw [the] river, about	90 "
From that place to Cobiesse, about	85 "
From thence to Meched Ali, about	110 "
From thence to Bassora, about	180 "

But this account is far from pretending to exactness; for as to the course, the irregular march of the caravan does not admit thereof, and the best means I had to judge of the distance was remarking the camels pace and their continual traverses, as food &c. inclined them, from whence I make

[1] Probably Kuwaibda. [2] Zubair.

account that in twelve hours travelling we proceed on our way about 20 English miles, and having travelled 327 hours the amount of distance will be as aforesaid 545 miles[1].

The pretensions before mentioned of the Arabs relating to our baggage we at last complied with, not only to avoid troubling the Government with trifles and most likely to no purpose, but also in attention to their plea of having made it their constant study throughout the journey to merit our favour; that [we] were answerable for the desart duties upon every freighted camel without regard to the quality of the load, and that finally we were witnesses how very hard what came to them was earned; and so we paid fifty odd dollars, besides some presents, which rendered them entirely satisfied and thankful. And having here particularly enquired concerning this matter, was informed by some that the demand had been contrary to custom, which exempted whatever was not merchandize from the common fees, and that only a small present was usual; but others declared the contrary and that the Arabs had rather been favourable in their demands than otherwise. However any dispute of this sort may easily be excused by adjusting the affair before the journey, I mean such who have many loads to transport; for as to a mean traveller, the difference can hardly ever be worth disputing, and as it is certain the Arabs are far from exorbitant in their demands or difficult to satisfy, it seems becoming every traveller, as well in gratitude for his own treatment as attention to the welfare of those that follow, to render by ample gratification the hospitable behaviour of the Arabs to strangers as agreeable to their interest as their duty.

We found no English vessels here or any other but a Dutch ship from Batavia, nor have the caravans such regard to the seasons of shipping as I imagined, being here informed their setting out is far from depending upon the will of the merchants, but entirely upon the pleasure of the Bashaw of Bagdat and the agreement of the principal tribes of Arabs; who having adjusted the desart fees and the number of their

[1] Beawes underestimated the distance; it is actually about 780 miles by his route between Aleppo and Basra.

respective people that shall be employed, they nominate each Shaick who governs the caravan to collect them; which manner of conducting the affair renders this road to Aleppo commonly more secure than any other, tho' not so safe, however, as to make unnecessary their going well provided with arms and ammunition, it being impossible to adjust with all the wanderers of the desart; nor do they think it worth while. But altho' the lesser tribes are generally awed by the greater, yet opposition sometimes happens, and whole caravans are plundered, as was the last year's [caravan] from Damascus to Bagdat; and such disasters may occur from either unforeseen difference, secret malice amongst the Arab tribes themselves, or the revenge of some particular tribe for injuries received from the Turks, which not long since provoked them to draw such a force upon this place as was expected would have sacked the town; and now lately the Bashaw's troops have so unmercifully dealt with these people that almost any revenge would be excusable.

There are two sorts of caravans that go from hence to Aleppo, the one consisting of camels only for sale and the other for merchandize, the former yearly, and generally constant with respect to time[1], whose permission is easily obtained, and tho' their carrying goods is prohibited, they so manage as never to go without. As to the latter, their setting out is not so certain, having difficulties to encounter, nor are they confined to any time, but merchants solicit license as occasions occur, and who now offer the Bashaw to pay him for permission the whole sum his duties would amount to, if they went by the way of Bagdat and Mosul, but are refused shipping bound from hence directly to Bengall or the coast of Cormandel. The utmost they ought to remain is July, least they should be retarded in their passage and not get round Ceylon before the N.W. monsoon; and if they have business at Surat they should be gone from hence in February at farthest, as lying in Surat Road becomes dangerous after the month of April. Wherefore a traveller bound to the farthest side of India ought to be here in

[1] Plaisted says mid-April to mid-June. Eliot says May or June.

December; he may be sure of his passage in a Bengall or Madras ship, or else to Bombay or Surat, and there find occasions enough to pursue his voyage.

The violent heats common to this place in summer are now upon decline, tho' still very uneasy and especially the night, which often reminds us how much better we passed them in the desart. The wind that brings extraordinary heat to this place is that they call Sherigi[1] or Southerly, and the cool refreshing wind Shimal[2] or Northwesterly wind; but of this latter are nevertheless those pernicious blasts or gusts in Arab Semeil[3], which begin in July and last 40 days, the danger whereof is well known about Bagdat and also in other places, but here it seems they never reach, nor to any part of the desart, because, they say, the river runs between, which as they pass entirely prevents their mischief, and that being upon the water is a certain security against them, tho' going a very little way from it on that side from whence they blow is attended with risque. Concerning which and how fatal these blasts are frequently to travellers, a Bagdat merchant assured me with instances to which he was an eyewitness. One whereof was, being upon the river in the season a Jew of the company, contrary to the persuasions of his fellow travellers, who repeatedly cautioned him of the hazard, walked up a small distance from the banks and in less than half an hour was brought back suffocated. The other instance he mentioned was a caravan that set out from Bagdat for Mosul in this perillous season of the year, of which in one day above one third were destroyed. These winds, he told me, seldom did any harm within the said city, because of the water about it, but few care to venture out that are able by remaining within to avoid the danger.

The Arabs it seems are not so apprehensive of those blasts, pretending, as I am assured, to perceive the approaching evil in time to guard against it by falling flat on their faces and covering close till the danger is past; and

[1] Sharqi: the south wind.
[2] Shimal: the north wind.
[3] Semail. Parsons gives a good description of this hot wind; *op. cit.* p. 93.

having enquired by what appearance [it] is given notice of, I find they pretend that bluish streams are seen in the air at some distance advancing, which always they say accompany the Semeil and are what infallibly suffocates, unless by the precaution mentioned they can be avoided; but if this was true, methinks the hint would be equally perceptible to others as the Arabs, and the pretended means of security as easily practised. However, their account is not altogether unnatural, for that sulpher does the mischief is highly probable and that the whole Semeil is not charged, from some in a company being destroyed thereby, whilst others remain unhurt; but that such sulpher is so apparent in bluish streams as to be a timely notice for providing against, or that any other hints precede the mischief so as to render it evitable, I am not inclinable to believe, at least that such previous notices are constant, for in such case the Semeil wind would be little more dangerous than any other, which is contradicted by the fatal accidents that have frequently happened to travellers, who, exposing themselves in such a season, can hardly be supposed to have suffered by either their ignorance or negligence of what so nearly concern their welfare; and as to their falling to the ground and covering when the danger arrives, it seems a good expedient, because a man may escape the first attack, and yet perish by longer continuing exposed.

The description of Bassora and the remarks occuring to me during my residence are elsewhere mentioned, wherefore, notwithstanding that paper has many uses and consequently the greater quality [quantity?] I presented my friends might be most esteemed, yet I beg leave to omit the repetition and should here conclude; but considering the universal weakness of a traveller is caring to manifest a peculiar capacity for judging of men and things, and the world commonly good natured enough to indulge them therein, I think myself obliged to behave in character, and ere I finish, express a due share of folly by making some remarks upon my fellow land leapers [adventurers or vagabonds], with whom I had occasion to be so long acquainted.

And first, their hospitality, with all imaginable care for

our welfare, a due respect in behaviour, a chearful readiness on all occasions to assist our servants, and lastly a faithful care of our baggage may be deemed as such. We have certainly the utmost reason to acknowledge that this virtue is possessed by the Arabs in the highest degree, and tho' it should be objected that what is here mentioned, their interest and fears might engage them to perform, and not any real attention to the rectitude and seemingly such a conduct, the supposition may be allowed without any deviation from the above character; for who is ignorant that in every other part of the world as the desarts of Arabia, fear is a natural curb to insolence and interest the common motive of respect? But yet there is [such?] a thing as hospitality, and infinitely more in my opinion amongst the Arabs than much politer people. And moreover it appears to me that whatever civility and security is to be purchased by strangers at the current price and an easy rate, such people should be esteemed hospitable and worthy the greatest commendation and particularly as the country [contrary?] is so often experienced and even without leaving Europe.

The Arabs are of Mahometans the most superstitious, exceeding greatly in formality and especially the punctual compliance with the set time of prayer, and almost incessant calling upon God and their Prophet; which being according to general observations a common practice with the worst of men, there is little reason doubtless to imagine such behaviour of the Arabs any indication of their probity; but considering that neither is excess in devotion an infallible token for deceit, and also the small share of knowledge acquirable by these people, I think their behaviour herein may be imputed to simplicity than, as by some, entirely hypocrisy.

These Arabs of the desart are particularly strict in abstaining from all intoxicating liquors; which whether a virtue or a weakness I leave to the judgment of others, but am certain every Christian traveller this way will note the forbearance, as thereby their stores of that sort are always secure. To this laudable scruple of the Arabs may also in some measure be attributed the grave and ceremonious regard that is observed amongst them, and exceeding few squabbles that happen, for they seem to be naturally a timorous people and more inclined to secret revenge than publick resentment. Yet if carousing was practised as elsewhere, we may reasonably suppose that rude, contentious, and noisy wranglings would be equally the effects; which I believe but rarely occurs, because I do not remember any in the whole journey. These people endure hardships with the least apparent concern or manifestation of fatigue of any perhaps in the universe; they are no more sensible of heat than if they were natives of the sun, and breathe the dusty medium free as the purest air; the forlorn waste that strikes a melancholy upon the minds of others affords to them delight beyond the gayest scenes, and it is certain that in all respects the Divine goodness seems in pity to have adapted their minds and bodies seemingly to their situation, as what appears to any besides a wretched condition is enjoyed by them with satisfaction.

They are excessively fond of money, and it may reasonably be supposed have great sums amongst them, their income being considerable from the produce particularly of camels and dates about Bassora; of which former came last year for sale to Aleppo eleven thousand, and of the latter, besides home and inland consumption, a considerable number of embarkation [*sic*] are yearly loaded therewith. And moreover their cattle and labour are no small articles of profit, and except by the extortions of the Turks, but little of these gains is returned. For as to apparel, the poor are content with a coarse manufactory of their own, and the richer are far from being extravagant, either in dress or any other ornament; and for food they are beholden to none but Providence and their industry, their delicacies being few, and what we deem luxury is in any shape a stranger to the desart inhabitants of the borders; whereof [wherefore?] with what view or whence proceeds so anxious a desire in them for wealth seems hard to determine, but we are to consider that the Arabs, like other people, covet ease and security, and moreover are fond of power and rising above the multitude, nothing of which is attainable without money. Nor are the distinguishing characters amongst them seemingly more than those of holy, rich and powerful, so that no wonder if those people in general express a greater eagerness in the pursuit of riches than those who abound in variety of characters to illustrate the desired superiority and that are procurable by species of merit, industry, policy and address, neither known nor practicable by the Arabs.

The greatest unhappiness of the Arabians immediately under the Ottoman tyranny is their disagreement amongst themselves; for were they united, such union would not only secure them from the insults of the Turks (with whom some or other are continually at variance), but render them a powerful people, and having the desart for a retreat might cultivate the borders, and vend their camels, cattle &c., exempt from the extortion and impositions they are now continually exposed to; for should any force be then too hard for them, their retreat might defy the Turks following them, and when safe, to come back might convince their enemies, by ravaging in turn, that to be agressors was neither politick nor profitable; whereas at present the Turks have not only reduced the wretches within their reach to the utmost misery, but constantly play the different tribes and petty bodies one against another to their utter destruction, who are nevertheless so infatuated as to be at continual variance amongst themselves, perpetually plundering and harrassing one another, and even value themselves alternately upon the common enemy to dispose and constitute a Shaick or ruler, whenever the discontended parties have not sufficient strength of their own.

But concerning this matter, I shall not presume to add. The Arabian politician is burlesque distinction [*sic*], I should unwillingly incur, nor am more desirous that the few particulars I have mentioned of the Arabs should be deemed an attempt to draw the character of a people from a months acquaintance, being sensible that such is ridiculous, and that men of infinitely superior discernment and experience have long since described the Arabs at large. But as by some means [*sic*] those descriptions where almost every inhumanity is laid to their charge, a traveller may to his disadvantage be deterred from passing the desart, or executes the journey with unnecessary suspicions and consequently uneasiness, I have thought it not amiss to declare the foregoing, and in gratitude to witness that, however barbarous the real character of these people may be or have been discovered from better occasions of knowing them, a man may travel a great way in their company without one instance to confirm it.

As the expences of this journey may be to some useful, I have hereunto annexed the account[1], and which concludes a journal as barren, I am sensible, of anything entertaining as the way it describes. But this is universally known so very common to such performances that I should be particularly impertinent to offer at apologizing for a defect which much the greater part of our voyaging fraternity consider as foreign to their obligations, wherefore shall only say that the foregoing relation is according to a general rule, and however incorrect, confide will be accepted as an expression of thankfulness for the many favours bestowed on me by the English gentlemen at Aleppo, to whom it is humbly presented, and I particularly desire may be acceptable.

Bassora, 2nd December 1745.

WILLIAM BEAWES.

[1] Not in the India Office copy.

§ II

ACCOUNT OF A JOURNEY FROM *BASRA* TO *ALEPPO* IN 1748

by

GAYLARD ROBERTS

PREFATORY NOTE

THE letter here printed for the first time is taken from a transcript in the Orme MSS. (India Office Library). It is found in the same volume as the narrative of Beawes, and the remarks made in the prefatory note to that section apply generally to this also.

Of Roberts himself little is known. His name occurs in some lists preserved at the India Office of the European inhabitants of Madras (1744–6). He was not in the East India Company's service, but was included among 'supercargoes and pursers' carrying on private trade. On 21 November 1744 the Court of Directors gave permission to Gaylard Roberts to go to his father, Captain Gaylard Roberts, at Madras, in order to be brought up in the seafaring way. Apparently both father and son were returning to England together when the journey now described was made; and it is evident from the account that the author was the father. It appears that Roberts had other companions on the journey, to whom he does not allude (he barely mentions his own son). Amongst them was a Mr Monro (see Plaisted, *infra*, p. 98). Now Munro (as it should be spelt) we know of from Alexander Drummond, who was travelling in Northern Syria at that date. When at Aleppo, he records that 'I had the pleasure of seeing Mr. Munro of Culcairn[1], who came from India'; and again 'Mr. Munro and some other gentlemen from India, coming through the Desart of Arabia' (*Travels through different Cities...and several parts of Asia*, etc., p. 239).

1 'John Munro, Esquire, of Cullcarn, late of Bombay' was one of the executors of the will (11 August 1757) of Andrew Munro, surgeon at Madras (Love's *Vestiges of Old Madras*, vol. II, p. 459). He had been on the Company's civil establishment at Bombay, commencing as a writer in January 1731 and ending as Third Member of Council in 1748.

MR. ROBERTS LETTER GIVING AN ACCOUNT OF HIS JOURNEY OVER THE DESART OF *ARABIA* IN HIS WAY TO *ENGLAND*

Aleppo, 1st *August* 1748.

Dear Sir,

The enclosed is a copy of the last I sent you. Since which I set out with the caravan from Bassora June 11th, arrived here the 16th ult., where I have received my principal and respondentia for the goods I advised you I had sold. I intended to have kept a journal of our passage hither, but was so excessive hot for the first four or five days that I expected to be transported to the other world, but they shaped their course another way (more northerly); we found the weather mend every day very sensibly. Near all that has been wrote by those who have journalized this way, has been that they set out such an hour in the morning, pitched their tents such an hour in the evening, that the ground was stony, or uneven, in some places gravel, sand, or level in others, that they met with pretty good water in some places, bad in others, and often get hares or antelopes, which the Arabs knock down with their sticks. This indeed is the greatest part of what a man can write of with any certainty who keeps a journal. A few have attempted to describe some exceeding grand buildings which we pass on the desart. But as it would require at least a month's time to take a survey of them to describe them truly, and as the caravan moving forward will not allow a man to do more than take a cursory view of them, all the attempts I have yet seen of those descriptions have been very imperfect. A palace[1] about midway between Bussora and Aleppo is the most solid and grand I believe of any in the world; but there is no taste or eloquence in it, nor

[1] This probably refers to Ukhaidir. He would see nothing else so 'solid and grand' as this structure anywhere on his route. It is actually 300 miles from Basra and 450 from Aleppo.

can the Arabs give the least account who built it or by whom it was inhabited, for as our companions were mostly of the wild sort, who live not in houses, the grandest structure they meet with seems to have no more effect on their curiosity than on the creatures they drive.

Palmera, a palace situated in a most delightful and spacious plain about four days from this place, has its walls of the finest free stone, and the best wrought I ever saw[1], and has been decorated with columns and cut capitals of the Corinthian order, with the entablature compleat, and many well turned arches; but as the former edifice was one fourth ruined, so was the latter three fourths ruined.

We past over a vast variety of country, some of it exceeding good soil, with some of the noblest and pleasantest valleys I ever saw, terminated with hills of easy ascents and not high; all which have been formerly well inhabited, but have been laid waste by the tyranny of their governments and the pilfering disposition of the worst of people (I believe) on earth, who have been rambling about in large herds for ages past, and still continue to plunder and destroy each other.

It would be worth no man's while to attempt this passage from Bengall unless he has a prospect of getting to Bassora the beginning [*blank*], as the caravan generally sets out from that time to the beginning of June[2], and if you get there after the caravan is gone, you lose the advantage of letting out your money on respondentia, for which they often give

[1] One would conclude from this that Roberts, at any rate, viewed Palmyra from a distance. But Plaisted, who chanced to have the same Arab servant as Roberts, was assured by him that Roberts had gone no further than Taiyibe (see Plaisted's narrative, 18 July; Taylor repeats this, pp. 229–30). Alexander Drummond, who was travelling in Northern Syria at that time, and was afterwards (1754–6) Consul at Aleppo, confirms this point. He says that 'Mr Munro, and some other gentlemen from India [Roberts was one of them; see p. 98] coming through the Desart of Arabia, passed by the ruins of Teybeh, or Tiera, as named by the Romans, *mistaking it for Palmyra*, which is but a little way distant from it.' It is interesting, but no proof of identity, that a 'William Robt' cut his name on the stones of Taiyibe (see Rousseau, *op. cit.* p. 155).

[2] Plaisted, on the other hand, says the 'Camel' caravans leave from mid-April to mid-June, but the 'Merchants' caravans await the arrival of ships from India, usually early in June, and the caravans leave accordingly about mid-July.

18 to 20 per cent, tho' you lose 10 per cent in remitting your money home by the lowness of the exchange here. But should the caravan be departed before your arrival at Bassora, you must proceed by way of Bagdat, where you will be plundered by the men in power at most places you come to, and is much more expensive than with the caravan, tho' it cost me for bare necessaries for myself and son from Bassora to Aleppo 1600 rupees; and amounts to full 2½ rupees per mile: a rate of travelling by far I believe the most extravagantly dear of any in the world. So that unless one has a fair appearance of getting well by goods he may bring to Bassora, which is hard to be depended upon, it seems by no ways adviseable to come this way. There is no other advice I can think of necessary to a person who attempts this passage, but that he ought to allow himself a bottle of sour shrub for punch and one bottle of wine a day, and to bring with him ten bottles of orange juice, very strong iron bound chests big enough to stow four dozen bottles in each, two of which make a camels load, 20 or 30 fowls in a strong coop well covered to screen them from the sun, to see they have meat and water given them at 11 every morning, and to recruit at Mushadali[1] what more you may want for the rest of the journey, as nothing is to be had beyond that place till you get hither. A few sheep may also be bought, each be put in a bag and stowed upon the chests. Hares (and mostly very good) you will meet with in great plenty. A good quantity of ghee[2] must be laid in; a few Bassora tongues; but pigeons and mutton we potted a good quantity, which the excessive heat spoiled in four or five days, and with them we lost a good part of our ghee. Cooks, bottles, rack, wine, and chests are not to be procured in Bassora, so that those you must bring with you. We rode on horses or mules from the time of setting out in the morning till ten and then going into the Kedgwa[3] (which are boxes to sit in on the camel with an awning over them) for the rest of the day, it afforded an agreeable variety of motion. I should advise

[1] Meshed Ali. [2] Indian butter.
[3] *Kajawa* (Persian), same as Beawes' *mihaffa* (Arabic). See p. 9.

the getting of good large Bassora asses to ride on in the mornings; which have an easy motion and cost but little, whereas they will not give here above one half what a horse or a mule cost at Bassora. The heat begins every day at eleven in the morning and continues till five in the afternoon; the rest of the time the air is delightful. Should you bring any bale goods with you, let them weigh 260 to 270 pounds each bale; which may save you the trouble and charge of repacking them, if you should find it advisable to bring them hither, for want of a good sale at Bassora, two such making a camel load. This is all I can think of concerning this affair that can deserve your attention, only that you ought always to have a servant by when they unload your liquor chests, to prevent their letting them go at once from the camels back like a bale, which will soon put an end to your store of liquor. Your packet for your uncle left Constantinople six weeks since, and I doubt not but is in [his?] hands before this. If any of our friends desire a sight or copy of this, please to let them have it. We are going to Cyprus to meet some French ship to carry us to Marseilles, from whence we may hope soon to get home.

Since writing the above we have taken our passage on a Dutch ship directly for England, who sails in a few days.

And am, Dear Sir, Your faithful
and most humble servant,

GAYLARD ROBERTS.

§ III

NARRATIVE OF A JOURNEY FROM *BASRA* TO *ALEPPO* IN 1750

by

BARTHOLOMEW PLAISTED

PREFATORY NOTE

PLAISTED first appears in the East India Company's records towards the end of 1740, when the Court of Directors granted his petition for leave to go to Bengal 'to get his livelyhood in the seafaring way there' (*Court Minutes*, 7 Nov. and 3 Dec. 1740). This means that he hoped to obtain the command of a vessel engaged in the local trade permitted to the Company's servants, and implies some experience in navigation. Later (1747) he declared that he had been at Genoa, Leghorn, Messina, etc.; so probably he had already made one or more voyages to the Mediterranean. Further, his assertion in 1748 that he 'was regularly brought up and educated in fortification and gunnery,' including apparently the elements of surveying, suggests that he had had some military training. And this is all we know of his earlier life.

His career in India may be traced in some detail with the aid of the extracts from official records given in Dr C. R. Wilson's *Old Fort William* (Indian Records Series, 1906). In July 1742 he assisted in surveying Calcutta with a view to putting it in a better state of defence; and on the death (July 1745) of the regular surveyor Plaisted was appointed to the vacant post. He was at that time captain and supercargo of a vessel named the *Kent*. A short experience of his new duties showed that the emoluments were far less than those to be earned at sea, and he accordingly resigned and took the command of the *Northesk*, belonging to the Governor (John Forster). Just as he was about to sail, however, news arrived (Sept. 1746) that Madras had been captured by the French; while at the same time came a message from Commodore Griffin, urging that Calcutta should be put into a posture to resist hostile attacks. Thereupon Forster prevailed upon Plaisted to give up the voyage and stay on shore as Engineer and Surveyor. To this post he was appointed early in 1747; and in February he produced a plan for strengthening Fort William by adding four bastions and digging a broad moat. Had his advice been followed, in all probability there would have been no Black Hole disaster nine years later, with its momentous consequences; but the scheme involved a sacrifice of private interests, and so it was rejected in favour of another by which a palisade was erected round the settlement, at a great cost and with little result. Plaisted had a quick temper and a rough tongue; and the animosities engendered by the dispute led to his being turned out of his post in the middle of 1748 in a peculiarly irritating manner. His opponents declared that he had never been regularly appointed, and they prevailed upon the Council to ignore him and appoint another man to the post. There was by this time a new Governor (William Barwell), who may have been unfriendly to Plaisted; but this is merely a matter of surmise.

Plaisted was not the man to endure calmly what he considered to be an undeserved wrong. As soon as he had finished the survey of Calcutta on which he was then engaged, he sent in (Dec. 1748) an indignant protest to the Governor, hinting an intention of proceeding to England to lay his grievances before the Directors. He seems to have lingered for a while, in the hope that he would be reinstated; but at last, on 27 September 1749, he applied for permission to return to England. This was granted, and the result was the journey now described.

Plaisted left Calcutta on 30 November 1749, passed Ceylon and arrived at Gombroon (Bandar Abbas), where the English and Dutch had factories. Here he considered travelling by way of *Spahawn* [Ispahan] in order to see, en route, Persepolis, and take a 'draught of the Ruins of a Place so celebrated by ancient Historians.' But he found this altogether impracticable, for although 'Shah Rook [Rukh] had been seated on the throne for nearly 15 months past, yet the whole Kingdom had not been reduced to his obedience.' As a matter of fact Persia was at that moment in the throes of the turmoil which followed the assassination of Nadir Shah. Plaisted observes 'It is easy to concieve what dreadful confusion reigned throughout the whole kingdom during these changes and revolutions, and therefore it will be deemed downright madness to have attempted to travel through the country at this time.' He therefore left Bandar Abbas in a native craft, and finally landed at Basra on 20 April 1750.

Aleppo was reached on 23 July. While awaiting an opportunity to resume his journey, Plaisted wrote, from Beilan, the hill resort above Alexandretta, on 6 August, a letter to Calcutta, to his friend Roger Drake (afterwards Governor of Fort William), describing his experiences in the desert. An incomplete copy of this document has been preserved among the Orme MSS. in the India Office Library, in the volume containing the narratives of Beawes and Roberts; but, since it adds nothing of importance to the printed account, it has not been reproduced here.

Plaisted embarked at Scanderoon (Alexandretta) on 11 August in a French ship bound for Marseilles, which was reached on 9 October, after calling at Cyprus, Rhodes, and Sardinia. From thence he proceeded by way of Lyons to Paris. After visiting Versailles, he resumed his journey to Boulogne, where, for a guinea, he got a passage to Dover, and arrived in London on 24 November 1750—nearly a year after leaving Calcutta.

Once in London, Plaisted had little difficulty in convincing the Directors that he had been badly treated. He seems, moreover, to have revealed to them some of the abuses prevalent in Calcutta and to have presented a plan for preventing these. The result was that he was sent back to Bengal early in 1752, and the Directors wrote censuring his dismissal and praising him as 'an honest, capable man.' However, they had recently dispatched Benjamin Robins to India as Engineer-General, and could not, therefore, order the reinstatement of Plaisted in his old post; but they expressed a hope that Robins would find a way of employing him, failing which, the Bengal Council were to provide for him in some other station, though not as a covenanted servant.

On arrival in Bengal, Plaisted found that Robins was dead,

and the way was thus cleared for his re-appointment as Engineer and Surveyor. This was accordingly done in September 1752. However, his quarrelsome disposition at once got him into fresh trouble. An altercation with a Mr William MacGwire, who accused Plaisted of maligning him to the Directors, ended in a scuffle during which the latter received a wound that laid him up for several months. His assailant was tried, and pleaded guilty; but the court evidently blamed Plaisted for the fracas, for MacGwire was only reprimanded and fined; while the Council declared to the Directors that he had acted under extreme provocation.

After a year's tenure of his post, Plaisted was dispossessed of it by the arrival of Colonel Scott, whom the Directors had appointed Engineer-General of all their Indian settlements. They were not, however, entirely unmindful of Plaisted, for in January 1754 they sent out instructions that he was to succeed to the post of Master Attendant at Calcutta on the next vacancy. This did not occur until November 1755, when he was duly installed in that office. Three weeks later he was suspended by the Council for insubordination, his offence being that he had forwarded to that body two violently worded memorials for transmission to the Directors, probably containing complaints of the treatment he had received. Thereupon he decided to go home once again; and upon his application a passage was provided for him in the *London*, which reached England in November 1756. MacGwire proceeded to England likewise, in order to defend himself against Plaisted's charges. This he did with such success that, in March 1757, he was allowed to return to Bengal. Plaisted, on the other hand, was refused permission to do the same, on the ground that he was of so turbulent a temper that it was inadvisable to grant his request.

Thus defeated, Plaisted occupied himself with the publication of his account of his overland journey, the proceeds of which may possibly have helped to provide for his immediate needs. Meanwhile he persevered in his applications to the Directors, pleading that he had been reduced to poverty in their service; and in the spring of 1758 they relented and dispatched him once more to Calcutta, with orders that he was to be appointed Surveyor of Works. He seems by this time to have learnt the wisdom of keeping on good terms with his superiors, and for the rest of his life his relations with them left nothing to be desired. In October 1761 orders arrived from London for his transfer to the Bombay establishment and he handed in his resignation of his Calcutta post accordingly. He was, however, engaged in some surveys at Chittagong[1], and the Bengal Council attached so much importance to his services there that they detained him until they could secure from the Directors the reversal of the order for his transfer. No objection was raised in London, and Plaisted remained in Bengal as Surveyor and Assistant Engineer, with in addition the rank and emoluments of a factor. The Directors had stipulated that he was not to rise any higher in the covenanted service; and although this was ignored by the Bengal Government in May 1765, when they gave him the emoluments (and for a time the rank) of a member of Council, his promotion had to be cancelled under instructions from London. All this time Plaisted was engaged in survey work at Chittagong; but a little later (August 1765) he was recalled to undertake similar work in Burdwan. He was now in high favour with the Council, who in the following March wrote home, recommending him to the favourable notice of the Directors. The end, however, was near. In July 1767 he was ordered to Lakhipur on a survey. Whilst there he seems to have been taken ill, for he returned to Calcutta on 1 October and died on the 27th of that month.

One small incident of his later years is preserved in a paper on 'The Ancient Geography of India' contributed by Lieut.-Col. Wilford to vol. XIV (1822) of *Asiatic Researches*. This says (p. 446): 'Mr B. Plaisted, whilst surveying some parts of the Sunderbunds, was carried away by an alligator,

[1] One outcome of his employment in this service was the 'Sailing Directions for the Coast of Chittagong,' written by Plaisted in 1761 and published as an appendix to Captain John Ritchie's *Directions for Sailing in the Northern Part of the Bay of Bengal* (1785). A letter from him, dated at Chittagong 1 May 1762, giving an account of an earthquake there, has been printed in *Bengal Past and Present* (vol. XVII, p. 162).

which he mistook for the rotten trunk of a tree. This was written at the end of his survey, where he thus left off, in the Surveyor-General's office, where I saw it about forty years ago.'

The first edition of Plaisted's book appeared in 1757, and contains the description of his journey from 'Calcutta in Bengal, by Sea to Busserah, from thence across the Great Desart to Aleppo, and from thence to Marseilles, and through France to England,' to which are added 'Directions by Captain Eliot Eliot for passing over the Little Desert from Busserah, by the way of Baghdad, Mousul, Orfa and Aleppo.' The second edition, published in 1758, is a reprint of the first edition, but has in addition chapters on the 'Account of Countries, cities etc. adjacent to Bengal etc.,' and the Journal of the Proceedings of the E. Indiaman *Doddington*. The English original was published in a French translation in 1758, and this latter version was reprinted (in French) in Thomas Howel's *Voyage en retour de l'Inde par une route en partie inconnue jusqu'ici*, etc., published in Paris in 1797.

Only that portion of the book relating to his passage over the desert from Basra to Aleppo and thence to Alexandretta is here included, and the text is that of the first edition.

PREFACE

THE following journal had remained for ever in obscurity from the little inclination I have of appearing in print, had I not been intreated by some friends who, by persuasion, have at last convinced me of the utility it may be of to future travellers, as a guide they may certainly rely on. For Tavernier, from whom I naturally expected very authentic accounts, has so far deviated from the true state of things in crossing the desart, that was I not aware his voyages were collected after he had done travelling (mostly from his memory) I should have been suspicious that many things, delivered as his, had been the produce of some of those chamber geographers who describe whole kingdoms, and their different roads, without ever having stept out of their mother-country, and are as little capable of judging of the authors from whom they make an extract. It was this induced me to be so minute in describing the different soils of the desart I passed over, because from thence appears the great error in Tavernier when he says that so many camels are loaded with firing; which had I relied on, I might have put myself to an enormous expence in carriage for an article that is to be found in abundance all the way you travel[1]. Many more such errors may be found, by comparing this journal with former ones. I have annexed, by way of appendix, an account kept by Capt. Eliot, a gentleman I well

[1] Tavernier's *Travels* have, at times, been held in doubt, and placed in the category of travellers' tales, but time is proving them to be more accurate than formerly believed. The more one knows the readier one is to forgive small errors, and the better able to appreciate the value of the whole as a contribution to knowledge. There is certainly nothing in Tavernier's account of the desert crossing to make one doubt his having endured it. He noted many things Plaisted failed to record—Ukhaidir, for instance. Read Tavernier with a modern map in hand, and every word falls into place. I can find no errors. The complaint which Plaisted makes regarding the fuel problem is a minor affair. Tavernier, as a diamond merchant, probably travelled *en prince*, and the first thing his town-bred cooks would have demanded if possible was a never-failing supply of the charcoal over which they had always been accustomed to cook.

knew, that the voyager may make his choice what rout[e] to take after his arrival at Busserah; and the short description of Aleppo is extracted from Dr. Russel, with whom I had the pleasure of being acquainted, without which it might have appeared somewhat defective. For the same reason I have added a few other things from undoubted authorities, to supply the place of my own inexperience; all which are sufficiently noticed, to avoid the imputation of plagiarism.

A JOURNAL FROM *BUSSERAH* TO *ALEPPO*, ETC.

ON the 20th of April [1750] I landed at Busserah, and was informed that there was a caravan ready to set out in fifteen or twenty days, which I was advised by everyone to wait for; but in this they were deceived, and consequently I was so too. However, this was not all my grievance, for I had other reasons which made me repent of waiting for it, which will be taken notice of hereafter. Here I was obliged to abide fifty-three days, in which I had a sufficient opportunity to make some remarks upon the place, if there had been anything worth observation; for though this city is large it has the meanest aspect and is the worst built of any I ever saw. The houses are generally two stories high, flat on the top, and constructed with bricks burnt in the sun, but in such a clumsy manner that the Governor's own house was no better than a dog-hole. There is not the least appearance of architecture in any part of the town except in the mosques, and they lean in such a manner that they seem ready to tumble down. The circumference is very large, which is in some measure owing to the great number of date trees planted within the walls; some think there are enough to supply all the inhabitants with dates, which are their principal food. It was built by the Arabians, who still make up the bulk of the inhabitants, and therefore it is no wonder they should make such provisions for themselves.

It is seated between the river Euphrates and the desert, which last is close to the walls; for you are no sooner out of the gate on the west side but you are in the desert. Authors have said that there is a canal, cut out of the Euphrates, which runs up as far as Bossora; which is a mistake[1], for the east

[1] The author is wrong. The present-day Asshar (Ashur) Creek did then, as now, run up from the Euphrates (Shatt el Arab) into the city, dividing it into two parts. Teixeira described it well in 1604 (see Hakluyt

end of that city is seated on the side of that river, and on which the Custom House also stands. There is indeed a canal from the Euphrates which runs from one end of the city to the other and divides it into two parts, between which there is a communication by bridges of boats. The ramparts are bad and greatly out of repair, and when I went round it as far as I could, which was about half way, in company with Mr. Pomfret, I counted ninety-nine bastions or round towers. Mr. Pomfret[1] was the gentleman I lived with all the time I was there, from whom I received great civilities, as well as from Mynheer Kruphausen[2].

This city is subject to the Turks and under the government of a Bashaw and a Musoleem[3]; though the first, who is a Turk, is the principal[4]. The garison consists of about three thousand Janizaries[5]; besides which there are five gallies under a distinct Bashaw[6], who is not subordinate to him of the city. These gallies are designed to keep the adjacent countries in awe. The Bashaw of the city has often acted in

Soc., Series II, vol. IX, pp. 27–8). The town itself was two miles or so from the river bank, but the customs house, etc., lay along the river front. *Old* Basra was farther away to the S.W., near the present-day Zubair, past which the Euphrates then flowed. The best contemporary description of Basra is Niebuhr's; see also his plan of the city (*Voyage en Arabie*, etc., vol. II, pp. 172 et seq., Tab. XXXIX).

[1] Nathaniel Pomfret was the East India Company's representative at Basra from May 1748 to March 1751, when he made over charge to Brabazon Ellis.

[2] Baron Kniphausen, head of the Dutch Factory, and a famous character. For a full account of his activities, see Wilson's *Persian Gulf*, pp. 179–81.

[3] Mutasallim—the Governor of the city. The Basha of course was the head of the province.

[4] Basra had been more or less under Turkish rule since 1668. It would appear that this was the critical moment between the departure of Sulaiman Abu Leilah for Baghdad and the revolt of the Qaptan (or the new Deputy Governor), for an independent Basra. Sulaiman Abu Leilah, a Georgian freedman of great parts, was given the governorship of Basra in 1748, and, according to Longrigg, 'under him we see Turkish rule at its best.' In 1749 he assumed the government of Baghdad, and Basra was left to the Qaptan.

[5] Abu Leilah, being a freed slave, relied upon his janissaries.

[6] Qaptan, or Lord High Admiral, in command of the fleet of local craft, chiefly used for keeping the Cha'ab pirates in order. See Niebuhr, *op. cit.* p. 175.

a very arbitrary manner[1], and by his exactions has been the occasion of mutinies and bloodshed; for the Arabs who are the natural inhabitants will not bear to be rigourously dealt with, for they are a people who are very bold, cunning and revengeful. There are many Jews here, who live by brokerage and exchanging of money, but they are kept very poor for political reasons. There are a few Christians of the Greek Church, who have no priest of their own, for which reason the officiating clergymen are Roman missionaries; but these are such mean, scandalous wretches that they not long ago made a tavern of their church, and debauched the people with the spirituous liquors which they distilled; and not only that, but provided mistresses for their customers, who were Christians, Mahometans, Jews and Gentiles. In 1691 this city was depopulated by a plague, of which 80,000 of the inhabitants died, and the rest ran away[2]. It was afterwards repeopled by the wild Arabs, who were about twelve months afterwards brought under subjection by the Turks, who are masters of the town to this very day[3]. But the trade is not now so considerable as when the Persians had it, because the Turks are very insolent to foreign merchants[4].

[1] This must refer to Abu Leilah's successful dealing with the local Arabs. 'He reduced the tribes, by rapid campaigns in his best manner, to an obedience unseen since he left Iraq. Muntafiq, and Bani Lam, tribes of Huwaizah and Arabistan, and Cha'ab pirates on the Shatt, felt his arm and obeyed' (Longrigg, *op. cit.* p. 168).

[2] This statement (as also the aspersions on the character of the Carmelite missionaries) was copied from Alexander Hamilton (*New Account of the East Indies*, 1727, vol. 1, pp. 83–4). The outbreak of plague occurred in 1690 (not 1691): see Longrigg, *op. cit.* p. 119.

[3] Basra was always the goal on which 'the wild Arabs' had their eyes fixed. Whenever an opportunity occurred they raided the city. Such a chance happened after the plague in 1690 and again in 1694, when a Muntafiq, Mani bin Mughamis, captured Basra, and destroyed the Turkish army sent to chastise him. Plaisted must refer to this temporary occupation by the Arabs, but it was *more* than twelve months before Basra was freed from the tribesmen. It was not till 1697 that the Huwaizah ousted Mani, and sent the keys of the city to the Shah of Persia, who in turn handed them to the Sultan of Turkey. See Longrigg, *op. cit.* p. 121.

[4] Hamilton, who described the Basra of 1721, makes the same observation regarding Persian encouragement of trade. For Turkish insolence to foreign merchants, see Longrigg, *op. cit.* pp. 157–58: 'Basrah was revisited by agents of the Honourable East India Company early in the third decade of the century [*i.e.* eighteenth] and its Factory opened as a permanent

I shall now lay down some necessary rules and directions for those who intend to travel for England by the way of Busserah or Bassora and Aleppo. And one of the first things to be considered, is the delay we may possibly meet with in taking this rout[e]; for, when any person has business to transact which requires his attendance at a particular time here, the difference of three or four months may prove a considerable detriment; while those who travel with other views, and are not afraid of expences, will be but little affected by it. The government in Persia, as has been observed, is so very unsettled that there is no passing now through that country without the utmost danger, and the Turkish Bashaws are so often changed and are of such different dispositions that there is no knowing what is to be expected from them till you come upon the spot. Hence the demands upon the merchants are arbitrary and many times uncertain, there being often no other rule for these things but the will and pleasure of the governors of particular places. For this reason caravans, which were ready to set out, have been retarded for a considerable time. Besides the Sheiks of the desert sometimes require exorbitant duties, which oblige them to deviate from the common track, whence they are longer on their journeys, and meet with greater difficulties therein.

There are generally two caravans which travel from Busserah to Aleppo, one of which consists of light camels for sale, and usually sets out between the 15th of April and the 15th of June. This is under a greater necessity of keeping to their time than others, on account of the great demand for camels in the Ottoman Empire; these are bred in the desert, and they generally sell three or four thousand of them every

station. Its difficulties—apart from the vagaries and private ends of its own staff, and their heavy death-roll—all sprang from the caprice and prejudice of the local government, whose sole aim, first and last, was to make immediate profit from the foreigners. In 1727 a vexatious tax was levied on their Persian servants. In 1728 a Company's interpreter was arrested for no offence. Farmans [letters-patent granted by the Sultan] were given and torn up by successive Governors, loans and presents demanded, claims unsatisfied, Capitulations unheeded, the customs rate altered at a whim.'

year, and make their returns in ready money. One reason of going so early is with a design of coming back with the merchants' caravan, if they cannot make one of their own. The other caravan, consisting chiefly of merchants, the time of their setting out depends principally on the arrival of the ships from India, particularly of those from Bengal; for the goods which these bring are principally purchased at Busserah, and are partly sent up the river to Bagdad, and partly carried over the great desert to Aleppo. The Bashaw always endeavours to prevail on the merchants to take the former road, because there is another duty to be paid at Bagdad, for he is always very desirous of fleecing them. However, when they come to an agreement with the Bashaw, they choose to go by the way of the great desert, the carriage being cheaper, and the impositions on the road less. The ships generally arrive from India about the beginning of June, and, when there is no impediment, the caravan usually sets out in the middle of July; but this may be either sooner or later, according to the time of the arrival of the ships.

Besides these there are four caravans which travel to Bagdad, which have no immediate dependance on the shipping, because they consist chiefly of merchants belonging to Bagdad and Persia; and therefore if a gentleman so orders his affairs that the ship he is on board of arrives at Gombroon[1] the latter end of January, or at Boucheer[2] the middle of February, he will probably find a trankey[3] at either of these places ready to depart for Busserah, and may have a passage on easy terms. And if he conforms a little to the customs of the country, as he ought in prudence to do, he will meet with great civility. However, he must take care to carry his own provisions along with him, for he will meet with nothing but sheep and fowls in his passage, and these he may have at every place he calls at. But as these people are not over cleanly, he may chance to meet with some bosom friends, or

[1] Bandar Abbas. [2] Bushire.

[3] Trankey (Teixeira's 'Tarranguy'): a small undecked vessel largely used in the pearl fishery in the Gulf.

rather unmannerly backbiters, which shifting once a day will scarce free him from.

He may chance sometimes to meet with no passage under a month or six weeks, and then he may hire a small trankey to himself for six tomans or thereabouts, and this he may be always sure of having at Kishmish[1]. The conveniences in one of these are but small, and his principal care must be to shelter himself from the inclemencies of the weather, which at that season of the year will be excessive cold. But then he will have a quicker passage, perhaps in fifteen days; whereas if he stays till the middle of March, waiting for a large trankey, he will find the North-Westers blow so strong that perhaps he will not get up in forty days time. And I desire this may be the more particularly taken notice of, because I fell into the same error myself, which occasioned me to arrive so late at Busserah; whereas had I gone in the little boat which set out sooner, I might have been there the latter end of February, and might have had a passage to Bagdad almost every week by some convenience or other; where, if you meet with no opportunity of travelling over the little desert, you may be certain of a passage to Mousul; and had it been my good fortune to have taken this method I should have been at Aleppo as soon as I got to Busserah. But as it was, I was obliged to wait for the desert caravan, because the stream of the river runs so strong at that season of the year that I should have been forty days in going up it to Bagdad, and after that I should have been fifteen or twenty days in travelling to Aleppo. However this road is the best when you get to Busserah in time, and from Bagdad you may proceed to Aleppo on horseback, before the weather begins to be immoderately hot. But if you take your passage from Bengal in the freight ship, you will not arrive at Busserah before the latter end of May, or not so soon, and then it will be best to join the merchants' caravan, though the time of their setting out is very uncertain.

However, upon weighing the whole, and considering the uncertainty of the departure of the caravans, it will be best,

[1] Qishm: an island near Bandar Abbas.

if an opportunity offers, to proceed to Bagdad, for you may get from Busserah to Imareck or Hella[1] in twenty days by going up the Euphrates, and then you may travel by land on horseback to Bagdad, which is seated on the Tigris.

The charges of this journey are likewise another thing which ought to be considered; for those of easy fortunes may not trouble their heads about the largeness of their expences, while others may be for living in as frugal a manner as possible; and yet all the money in the world will not free him from the inconveniences and fatigues which necessarily attend such a journey. It may cost a gentleman who spends his money freely 1500 or 2000 rupees; for I believe Mynheer Canta, who was in our caravan, expended a great deal more, for his carriage alone amounted to 1000. But my own charges were as follow:

	Mamoodies
For the camel which carried my cajavas[2] 75 piasters, and for 3 more at 25 each, which makes 75 more, and amount to	900
The two cajavas, with everything belonging thereto, as also 4 saddles and 6 skins of water, cost me fitting up ...	246
Two maunds of bread, being 190 pounds	165
Two maunds of rice, the same weight	104
28 pounds of sugar	55
Three okar of coffee	18
Twelve okar of ghee, a sort of butter	72
A dupper or large leather bottle	12
Two matarras or small leather bottles for water, which are exceeding useful	16
Onions, pepper, &c.; as also a carpet	64
Asses to carry my luggage to Zebar	20
Spent about 40 rupees at Zebar, and in the desert for hares, &c., the particulars of which would be too long to insert	216
To my servant who attended me, 50 piasters	300
Total Mamoodies	2188

All which amount to 48 pounds sterling, without reckoning anything for liquors, which were supplied gratis by Messieurs Pomfret and Kniphausen. The former lent me likewise a travelling kitchen and a tent, which were particular favours.

[1] Hilla.
[2] For this word see a note on p. 9.

Some are very desirous of taking a horse over the desert; which cannot be had at Busserah under 500 rupees, and the carriage of his water and provisions will cost 100 more. If the horse gets safe to Aleppo, which is a great question, he will not sell it for above 300 rupees, so that the certain charge will be 200. Besides, there is no riding a horse after nine in the morning on account of the heat. Therefore, upon the whole, I think it a needless expence; and as for my own part, I always walked till that time. The carriage of every six dozen bottles of liquor will cost 25 or 30 dollars.

A tent will be absolutely necessary, for sometimes the caravan will encamp in the desert for two or three days together. With regard to provisions, there is no carrying of potted meat, for the sun will spoil it the first day; nor yet butter. But you may provide yourself with ghee, or boiled butter, cheese, thirty or forty tongues well cured, and a little salt, and with these you may make a delicious repast. Onions should be never forgot, because you will meet with hares almost every day, and these are all the fresh meat you must expect. Your cups and plates must be of copper tinned, unless you will go to the expence of silver; but chinaware will be very improper for this journey. Those who come from Bengal may make use of their rattan hampers for provisions, which they may lock up; and their wine must be put in chests which will hold about three dozen each, one of which is to be hung on each side of a camel. The skins for water must be bought at Busserah, which will be best done by yourself, for there is no trusting the Arabs. Let them always be kept full of water till you set out; and frequently change it, by which means they will hold the better, and become sweet and clean. You cannot be too careful in this respect, for water is principally to be minded. You should likewise have a kettle which will hold about five gallons, with a cock about an inch from the bottom; for the water in the desert is so muddy, that there is no way to make it fine, but by filling the kettle with water over night, and drawing it off into your matarras[1] in the

[1] Arabic *matara*, meaning either a water-skin or (as here) a leathern vessel.

morning; unless you can think of a better contrivance. And to say the truth, you would not make use of this water at all, if extreme thirst did not oblige you.

A person who wants to travel as cheap as possible, may make shift with two camels well enough, which are thirty piasters each; which will reduce the first article in the former account from 1146 to 284 mamoodies, excepting four dollars for two saddles, and two skins for water. Besides, half the provisions are full enough for a man and his servant. In this case I suppose him to ride on the camel and not in cajavas; which I would do myself if I was to perform the same journey over again. For there is no more inconveniency in the motion of the animal than there is in the cajavas, as I have found upon trial; the only difference is being a little covered from the heat. However, the heat of the sun is not the most incommodious circumstance you will meet with on the road, but that of the north-west wind; for this blows directly in your face, and is as violent as if it came from a glass furnace, and penetrates into your very lungs. This may be probably owing to its passing over such a vast tract of barren land heated by the sunbeams. The Arabs turn a part of their turbant [turban] before their mouth and nostrils, by which they find a small alleviation. It likewise greatly affects the eyes; which perhaps might be remedied by green glass, worn like spectacles, and tied behind the head to keep them fast.

It is not worth while to carry a great quantity of liquor, for the bottles will be apt to break. And the utensils may be reduced to a small tea-kettle, two kettles, which will equally serve for boiling and frying, three copper plates and two sneakers of the same. By thus retrenching your expences, you may pass over the desert for two hundred rupees, and, if you associate with a merchant, for one hundred. For he perhaps will find you with provisions all the way for thirty piasters, and probably in a better manner than you can do for yourself; but you must never forget tea and coffee, and the equipage belonging thereto.

I now proceed to my journal of my journey over the desert,

which begins on June the 12th, the day when the caravan began its march from Lassar[1] to Chubdar: as for my own part I set out early in the morning for Zebar[2], a village about three hours ride from Busserah, having sent all my things thither yesterday, and was forced to take up my lodging in a mean dirty house, where I waited three days. Here the merchants are supplied with camels for carriage.

June the 15th. We set out at half an hour past eleven for Chubdar[3], the place where the caravan was to rendezvous. We had scarce advanced half a mile in the road before my cajavas broke down. However, they were soon set to rights again, and we overtook the caravan about four; having had a spice of strong north-west wind, which was excessive hot by blowing over the burning sands of the barren desert. It had a bad effect upon my eyes, for it made them so sore I could hardly see, though I had covered them with muslin by way of prevention. Here I met with Mynheer Canta, his clerk, and Padre Prosper. At this place there is water, and the ruins of four small forts, but no inhabitants. Here I would have the reader take notice once for all, that I intend to distinguish the days on which we proceeded on our journey from those in which we were encamped, and to set down the number of the former at the end of each day's march, that the distance from Bassora to Aleppo may more readily appear. Thus on this day we are about half a day's journey from Busserah.

June the 16th. At half an hour past six in the morning the caravan began to move, and we were soon joined by the Mufti[4], who was travelling to Bagdad. I judge the whole number of our camels to be about two thousand, and I was

[1] Read 'the caravan from Lassar began to march to Chubdar.' Lassar is El Hasa in Arabia, where the camel convoys originated (see p. 93).

[2] Zubair.

[3] Kuwaibda. It seems to have been the usual rendezvous for outgoing caravans. Della Valle records that 'an Arabian Sceich resided there who receives a Gabel [baksheesh] for the Caravans and Burdens that pass that way.' In those days it was 'a town.' Capper, who passed through it eight years after Plaisted, at the time of the Persian occupation of Basra, records it as a village which had been ruined by the Persians. Taylor in 1789 found it still deserted.

[4] Mufti: doctor of (Islamic) law.

told there were three hundred musqueteers, but I do not believe there were above half so many. About noon my cajava broke again and I fell through the bottom of it under the camel's belly. In the evening a great many empty camels joined us from various parts of the desert. At our first setting out the soil was gravelly and sandy; but for the greatest part of the next day it was chiefly gravel, with brush-wood growing thereon. We encamped at sunset. Days one and a half.

June the 18th. We set forward again, at sunrise, having bent our course yesterday and today nearly towards the setting sun, and struck out of the usual track more into the desert. The country was nearly upon a level and the soil gravelly, with plenty of shrubs and a great number of hares. At four in the afternoon the desert assumed a new face, for we found ourselves in loose sand with shrubs, and one of our people killed a land tortoise. My cajava breaking down again, I rode on the back of a camel the whole afternoon. We encamped in a loose sandy soil about eight in the evening. Days two and a half.

June the 19th. We got under march at four in the morning, continuing our course towards the same quarter; but at eight we came into an uneven country, being nothing but hills and dales, which we first perceived by going down hill. Here the sand being loose it lay in[1] heaps, just as it had been driven by the wind. However, there was here and there some large bushes, but no hare-holes that we could perceive. At noon we encamped near a tribe of Arabs who had there pitched their tents, which are their constant habitation; and these they remove from place to place, according to their conveniency. Here we had water for our camels, they having been without in eighty miles journey. The name of this place is Khunigha[2], at which we bought sheep at three piasters each. Days three from Busserah.

June the 20th. We still continued encamped at Khunigha, the caravan being busy in purchasing camels. Here Monsieur

[1] The sand bed—El Umaighar; see *Carte Internationale du Monde au* 1,000,000, Basra, Jan. 1927.

[2] A watering-place close to Qasr Naba. See further, p. 70.

Falquir, a Frenchman, who was brought to Busserah by the *Rose* Galley, and to whom I spared half of my tent throughout the whole journey, would needs make an excursion out of curiosity to the tents of the Arabs, and was so rash as to enter into one of them. I was sat down to dinner, thinking he was only gone to Mynheer Canta's tent, to which I sent my servant to call him, who brought word back he was not there. Then I began to imagine some misfortune had befallen him; therefore, in conjunction with Mynheer Canta, I sent three Arabs on dromedaries to seek him, supposing he had wandered out of his knowledge. These hired a man belonging to the tribe, for two piasters, to direct them to the tent where he was to be found. Here they met with him, surrounded by people who had robbed him of all the money he had about him, which was seven piasters. However they brought him away, and very probably saved his life; for it was the opinion of our own Arabs, they would have murdered him if he had continued there till night. This place has been noted for crimes of this kind, for Khunigha in the Arabic language signifies to throttle[1].

June the 21st. We still continued at Khunigah, because the Sheik who was our Caravan Bashi wanted money, on pretence of defraying the expence of the caravan, affirming his soldiers would go no farther without being paid; though it had been customary to stay till the end of the journey, and then make everyone contribute by a proportionable assessment, to which those who were merely passengers paid but little for themselves and necessaries. But our Sheik, who now shewed himself to be a very dishonest scoundrel,

[1] Teixeira gives the meaning of the word as 'drowning' (*op. cit.* p. 42). Taylor describes this region in detail, and says: 'Khanega is a species of wadi, which from its low level collects rain water in considerable quantities; when completely full it bursts over the country' ('Notes on Abu Shahrein and Tel el Lahm,' by J. E. Taylor, Esq., *Journal of the Royal Asiatic Society*, vol. xv, 1855, p. 404). This is the most likely meaning of the word. Several wadis coming from the south do actually meet here, but have their passage northwards blocked, or partially blocked, by a ridge of sand and pebbles. There is a similar feature, on a larger scale, in Qasim, described by Doughty (see *Arabia Deserta*, vol. II, p. 392).

instead of protecting the caravans, as his office should have obliged him to, attempted to plunder it, especially us who were strangers and some few merchants, whom he designed should pay the whole demand. For this purpose he made me a visit and told me he wanted to borrow of the Frenchman and me an hundred fundiklees[1], which is about fifty pounds, promising to give us an account of this money when he came to Aleppo. I was unwilling to comply with this exorbitant request, though I knew some of the merchants had submitted to pay what he had allotted for their share. I told him we were no merchants, nor had brought any money to lend, but were willing to pay our proportion, if he would tax the whole caravan to raise the money which he wanted, and which ought to be in proportion to the number of camels belonging to each person in it. This answer was very far from satisfying the Sheik, for I was to understand before he left us that, if we did not advance the sum which he demanded, he would leave the Frenchman and myself in the desert. This threat of his, I must confess, startled me a little, and made me reflect that he had the law in his own hands, and that it would be best to make the matter up as well as I could. With this intent I desired the Frenchman to lend me fifty fundicklees out of the sixty which he was possessed of, for I had only fifteen dollars of my own, hoping we might have got off for one half. But the above sum being Monsieur's all, he declared he would stand it out and not lend the Sheik a single fundicklee on his own account, but that he would trust me with the whole and to do what I pleased with, provided he run no risk himself.

Upon this I accepted of the fifty fundicklees, and put them into the hands of a merchant as so much lent to the Sheik, to supply his present exigency, expecting to have it returned when we came to Aleppo; and at the same time used all the arguments I could to excuse the Frenchman from paying anything. But this proposition the Sheik would by no means comply with; for though he himself did not understand what

[1] Arabic *funduqlı*, a small Turkish gold coin (see *Encyclopaedia of Islam*, s.v.).

the Frenchman and I talked about, he could perceive by our gesture that the Frenchman was more unwilling to advance money than I. Besides, as we were obliged to talk Portugueze, that we might understand each other, my Arab servant, who was present, betrayed our conversation to the Sheik, and instead of being a true interpreter, I have reason to believe, made some additions of his own. This put the Sheik into such a passion that he ordered my comrade to be laid hold of, which they did, and stamped him under foot, not forgetting to ply him with blows, to force him to a compliance. At length, upon my assurance that he had no more than ten fundicklees remaining, they were contented to take them, provided I would give them a note for the other forty, for he would accept of no security from the Frenchman; to which Monsieur thought fit to agree, finding it in vain to stand out any longer, as there is no resisting superior force.

I was greatly at a loss how to reconcile this proceeding of the Sheik to his first pretence of his wanting money to pay the soldiers, or for any other occasion he then might have; and more expecially as he promised to return the money at Aleppo. However, this affair was cleared up when I afterwards demanded the return of my note: he altered his tone, and strongly affirmed that it was a present to him for his care of the convoy.

Most of the caravan, and even some of the Arabs themselves, looked upon this as an extortion never practised before; and all that he could allege by way of excuse was that Mynheer Canta had made him a present of one hundred and fifty fundicklees at first setting out; which indeed was true enough, but then our cases were quite different, for he had a considerable sum of money to be taken care of, whereas we had nothing but our cloaths and provisions, as passengers only, as in reality we were nothing else, for we had no merchandise nor any other thing which could be a sufficient foundation for his extraordinary demand. I had, it is true, a bill of exchange for two thousand piasters, but this did not come under his cognizance, whatever it might have done if I had carried the money with me in specie. But this was a distinction that he had not honesty enough to make, and it was sufficient for him that we were Franks, who are generally looked upon in this part of the world to be as rich as princes. The best terms I could perswade him to make was an offer of a receipt that I had freely made him a present of the money and note in question, with a promise to make no farther demand during the remaining part of this journey. It was in vain to attempt at present to procure any farther redress, and therefore we were forced to be content till our arrival at Aleppo.

In the evening one of his people came, in a very abrupt manner, to demand two fundiclees for having had so much trouble with the Frenchman. And here I cannot help observing that the Arab to whom we paid two hundred and seventy five piasters for seven camels seemed to have had a principal hand in the oppression we had been under; for he was one of the Sheik's council during the whole time of the debate, and made no scruple of sacrificing those who had paid him so handsomely for his camels, with an intention, as I suppose, of escaping scot-free himself. Therefore let those who shall pass this way hereafter put no trust in any Arab, especially those of the desert, for there is not one of them but is villain enough to cut your throat for ten piasters, if he had a fair opportunity; and therefore the utmost care and caution is necessary whenever there is occasion to transact anything with them, or when you in any sense come under their power.

June the 22nd. We began our march at half an hour after sunrise, and about eight we left the loose sandy soil behind us, and were got among some low hills. We now found a change of the soil every hour, for it was sometimes gravelly, sometimes stony, and frequently a firm sand with bushes. At nine we crossed a place which resembled the bed of a river which had been dried up; and at two in the afternoon we arrived at Ghurare[1], which is an old ruined fort, where there is pretty good water. Here we met with Seid Tallub with

[1] I cannot identify the name. There are many ruined forts in the district.

the merchants' caravan, who had pitched their tents at this place, and we did the same close by them. Three days' journey and a half from Busserah.

June the 23*rd*. We proceeded on our journey at sunrise, as did also Seid Tallub's caravan. The soil was gravelly at our first setting out; after which we came to a heath, and then to stony land. At nine we arrived at wells of very bad water, and so bitter that our camels would hardly drink of it. Then we continued our course over a thick heath; and afterwards we had very barren, stony land for the rest of the day, till the time of our encampment, which was half an hour before sunset, in a spot full of shrubs. Four days' journey and a half from Busserah.

June the 24*th*. We began to move before sunrise; and our road, for the greatest part, lay through such stony ground that the camels could hardly find proper places where to set their feet. At eight we past over a piece of ground all bestrewed with flint-stones. This day the people belonging to the caravan killed a great number of hares; and we came to a place where we found water and filled our skins, but did not stop to let our camels drink. After this we entered a heath, the soil of which was damp; and there were several spots both yesterday and today which seemed to have been flooded[1]; whence I conclude that in the winter season it must be so marshy and full of water that there is no passing this way. At five in the afternoon we came to a place called Ghudary[2], where we met with wells about six feet deep, the water of which was just sweet enough to dress our victuals. What connection there may be between these wells and the marshy places above mentioned is hard to say; but probably they both were supplied with water from the same cause. Five days' journey and a half from Busserah.

[1] In a recent letter to *The Times* (6 Sept. 1928) on 'Wild Life in Irak.' Mr Norman L. Corkill describes this little-known region. He says, 'Many old disused wells are scattered about, and I know of at least one perennial pool further north....The Wadis are here thickly covered in places with vegetation, even *nebuk* trees occurring.'

[2] This must be Niebuhr's *Ghadâri*, but we have no modern equivalent.

June the 26th[1]. The caravan proceeded on the journey at sunrise, through marshy ground full of shrubs, and afterwards over stony land. At length we arrived at a kind of a heath overspread with wild thyme: but all the rest of the day our road lay through a barren gravelly soil, where there was scarce a shrub to be seen, unless in some few places now and then. At sunset we encamped on a barren spot. Six days' journey and a half from Busserah.

June the 26th. We began to march at sunrise through a country which was mostly barren, and at nine we came to a little hill covered with red stones; afterwards the land was gravelly and full of stones, and the hills in some places were very steep. At half an hour past four in the afternoon we encamped at a place called Alathla[2], and encamped near the wells, close to which were five trees, which in the desert is a very extraordinary sight; for these are the first we have met with hitherto. Seven days' journey and a half from Busserah.

June the 27th. In the preceding night we were alarmed with the noise of thieves, who had robbed the Mufti and carried off all his baggage. This, as appeared afterwards, was contrived by the order of our Caravan Bashi. This perhaps had been done before at Khunigha, if he had thought the place had been as convenient for the undertaking. However, he was now determined the Mufti should not escape scot-free, notwithstanding his sacred caracter, which should have been had in some veneration, at least by one of the same religion. But men so wickedly inclined as these Arabs, whose godliness is gain, will stop at nothing to enrich themselves. When the Mufti was about to take another road[3], the Sheik gave him

[1] An obvious error for '25th.'

[2] Alathla is noted by Niebuhr (*Eläldthe*), Capper (*Alathe*), Taylor (*Alataly*). It is difficult to identify the site. It must be on, or near, the Darb Zobeida. Taylor saw it from a distance as a ruined village, not far from Rahba. Capper records it as a hill, with two small forts, a spring of water and some cultivation, about four or five hours S.E. of Rahba. Kiepert marks a ruined site, *el-Adhle*, at the north-west corner of Bahr Najaf (see *Zeitsch. Gesell. für Erdkunde zu Berlin*, 1881, Taf. I, also 1883, Taf. I).

[3] This shows the position of the caravan at the moment. Meshed Ali (Najaf) was probably in sight and it was the natural parting of the ways for anyone going north to Baghdad.

to understand that he expected some present for his care and diligence; which the former perhaps thought he did not deserve, or was unwilling to comply with. The road to Bagdad lies through Meshed Ali, and the Sheik pretends there was greater danger between the place where we were encamped and this last town, and therefore advised him to take a guard of his soldiers, for whom he expected to be well paid. However the Mufti was unwilling to swallow the bait, and told him he was determined to run the risk. The Sheik, finding that the Mufti saw through his thin pretences, made use of this stratagem to bring him to his own terms. Whether the Mufti thought himself really robbed in good earnest or otherwise, is very hard to say; agreed for part (some say half) of his goods, and accordingly had the remainder returned, and soldiers allowed him for a convoy.

This affair taking up some time, we could not proceed on our journey till half an hour after six. Our road sometimes lay over stony ground, sometimes in sandy soil, but chiefly among hills, some of which were as white as chalk. However, in the valleys there were some large bushes. We encamped at one in the afternoon, at a place called Hufnie[1], near a pool of rain water, which was sweet but muddy. Here we waited for the return of the soldiers. Eight days' journey from Busserah.

June the 28th. We proceeded on our journey at half an hour before sunrise, in a country which was barren and stony, and where scarce a shrub was to be seen. The road was very uneven, for we were constantly ascending and descending. In the vallies there were a few green bushes. At nine we came to a place covered with stones of the colour of pitch, at the same time that a little hill close by was of the colour of chalk. From thence we passed through a gravelly plain, where we met with shrubs; and at five in the afternoon we ascended and descended two very rugged places, which were

[1] This must be in the neighbourhood of Tuqtuqana, which most travellers mention. It would be the natural place for the caravan to wait for the return of the soldiers from Najaf. It is 30 miles from Ukhaidir, a journey which Plaisted's caravan accomplished in a day and a half.

UKHAIDIR.

very difficult for loaded camels to pass along. We were soon after alarmed with a small party of Arabs, which put us upon our guard. I believe there was not above twenty, though the fears of the caravan had magnified them greatly. We encamped before sunset in a place surrounded with little hills. Nine days' journey from Busserah.

June the 29th. We began to move a little before sunrise, and in the first part of the day we travelled through a country full of gravel, and stones like shingles; then stony, and last of all sandy. However the country in general was not so barren as that we passed over for three days last past, there being plenty of shrubs, some of which were very green. We encamped at two in the afternoon, three miles short of a ruined fort called Akayathar[1], near a standing pool of water, which was so muddy it was not fit to drink; for which reason three wells were dug pretty near it, wherein they met with water which was very good. If this method was put in practice oftener, especially where the situation of the ground gave some hopes of success, I am persuaded the scarcity of water so much complained of would be greatly lessened; and perhaps in the most improbable places it would not be wanting if they were to dig deep enough. But it is no wonder that there are no persons have public spirit enough for these performances, since they have no other care but to serve themselves, without endeavouring to render travelling over the desert more commodious to others. Here we remained encamped, in expectation of merchants from Meshed Ali. Nine days' journey and a half from Busserah.

June the 30th. We continued encamped in the same place, and for the same reason.

July the 1st. The caravan began their march before sunrise, bending their course directly into the desert, over a

[1] Ukhaidir. This makes Plaisted the third Englishman to pass in silence these famous ruins. It remains for our fourth traveller—Carmichael—to reap the reward. Tavernier, whom Plaisted rather scorns as an armchair geographer, *did* describe 'the Great Palace built of brick' in some detail. He refers to the 'pool lying before the door of this Palace,' and adds that there was also an aqueduct which the Arabs told him once brought water from the Euphrates.

sandy soil with shrubs in abundance. After we had travelled five miles we pitched our tents, our Caravan Bashi having received advice that the loaded camels from Meshed Ali were set out on their journey. About five in the afternoon about an hundred of them arrived.

July the 2nd. We began to set forward half an hour before sunrise, at first through a sandy soil, and afterwards over gravelly and stony land. At nine we passed between a hill and a chain of hills; and near eleven we arrived at a place which had a very singular aspect, it consisting of nothing but sandy hillocks, over which the travelling was very bad. At one in the afternoon we enterd into a very spungy plain, full of shrubs, which we continued passing over till about five; at which time we encamped at Ruselain[1], near a pool overun with reeds. In the night the Arab of whom I had my camels lost five of these animals. Ten days' journey and a half from Busserah.

July the 3rd. The caravan was in motion before sunrise, and for the greatest part of the morning we passed over hills and vales, but in the afternoon through a champion country, the soil of which was a firm and hard gravel with shrubs. At half an hour before sunset we encamped near a small mud-redoubt called Themel[2], said to be built by the Turks, but now abandoned. At this place there is a spring, the water of which runs into a pool, full of reeds, and is very bad. Close by it there are two or three acres of ground, which appeared to have been lately tilled; for the stubble, perhaps

[1] As regards the term 'Ras el Ain,' it is often used in these regions, where a spring-head is of rare occurrence and of great consequence. Unfortunately the name does not help one to identify the site. We know of one Ras el Ain, the sulphurous spring at the extreme west corner of the oasis of Shithatha, but as Plaisted makes no mention of this considerable oasis (160,000 palms), and as its evil reputation caused most caravans to avoid it, I think that his Ras el Ain is more likely to be one of the many in the 'low lying marshy ground rich in springs' (Bell) to the west of Shithatha. Compare Carmichael's diary, 16 November.

[2] Qasr Thumail. Gertrude Bell's description agrees with Plaisted's. 'The mound of Themail is crowned by a fort built of mud and unshaped stones. . . . The existing building looked to me like rough Bedouin work, though I suspect that it has taken the place of older defences. A copious sulphur spring rises below it and flows into the cornfields of the Deleim.' (*Amurath to Amurath*, pp. 129–30).

of wheat, was still remaining, and was still to be seen on the ground. I went to view the redoubt, and found it consisted only of two parapets. Days' journey from Busserah, ten [*should be* eleven] and a half.

July the 4th. We proceeded on our journey at sunrise, through a country which had much the same appearance as yesterday; generally gravelly, but in some places stony with ascents and descents. We encamped at six in the afternoon, and sent messengers to Cubessa[1] to learn news of the Bagdad caravan, and to know whether it was ready to set out or not. In the meantime water was fetched from a place about two miles distant[2]. Twelve days' journey and a half from Busserah.

July the 5th. We began to march at half an hour before sunrise, in a soil for the most part gravelly, and in some places stony, leaving Cubessa to the right, or eastward four miles. We afterward came to rough stony ground bad for travelling, and encamped about eleven in a valley surrounded with rising ground. Here we found some springs, but the water had an intolerable smell[3]. At the bottom of the valley there was grass which had not lost its verdure, which the camels soon made an end of. Cubessa is a small town or village seated in the desert to the west of the Euphrates, and four days' journey from Bagdad; it is inhabited by Arabs, and is under the dominion of the Turks. I viewed it with my glass, and perceived it was surrounded with date trees[4]. It lies in the direct road from Bagdad to Aleppo, and here we waited again for the Bagdad caravan, part of it being arrived at Cubessa, and the rest not far off[5]. Thirteen days' journey from Busserah.

Here our Sheik had the modesty to make another demand of money, though at Khunighah he had promised to be

[1] Kubaisa.

[2] Possibly Bell's Ain el Asfuriyeh, or Djelib esh Sheikh.

[3] This may be Bell's Ain Zazu—'water drinkable but far from sweet,' but there are many other springs in the neighbourhood, all within sight of Kubaisa.

[4] See Carmichael's description, 12 November.

[5] Niebuhr gives a full list of the stages from Baghdad to Ain el Arnab (*op. cit.* vol. II, p. 194).

content with what he had already got, and ask for no more. I had brought a seaman from Busserah, and had entertained him as my servant, letting him ride in the other cajava to balance my weight; otherwise I must have put in a bag of rice to answer the same purpose. This man the Sheik had dignified with the title of merchant, but I desired him to look at the seaman's habit, and then judge of his station. I likewise informed him that his business was only to serve me as cook, and that as it was not customary for servants to pay anything for their passage in the caravans, if he persisted in his demand, I would send him to Cubessa, and procure him a place in the Bagdad caravan. His demand indeed was no more than ten fundicklees; but I told him he might as well skin a flint, or extract oil out of a stone, as to extort money from one that had it not. However after some debate he was contented to say he forgave him.

July the 6th. We continued at the same place, still waiting for the Bagdad caravan. This day one of the Sheik's soldiers came to ask me for money, telling me Mynheer Canta had given them some; but I resolutely refused to comply with the request, being determined to go to Cubessa rather than to submit to any more of their extortions. This made them quiet for the present. I was afterwards informed that Mynheer Canta had given them ten fundicklees. At about eight this morning part of the Bagdad caravan arrived, the rest being on the road.

July the 7th. We remained still encamped, and at half an hour past five in the afternoon the remainder of the Bagdad caravan arrived, being in all about two hundred camels with fifty soldiers. This recruit made our caravan very strong, and perhaps the strongest which has gone this road [for] a considerable time. It consisted now of about five thousand camels, four hundred of which were loaded, and the rest were designed for sale. The men were about ten or eleven hundred.

July the 8th. We began our march a little before sunrise, and the road was at first rocky, then stony and afterwards gravelly, till about nine, when we entered into a plain surrounded with hills, which was full of shrubs and wild thyme. Our way out of it lay up an ascent which was scarce passable[1], for being rocky it was very difficult of access; after which we got into a gravelly plain. About nine we passed by a ruined building of unhewn stone; some of the caravan told me it was formerly built by a Sheik, with a design to extort customs of all the merchants who passed that way. It is called Husur Tahusha[2]. From hence the soil was variable, sometimes a large gravel, and at other times a firm sand. We pitched our tents about an hour before sunset. Fourteen days' journey from Busserah.

July the 9th. We pursued our journey about half an hour before sunrise, and travelled the whole day through a level country, with not so much as a hill, and the soil was firm sand and gravel. At ten we passed by an old ruined building[3], there being nothing left but a door. Soon after an ostrich[4] crossed our caravan, running southward; some of our men pursued her, but she was too nimble for them. However

[1] Probably the Wadi Turaif. Taylor camped in the same 'deep ravine' two hours from Kubaisa (*op. cit.* p. 235).

[2] There is no other mention of this site, and no modern equivalent for it.

[3] Probably identical with the *Jacabjamus* of Carmichael (see p. 152, and n. 1).

[4] Plaisted's mention of the Arabian Ostrich is of considerable interest. Teixeira had already reported them in 1604, about two days W. of Basra. General Sir Eyre Coote in 1771 saw them two days E. of Palmyra. Irwin found a nest at a point half-way between Palmyra and the Euphrates in 1781, whilst Taylor in 1789 saw several ostriches and found their eggs in about the same locality as where Plaisted saw them. Olivier recorded them in 1797 still further N.; finding them W. of Rahba and S. of Deir ez Zor, on the 35th parallel. But Abraham Parsons, in 1774, had 15 warm eggs (containing chicks) brought to him at a point which must indeed have been the most northern limit of their range, namely N. of Taiyibe, and not more than five days S.E. of Aleppo. Since those days the ostrich has retreated farther into the desert. But it is still to be found as far N. as parallels 33° and 34°. The late Col. Leachman said: 'It is found to a certain extent north of Jauf, at the heads of the Wadis which drain into Mesopotamia as far north as the Damascus-Baghdad direct route. I have eaten fresh ostrich eggs in the desert 100 miles west of Kerbela, also 200 miles west of Basrah.' The Nafud sand-bed is their principal refuge in Northern Arabia, and they range as far west as the Hejaz railway. The species has been distinguished as separate from the Sudan race and named *Struthio camelus syriacus* (*Bull. Brit. Ornithologists' Club*, vol. XXXIX, p. 83). For further accounts of the Arabian Ostrich see articles by Prater in *Journal of the Bombay Nat. Hist. Soc.* 1921, 31 March; by Carruthers in *Ibis*, July 1922, pp. 471–74; and by Cheesman in *Ibis*, April 1923, pp. 208–11.

we afterwards killed an antilope[1]. We pitched our tents an hour before sunset. Fifteen days' journey from Busserah.

July the 10th. We were in motion by two in the morning, our camels having been two days without water and having met with little to eat. Our road all the way was stony and rocky, among hills or rather mountains; we passed through defiles where only two could go abreast[2]. The soil in some places was good red and yellow oker. About nine in the morning we were got through the very worst of them; when we perceived a wall with an arched door[3], which seemed to be but lately built. Near this place there was good water, where the Bagdad caravan let their camels drink; but we proceeded about a mile farther to other wells[4], where we encamped about ten in the morning. The soldiers renewed their demand for money, but with the same success as before. Fifteen [*should be* sixteen] days' journey from Busserah.

July the 11th. We continued still in our camp.

July the 12th. We proceeded on our journey an hour before sunrise; and our road for the first two hours lay over a stony hill, after which we entered into a champain country with gravel and shrubs. This lasted till two in the afternoon, when we entered a flat valley which abounded with shrubs and patches of high grass[5]. This continued till we encamped, which was about five in the afternoon, with a design to let the camels feed. Days' journey from Busserah sixteen and a half.

July the 13th. We began our march about three in the morning, and soon perceived the valley to enlarge into a plain, which was the most fertile of any part of the desert we had

[1] Probably gazelle, it is very doubtful that the Arabian Oryx ever ranged as far north as this.

[2] The hill country to the S. of El Qaim on the Euphrates. Rousseau notes it (*op. cit.* p. 131).

[3] There is no other mention of this.

[4] Teixeira is the only other traveller who watered hereabouts. He found the three wells of *Muy el Mecenah* or *Methenah* in a channel surrounded by hills.

[5] This must be the lower portion of that big drainage from the North Syrian Desert, which enters the Euphrates at Abu Kemal, the Wadi Rathqa. Nearly all travellers were struck by its size; Teixeira noted it as 'a ravine and channel of a wondrous great watercourse.'

yet passed through, and is terminated by two chains of hills[1]. And here it will not be improper to observe that, since we passed the hills mentioned on the tenth, we found the climate greatly altered for the better, being much more mild and tolerable, and consequently the shrubs were not so much scorched as before; besides the ground was frequently covered with a particular kind of soft grass. At the end of this plain we arrived at wells of good water, which were very deep, and walled round the inside of the borders with stone[2]. We encamped a little before nine in the morning, where we continued the remaining part of the day.

July the 14th. Our caravan was in motion a little before sunrise, and we travelled the greatest part of this day among hills and valleys with a gravelly soil; and yet we found less inconveniency here than in the southern part of the desert, for in many places the earth was covered with a thin coat of grass, and the hills there abounded with shrubs, which I never saw before.

In our journey I had frequently seen an animal I could not tell what to make of. But this day one happened to be killed, which enables me to give you a description of it, which I rather choose to do, because it seems particular to this part of the world. The head, body, fur and colour are exactly like a hare, and the tail is long and tapers like that of a rat, only it is bushy at the end, and is carried erect when this creature is in motion. The shape and position of the tail made me suspect it to be at first a kind of squirrel, till I had a nearer view of the whole proportion; for then I perceived that the hind legs were five times as long as the fore ones. This occasions it to jump when pursued in a very surprising manner. The size is much the same as that of a rat. There are a great number of them in the desert[3]. We encamped at five in the afternoon on a little spot of ground. Days' journey from Busserah eighteen.

July the 15th. We set out about three in the morning, and

[1] Jebel Sughur and Jebel Rathqa (see Cernik's map, Ergänzungsheft No. 44, *Pet. Mitt.*, 1875, Taf. 2 and 3).

[2] The steined wells of Jubb el Ghanam (see pp. 16, 146).

[3] A remarkably good description of the Jerboa (see also p. 31).

for two hours we continued ascending and descending over stony eminences, which at length were enlarged into hills; but a little after sunrise we arrived at a small plain where we found wells[1], but not enough to water all our camels, and therefore the much greater part went forward, for those that stopped were only some few of the Bagdad caravan. Two hours after we had passed these wells we entered into a spacious plain, and after that we arrived at hills. Then we travelled over hills and plains alternately the rest of the day. The soil was sometimes stony, but chiefly gravel and firm sand with shrubs. We pitched our tents three quarters of an hour before sunset. Nineteen days' journey from Busserah.

July the 16th. We proceeded on our journey an hour before sunrise; but the Bagdad caravan was in motion much sooner. At first we passed over a barren gravelly plain, at the end of which was another almost surrounded with chains of hills[2],

[1] This part of the Syrian desert is as yet little known; we are in fact still dependent upon these early travellers for what knowledge we do possess. Three stages (accomplished in two or three days according to the season) lay between Jubb el Ghanam and the first waterings in the neighbourhood of Taiyibe. As often as not these stages were waterless. It is about twenty-five hours' journey, over easy country. This district is not altogether featureless, nor without water. In addition to these nameless wells of Plaisted's, we know of the wells of *El Djehar* and the *Wadi el Mia* from Rousseau; of *Jebul Serhim*, eight hours beyond Ikhwan, and *Khuder* (*Khuder* may stand for Ghadir, water-pan; Cernik calls the district *Chabra Hochthal*, and in it he places the *Chadr* (Ghadir) *el Gaura*), halfway between Ikhwan and Jubb el Ghanam, from Irwin; of five wells cut in the rock about midway, recorded by Coote; of two sites named *Lachadamie* and *Lachadier*, of *Alhadrat ul Muy*, from Taylor; of the Valley of *Garer*, from Evers, which is probably a central depression where wadis collect from north, south, and west before flowing eastwards into the Euphrates. From Holford we know of wells called *Ferrash*, a little to the south of the general line. Teixeira, who was also to the south of the usual route, passing in a direct line between El Qaim, at the bend of the Euphrates, and *Sucana* (Sukhne), notes *Gadyr a ther*, 'a channel famous in those parts,' which is the Ghadir et Teir, the basin which receives the Wadi el Kebir of Sukhne; *Ketef el Hel*, probably in the Wadi Hail which we know of from Fowle's journey in 1910; *Ragem el Kayma*, a Rijm, or cairn of stones in the shape of a tent. It is possible that these cairns may be identical with the Turkoman burial-place noted by Della Valle in 1614. The locality is the same. Anyone acquainted with the tombs of nomadic Central Asia will appreciate the simile.

[2] Outliers of the Jebel Dhahik, or Jebel Bishri. The watering might be the Ghadir et Teir. For this region see Cernik's map, Ergänzungsheft No. 44, *Pet. Mitt.*, 1875, Taf. 2 and 3, and Musil's *Northern Arabia*.

which was fertile in shrubs, and had at the end wells of water, which we were deprived of by the Bagdad caravan, which had risen early for that purpose. We proceeded over hills which brought us to another plain fertile in shrubs, and encamped at sunset in a low valley. Twenty days' journey from Busserah.

July the 17th. We began our march an hour before sunrise, and continued ascending and descending for three hours together, and then passed over hills which led us to another plain as smooth as a bowling green, but barren. At the end of this we passed over rising ground, from whence we had a view of Tayba[1], and encamped close by it at four in the afternoon. Here is a pool of water thick set with reeds, and Tavernier mentions a spring which runs into this pool, but I did not see any there was, whatever might be at the bottom. Our camels had been now four days without water, which made some of them lie down frequently with their burdens. Days' journey from Busserah twenty one.

July the 18th. We continued at Tayba to give the camels rest. Captain Roberts, in a letter of his, says he saw well wrought capitals of the Corinthian order, without naming the place; which made me imagine he had meant Palmyra; but my Arab servant, who travelled with him, assured me that he came the same track with him over the desert, that he visited this place, and took a drawing of some parts of it with a pencil. Add to this that Palmyra lies sixty miles south-west of this place[2].

Tayba[3] is a walled town, seated on a rising ground, and

[1] Taiyibe.

[2] See note to Roberts' narrative, p. 45.

[3] Taiyibe was first recorded by Tenreiro in 1523; he described it as a walled city in the desert with 500–600 inhabitants, who lived by hiring out camels to caravans. He passed through it again in 1528 on his return journey. Teixeira was the next visitor; he found it a village of '250 houses founded on ruins of an ancienter that belonged to French Christians'; he also mentions gardens and orchards. Della Valle, in 1614, found Taiyibe worthy of its name, for it was 'good' to discover, in the midst of the wilderness, a place producing fowls, cucumbers, citrons and other delicacies. He remarks that 'in the Neapolitan Kingdom it would be a hamlet, but in Arabia it is a town, for it is a "walled settlement."' He explored the ruins, noting the 'belfry,' of a size and workmanship which

makes a tolerable appearance when you come within a proper distance. The English merchants[1] who were here in 1691 observed the prospect was helped by a well built steeple, to which the Mahometans had joined a mosch, supposed to be the remains of a Christian church[2], because it was built with more art and beauty than is generally to be met with in Turkish fabricks. The people that inhabited this town seemed to be more civilised and of better fashion than they had hitherto met with in the desert; but it is now desolate, and the houses in ruins. The gateway is arched and very

bespoke Christian origin, and also a Greek inscription, and another 'in strange character.' On his return in 1625, he observed that the 'Franks' of Aleppo kept a native agent there. Bernardino passed through Taiyibe in 1606, and recorded stone aqueducts and other ruins in the neighbourhood. The English merchants of the Aleppo factory, Lanoy and Goodyear, visited it on their second journey to Palmyra, which they had rediscovered a few years before. In their days Taiyibe was still an inhabited village, 'pleasantly situated, and makes a good appearance.' Soon after this it fell into decay, for in Niebuhr's itinerary it occurs as a village entirely destroyed twenty to thirty years before, *i.e.* 1730–40, and Beawes reported it deserted. Bischoff, however, in 1873, found it reoccupied, ten or twelve families having recently settled there; while Ostrup, in 1893, estimated it as a village of thirty houses. Plaisted gives a fuller account of Taiyibe and its ruins than any other traveller to date. Subsequently Carmichael and Taylor saw it from a distance, but Coote, Olivier and Rousseau actually visited it, Coote remarking 'the walls of stone were about half a mile in circumference.' Ostrup suggests that the little walled village of the present day occupies the site of the Acropolis of the ancient town, which covered a much larger area. The village is built on a curious plan, all the houses turning their backs to a common circular wall, so that in the middle there is an open space, like a market-place. In the centre of this there is a Watch Tower. Most travellers mention this tower, steeple or belfry, on to which was built 'a filthy mosque,' also the ruined fortifications, and 'citadel'; several note an inscription 'in an unknown character,' or, according to Olivier and Rousseau, in Kufic. Taiyibe has springs of sulphurous water, there being no evidence of the excellent water from which it is supposed to take its name, '*Tiebe*, so called from the goodness of the waters, which however we found not extraordinary' (Lanoy and Goodyear, *op. cit.* p. 56). Probably the more abundant source is at Ain el Qom, which was the source of supply for the ancient settlement of Qusur el Ikhwan and others farther south. See also Musil's *Palmyrena*, p. 76.

[1] Timothy Lanoy, son of Benjamin Lanoy, Consul at Aleppo, and Aaron Goodyear (mentioned by Richard Bell in August 1669 as one of the 'Factory at Aleppo'; see *Indian Antiquary*, 1908, vol. 37, p. 163). They were accompanied by the Rev. William Halifax, Chaplain to the Factory, who, as noted in the Introduction, wrote an account of their travels.

[2] Ghassanide Christian.

strong, with marks of its having been cannonaded. Just at the entrance there is an inscription on a wall, the characters of which I did not understand, though they might probably be Palmyrene, for Dr Bernard[1] affirms he met with some of that kind when he visited this place. The most remarkable building which I saw was a square tower, which, doubtless, was the steeple above mentioned; it is built of hewn stone, and is pretty entire, only the upper part is out of repair. There are one hundred and fifty-five steps on the inside to go up to the top of it[2], and adjoining thereto are the ruins of a chapel, but the parts which are left are not sufficient to give a just idea of its dimensions or architecture. However, there is a part of a room yet standing, whose dimensions may be about as large as a bedchamber, and in it are two Corinthian capitals, one of which is very badly wrought; but the other seems to be pretty well executed, and may probably give rise to the encomiums of Captain Roberts. I should have been very particular in measuring all its members, if the Sheik, who now pretended to have a great regard for me, had not sent to acquaint me I was in danger from some concealed Arabs. However I observed that the triglyphs[3], which bend backwards in our modern capitals and stand upright, lay flat in this, and leaned on one side. The stone or alabaster of which it was made seemed to be a very fine sort; but the other, and three or four shafts or columns, were only of freestone. There were two shafts of pillars fixed in the wall, which had the appearance of marble, about four feet long, and eleven inches in diameter; but they were without bases and capitals. Over these there was an arch, turned with the same sort of bricks of which the rest of the building is constructed.

[1] Dr Bernard, an Oxford don with Oriental leanings, never visited Palmyra himself, but wrote, in collaboration with Thomas Smith, *Inscriptiones Graecae Palmyrenorum*. Halifax sent Bernard the account of the second expedition (1691), which appeared eventually in the *Philosophical Transactions of the Royal Society*, vol. XIX, p. 83.

[2] Ostrup calls it a 'watch tower, as at Kasr el Hir.'

[3] An architectural term for an ornament consisting of a tablet repeated at regular intervals along a frieze, and having three vertical grooves, two perfect and the third divided.

Two miles to the westward of Tabya there are high hills, on which stands a building resembling a chapel[1], and nearer the town is a noble quarry of white transparent alabaster, of which the capital above mentioned was most probably made. This place and the adjacent country gave me more pleasure than anything I had met with since I left Busserah.

We were alarmed yesterday with about fifteen horsemen, who rode towards us on full gallop. Our people went out to meet them with their musquets, which prevented their doing any more harm than carrying of[f] a straggling camel. But at midnight we had another alarm which put us into greater fright, occasioned by the arrival of the Bagdad caravan, which we had left at the watering place, and which we at first apprehended to be an enemy. From hence we dispatched an Arab to the Bashaw of Aleppo to acquaint him with the near approach of our caravan.

July the 19th. We proceeded on our journey just at sunrise, and passed between Tayba and the hills, and then entered into a gravelly plain. At nine we came among other hills, where the soil is as yellow as oker. After this we advanced into a plain surrounded with hills, and marched through an opening at the farther end, which led into another plain, where we encamped at five in the afternoon. Days' journey from Busserah twenty two.

July the 20th. This day we were in motion half an hour before sunrise; and at first we passed through a barren plain to the westward of which is a hill, where there is a white house or fort. At the end of the plain the country is uneven, but not hilly; and so continued till three in the afternoon, and then we entered another plain abounding with shrubs. We encamped a little before sunset. Days' journey from Busserah twenty three.

July the 21st. We began our march at half an hour before sunrise, and passed over a rising ground till nine, very full of holes. The soil was chiefly hardened sand, which con-

[1] The shrine of Sheikh Ibrahim, a local saint; it was still standing at the time of Musil's visit in 1908.

tinued till we approached certain hills, which lay to the left[1]. At noon we passed by them, and came into a sandy plain covered with salt, which was about five miles in breadth. Soon after we left it we got to the back of the hills, where we encamped at four in the afternoon. This place is called Hugla[2], where we met with a standing pool of water; and about two miles to the north-west of it there is a village called Jubone[3]. Here the caravan is always obliged to stop and wait for the Bashaw's orders, which now is subject to his sole direction, who appoints a place at which they are to rendezvous, to which the Shabander and his people advance first, and when all are ready they proceed on their journey. Days' journey from Busserah twenty three and a quarter.

July the 22nd. This day the Arab who was sent from Tayba returned back; as also a party of horse to conduct us to the place of rendezvous. We were in motion at eleven before noon; and at first marched over a gravelly soil, with a chain of hills on one side, and the salt plain on the other. Then we came soon after to fields fertile in clover, and then to others quite green. We passed by two villages, the first of which was deserted but the other was inhabited[4], and all the houses had domes in the fashion of bee-hives[5]. Then we proceeded to the place of rendezvous, where we found about twenty custom-house officers in their tents, near a spring and a stream of water. We encamped about three in the afternoon. Days' journey in all from Busserah twenty four. We are now about twelve miles from Aleppo.

On the 23rd of June[6] the officers made a stricter enquiry into the commodities belonging to the caravan, and were very strict in searching after pearls, which pay a double duty when concealed. One of the caravan, an Armenian, whom I took

[1] Jebel el Hass (Sachau). [2] Hiqla (see also p. 136).

[3] El Ghubtin (Sachau) or Jubben.

[4] Sfira—the inhabited village, and probably El Melluhah—the deserted one.

[5] These are the domed mud houses, peculiar to the treeless district around Aleppo. The conical domes are said to be of very early origin, appearing in the same form on the bas-reliefs at Nineveh and also on Egyptian monuments.

[6] An obvious error for 'July.'

to be a servant, wanted to have kept his money private, but was detected, and found to have 200,000 rupees (which amounts to about 25,000 pounds of our money) in pearls, for which they demanded double duty. This day Arthur Pollard, Esq., our Consul at Aleppo, having had notice of my coming, sent me a letter by a priest, which contained a very kind invitation to his house; whereupon I took horse and rode to Aleppo. The loaded camels followed next day, and went with their cargoes to the custom-house.

General Remarks on the Passage over the Desert.

I have been the more particular in making my observations on the nature of the soil as we passed along, because this desert has generally been represented as a level sandy plain; whereas in reality the greatest part is a hard sandy gravel like some of our heaths in England. In some places it is full of large loose stones, and in others full of small hills, which are more barren than the valleys or plains, for these are generally full of shrubs, and the lower the situation the more green they are. However, these are but few in comparison of the rest, for the greatest part are dry and parched by the heat of the sun, insomuch that they will take fire as readily as shavings; and yet these are all the food the camels have to live upon. All the hills between Busserah and Tayba seem to be little else but stones.

There is no want of water, as is commonly supposed, when you travel the common track; but then it is generally bad, and therefore it is the quality but not the quantity that is most to be complained of. Even the very best is soon rendred unfit for present drinking; for when you come to a pool, everyone is for taking care of his own camels, and therefore as many of these plunge in at [a] time, that the water soon becomes muddy and unfit for use. However, necessity has no law, for I have been forced to take up with it, and have drank it as thick as Turks do their coffee, who, it is well known, always shake the pot before they pour it out; insomuch that I am not certain whether or no I have not swallowed my peck of dirt, which, according to the proverb, everyone is obliged to eat before he dies. However, I guarded against this as well as I could by straining it through muslin thrice doubled, which I put over the mouth of my matarra. Those pools or ponds which were surrounded with plenty of reeds were generally better than the wells; for the water of those we stopped at on June the 23rd was as green as grass; that of Ghudary on the 24th was very bad, and both were exceeding bitter; that of the wells at Alathla had a very offensive smell, and yet we were obliged to drink it; but that of Themal, which we arrived at July the 3rd, was much more abominable. When we waited for the Bagdad caravan, on July the 5th, the water was so insufferable that Mynheer Canta gave twenty five piasters to a man to fetch him two skins of water from the river Euphrates. However, it is observeable that this became sweet in twenty four hours time, by its agitation in the skins on the back of the camels; but this was but a small compensation for our having been forced to drink it for three days before. The water of the pools was generally very good but muddy. For further particulars you may consult the journal.

The greatest distance between the watering places was two days and a half, and happened at the first setting out, that is between Chubdar and Khunigha. Our camels, indeed, when we came to Tayba had been four days without water; but then we passed by some twice during that time, where we filled our skins for ourselves, though we did not stop to let the cattle drink. I have before observed that it is owing to the laziness of the Arabs that water is not to be had more frequently, for there is little room to doubt that, where the shrubs were green, this necessary fluid may be found, especially since where they are already dug the soil is much less promising. It is well known that those who dig deep enough to stratum of clay will seldom lose their labour, as appears from the wells we met with on July the 13th. The many fragments of ropes on the stone edges, and other signs, demonstrate that these had been long made use of; and it is plain their being sunk in that place was owing to great necessity, for there did not seem to be much probability of finding water in that place, because the soil round about them was dry. Whence I conclude that there can be no want of it in the plains and valleys throughout the desert, if the Arabs would be at the pains of opening the ground to a proper depth.

But though the water is so bad, the air, except in the rainy season, is always pure and serene, insomuch that there is no manner of danger in sleeping on the ground; for there is no dew in the night, though the weather is excessive hot in the day. Those of the caravan who exposed themselves to the open air, almost naked (as is the custom in this part of the world), never caught the least cold or were attacked with the least disorder; which is a plain proof of its being wholesome. And if they happened to wake, had the pleasure of beholding a serene sky and brilliant stars without the least scintillation. If there had been any dew in the night, I must have known it by my fuzee[1], which always lay by me on the ground, and continued as bright as ever without any appearance of rust; which it could not have done had there been any moist vapours fallen upon it.

The animals in this desert are but few. However, we met with hares frequently, that ran cross the caravan. These the Arabs endeavoured to knock down with the bludgeons they drove the camels with, and sometimes they would kill twenty or thirty in a day. These burrow in holes like a rabbet, which holes were as numerous all over the desert as those of a warren in England. To say the truth, I could not help suspecting that there were other animals concerned in making these subterranean habitations, though I had not the good luck to see them. Besides these I saw but one antilope, and the creature described on July the 14th. We met with lizards of various kinds, and some few snakes or serpents, which seemed to be a sort of a viper. There was no want of insects, such as beetles, locusts, &c., and when we drew near Aleppo, the scorpions were of a monstrous size. The birds are very few, for we saw none but ostriches, partridges and eagles, of which last we killed two or three.

[1] An old term for a musket.

The caravans which cross these deserts are of two sorts, the caravan of light camels, and the merchants caravan, of both which I shall give a description. The first is chiefly made up of young camels which are sent by the Sheik of Lasser, or Ahsa[1], a town in Arabia, who is a potent prince, and appoints one of his dependants to be the Caravan Bashi. This man has the direction of the whole caravan, and all who join it must submit to him. He has a guard for its defence, which consists of about 150 men, mounted on dromedaries, which is a lighter and swifter sort of a camel, but not a distinct species, as some have imagined. When the time of the departure of the camels sent from Lasser is known, the rest belonging to other tribes who have any for sale are ready to join them, insomuch that in the first five or six days from their first setting out they double or triple their number, as they pass along. Besides, when there are any merchants who want to go to Busserah, and cannot make up a caravan of themselves, they make use of this opportunity and join the caravan of camels, which sometimes proves very advantageous; because at this time the carriage is much cheaper. However, the Arabs, being of the same country, or at least of the same original, are generally much better treated on that account, and travel much cheaper than Greeks, Armenians, Europeans, or even Turks themselves. When there is any considerable number of merchants they generally pay the whole expence of the convoy, though the Sheik should demand no more than what is customary to pay. Whereas, in the merchants' caravan they agree beforehand to pay only so much for a loaded camel. This will, in some measure, explain the behaviour of our Sheik at Khunigha, who there took money from the merchants as well as from us. He pretended to borrow money, for which he gave his note, to pay all back again that should be more than they had agreed to pay. But as we had made no contract, because we had no merchandise and consequently had no occasion to make any, he had no pretence to require any from us;

[1] The Sheikh of El Hasa, a district, not a town, on the Arabian coast opposite Bahrain Island. The chief oasis is Hofuf.

which put him upon the expedient of borrowing, or rather extorting what he pleased under that pretence. Among other artifices, he told us he had paid several sums of money to the Sheiks of the desert for letting the caravan pass. But we knew this to be a falsity, for there were no such persons seen throughout the journey. But enough on this subject.

The bulk of the caravan is made up of Arabs of the desert, who are an ignorant, brutish, low-lived set of people; which is no wonder, considering their manner of life, and the meanness of their education, in a place where they can have little or no knowledge of the rest of the world. They have no acquaintance with politeness or social virtue, and consequently have little regard for the distinctions among mankind, or the difference which is due from inferiors to their superiors. There is very little difference, either in dress or behaviour, between the lowest camel-driver and the Sheik himself. Add to this that, they being bred in a hardy manner themselves, and always exposed to the inclemency of the weather, they are apt to imagine that others, though brought up never so delicatly, are able to endure all the inconveniences which they are exposed to as well as themselves; nor will they serve you one jot the more or better for paying them well for what they do. When I was at Busserah I gave my camel-man six dollars for six skins of water, and for a camel extraordinary to carry it, that I might always be well provided with that necessary article; and yet when I came on the desert I was obliged to drink out of the same skins with their [*sic*] own servants, and could not have an advantage which I promised myself, because I had paid for it, and therefore had a right to it. The only way for those who travel this way will be to purchase skins of their own, and then they can have no pretence of depriving you of your property.

When you are upon the road the Caravan Bashi makes a signal in the morning to load the camels, and then every one goes to work with all possible speed. However, this business belongs to the camel-men and their assistants; so that you yourself have not the least trouble about it. When the Bashi judges every one to be ready, he gives the signal for marching; and then two men, who are hired for that purpose, advance half a mile ahead, and the rest follow in the same track. The soldiers, unless there is any immediate danger, keep about the middle with a small flag; but if there is any alarms they divide themselves, part on one side and part on the other. When the caravan comes near a hill, or any suspicious place, they send out scouts to reconnoitre the road, and see whether any men lie in ambush. When there are any people appear in sight, part place themselves between them and the caravan, and halt till the rest come up. Then all the camel-men light their matches, and drive up all the straglers into a body. These make up the chief strength of the caravan, for not only they, but their servants are obliged to be as vigilant as possible; because if the enemy should get the better, they would suffer as much as the merchants. These robbers always appear on horseback, and though their numbers should be no more than thirty, they will be able to do a great deal of mischief to such a caravan as ours, and carry off a great booty; for they endeavour to come upon you unawares, and fall upon that part that is the least guarded, putting the camels into confusion. These being of a very timorous nature, some will run one way, and some another, dispersing themselves in the desert; and this is the very thing they aim at, for they can pick them up at their leisure. Besides those of the caravan who escape themselves give themselves little trouble about what becomes of the rest; or, if they did, they know it would be impossible to recover the loss. Besides, while they were assisting others, they themselves would be in danger of losing their own property. When they have advice that these freebooters intend to intercept them, or that they are like to meet with men on horseback, they judge it best and safest to deviate from the common track in order to avoid them. But if the men are mounted on camels or dromedaries the danger is not so great; for thirty of the former are able to do more execution than three hundred of the latter. For this reason they never are afraid of meeting people with camels only, unless they are much superior in number. When they are like to be attacked by a gang of this sort they make the camels lie down and tie their legs together to prevent their running away or even rising up, and then the men, armed with firelocks, advance to meet the enemy. This generally obliges them to retreat, for they, having nothing but lances and swords, dare not stand the fire of men on foot who are able to take good aim. When the caravan is out-numbred, they make the camels lie down in a ring, and as it were intrench themselves in the middle; insomuch that they generally come off conquerors, unless they are surprised at unawares; but this seldom or never happens to be the case.

The camels in this caravan are not tied seven or eight together, as in Persia, but are loose and march along without observing any order, like a drove of cattle in England going to market. Their usual pace is only walking, nor can a camel or dromedary with a man on his back be easily put out of it. And though their legs are long and they take great strides, yet they rid[e] no more ground than a man in his ordinary method of travelling on foot, as I have often experienced when I have walked for three or four hours together. One thing that makes them so slow is their nibling at every shrub they meet with, which makes it no wonder that a man who walks a common pace should get to his journey's end before a camel. Hence upon due deliberation I have estimated that a camel may travel thirty miles in a day, one day with another, if he is upon the road thirteen hours together, as was our case, for we never halted or stopped to dine, as many other caravans do. Now, as we were twenty four days on our passage, the distance between Busserah and Aleppo must be about 720 miles, which agrees very well with the best maps of this part of the world[1].

The time of stopping, in order to encamp, is at the will and pleasure of the Bashi, and this is done without order or regularity; only the owners of the camels take care to keep those together which belong to themselves. The loads are then taken off, and they are driven out to forage for an hour

[1] Plaisted made one of the quickest recorded passages of the Great Desert.

or two. When they return, they are made to lie down with their saddles on, and only one leg tied; but they sleep but little, and less than any other creature I am acquainted with. The camels have no other sustenance but the withered shrubs which they meet with in the desert. Only those that are loaded have a lump of dough given them every night.

After what has been said, it is easy to see how necessary and useful camels are in passing over these vast deserts, where no other beasts of burden could live without being supplied with provender from other places. No quadrupede but this can live so long without water. Four days I know they can, and have been told fifteen; but this I do not affirm for truth, though those that told me asserted it from their own knowledge. They pretend this was occasioned by having gone out of their way, and from having followed an unfrequented track. However, this is certain, that almost all the men and many of the beasts died. Camels are enabled to bear thirst longer than other animals by means of a bladder which is placed near the entrance of the throat, which may be seen very plainly when they are loading, for then they grumble and growl, and throw the bladder up in their mouths. This I suppose is always filled at the time of his drinking, and with this he must needs moisten the dry food which he meets with on the road, and expends it very gradually; and yet I observed the day before we came to Tayba it was quite empty, when they had been but three days without drinking, which occasioned them to eat very little on the following days. The genital parts are seated quite different from those of other animals, for which reason they always void their urine backwards. In winter the camels are clothed in long wool like a sheep, which falls off in the spring; and in the summer they look so sleek with their short hair, that you would take them for a different kind of animal. Besides, those that are bred in the southern parts of Asia are of a slighter make than those that travel between Constantinople and Persia. For these last will carry a thousand pounds weight easier than the former can six hundred. Those which are called dromedaries are small clean limbed beasts, the best of which are bred at

Muskate, and only differ from other camels as a cart-horse does from a racer. In Tartary and other places there are dromedaries and camels with two humps on their backs; but these I never saw.

The merchants' caravan consists of merchants or traders, who agree among themselves who shall be their Bashi; by which means they avoid impositions, and pay no more than what is necessary for the good of the whole company, and every one contributes his share in a just proportion. When their expences are extraordinary, on account of any danger they may meet with, they are all assessed alike. The Bashi they have chosen for several journeys is Seid Talub, a man of great worth and reputation, and who is generally respected by all the sheiks of the desert. He always acts with great integrity and honour, and would not forfeit his character for any consideration. He is in great credit from one end of the desert to the other, insomuch that his letter is said to be a sufficient passport alone to carry a man safe through it. He is said to be a descendant of Mahomed, and to have the strictest regard for the moral part of his religion. Captain Roberts, Mr. Monro[1], &c., went with his caravan, and were so pleased with his extraordinary civility throughout the whole journey, that when they came to Aleppo, they made him a present of a gold watch and some other things of value. However, what I have said concerning the behaviour of our Sheik is sufficient to prevail on all those who travel over the desert to be very cautious to whom they commit themselves to the care of.

As for the Arabs of the desert, I cannot see how they can be trusted; for they make a trade of robbery, and are brought up to it from their infancy. They are continually wandring from place to place seeking whom they may devour, and make no scruple of pillaging their own countrymen when they have a superior force. How then can others expect to escape scot-free? Nay, it will be very well if they can save their lives. However they pretend to stand much upon their honour; and if their wives or daughters happen to make a

[1] See p. 45.

slip, they make no more ado but take them on one side and strike off their heads. Nor will the man with whom they were great come off any better, if ever they get him within their power. What their honour is in other respects, the following instance will give you some idea of.

A caravan which set out from Busserah about seven months sooner than ours, were under a Sheik, put in by him of L'Assah before mentioned; who after he had taken money from the convoy, sent advice to another on the road, assuring him he would make no resistance if he should be allowed half the booty. By this means the merchants were deprived of all they had by the treachery of their own Caravan Bashi; only a camel was allowed for every two to pursue their journey to Aleppo. However, this scheme was not conserted in so private a manner but it was found out; insomuch that the Arabs themselves, who had lost their camels, refused to go any more under the direction of so villainous a Sheik; upon which the man who conducted us was chosen in his room, who for honesty was much of the same stamp, for it afterwards appeared he had some of those very goods which the merchants had been deprived of, and carried them with him for sale, upon which account an accusation was brought against him at Aleppo. Thus you see how hard it is to find a man you can confide in among these sort of people. However, that there are some of greater honesty among them appears from the character of Seid Talub abovementioned, who always took the utmost care to preserve his caravan, though he once undesignedly brought it into the utmost distress. For as he was conducting the last caravan, and was advanced pretty near Meshid Ali, he had advice that the Bashaw of Bagdad intended to intercept it with a body of horse; upon which, in order to avoid him, he turned off to the left farther into the desert than the common road lay. He likewise sent out four of his people every night different ways, to give him notice, if they should happen to see them or hear where they were. One of these who had been employed on this errand one night never returned, which gave him room to suspect he was betrayed; upon which he turned off directly into the desert, and kept the same course for two days together, and got entirely out of his knowledge. But the worst of it was he could find no watering place, and was forced to wander about, as some say, for fifteen days, till they were reduced to the last extremity, and then they providentially met with what they wanted. This was the time hinted at above, when the camels were so long without water. It seems this Sheik had some dark intimation of the Bashaw's design before he left Busserah, and had given the merchants his word he would run any risk rather than let them fall into his hands. I have insisted the longer upon these things, to shew the necessity of inquiring into the character of the Sheik to whom the care of the caravan is intrusted, that those who travel this way may be less exposed to the treachery of those designing Arabs. Besides, if you are under the direction of a man of integrity like Seid Talub, he will not only use you well himself, but he will hinder every other person from doing you any injustice, for he is not only the sole governor but judge.

The merchants' caravan proceed on their journey much in the same manner as the other, only they stop a little at noon to take some refreshment; and they are much more sociable, taking each other's part when the camel-men are insolent. Besides, no man is oppressed or excised for having more and better conveniences than the rest. Though indeed all the merchants are provided with tents; whereas in our caravan none had any but Mynheer Canti [*sic*] and myself, not even the Bashi. It will be best for every one who can afford it to be provided with a tent; and yet they are not so absolutely necessary as many may imagine, for their greatest use is when you encamp for a day or two together, they being always struck at night after sunset.

Before I entered on the desert, I apprehended there would be great difficulty in travelling such an extent of ground; but I soon found myself mistaken, for the road is easily found, unless you are obliged to leave the common track. Their rules are always to call at the same watering places, to which they are guided by the hills and valleys, which are well known to those who have often passed that way. Besides they are assisted by the sun; and in many places the way is beaten like our footpaths in England, particularly between Chubdar and Aleppo, where the tracks made by the camels are very visible. Indeed, in some places there is no such thing to be seen; but then it is where the land is marshy or the soil loose and sandy, and then they are directed altogether by the sun and hills. Sometimes, perhaps, they may stray a little out of their direct way, but they soon get into it again. The tracks are very easily known, for there are many of them running parallel to each other for several miles in breadth; insomuch that it is almost impossible to make any mistake. Besides there are single men who carry letters every month from Busserah to Aleppo, which could not be so easily performed if the road were difficult to find. Add to this, that there are other tracts which run across the desert from one watering-place to another. In short, there is not the least danger in mistaking the way to those who are the least used to the road; but if a caravan is obliged to wander out of their knowledge, then they may be reduced to the greatest extremities for want of water.

I make no doubt but many of my readers will think this to be a barren description of a very barren country, and indeed I am sorry it afforded nothing better; but this, which may seem very tedious to some, may be very useful to some of my Bengal friends, who may possibly have an occasion to make the desert in their way in travelling home to their own native country. This made me very unwilling to forbear mentioning anything which might possibly be to their advantage, in directing them to take the best measures in prosecuting their journey, and by shewing how to avoid all those dangers and distresses which some have often been exposed to in this inhospitable country. I know that letters have been sent from Aleppo by a few who have past this desert, but without many particulars of their journey over it, either because they kept no journal, or because they were so immersed in pleasures at Aleppo that all their former hardships vanished out of their mind. However I am the first who crossed it with the camel caravan, and probably have been the greatest sufferer on that account; and perhaps am the only person who was at the trouble of writing each day's occurences, after having been cooped up in a cajava for thirteen hours together.

I shall now conclude what I have to say on this subject by giving some farther advice to such as out of choice or necessity are arrived as far as Busserah on their passage home. When you are got to Busserah it will be very lucky if you meet with a caravan which shall set out in ten or fifteen days time; and then the opportunity is by no means to be neglected, because then your arrival at Aleppo will be more speedy, and at less expence. Bagdad, it must be owned, is considerably nearer Aleppo than Busserah; but the carriage is dearer, because camels are more scarce at Bagdad, for the caravan that joined ours gave fifty dollars apiece. At the usual rate of travelling you will get from Busserah to Aleppo in thirty two days, though you are actually upon the march but twenty four days and one third. Now we will suppose the distance from Bagdad to Cubessa to be four days' journey, and from Cubessa to Aleppo fifteen and one third; yet the time of resting by the way will make this last distance twenty days. But if you go by Kerkut, you will be much longer, as appears from Captain Elliot's journal, added to the end of this. And here it will not be amiss to give you the length of time which each of these roads will take up.

	Days.
From Busserah to Aleppo across the great desert is ...	24
The time from Busserah to Bagdad is very uncertain, because it depends on the strength of the current, which is not so swift in March as at some other times, and the time of the passage may be ...	15 or 20
Then 20 from Bagdad to Aleppo makes the whole ...	40
From Bagdad to Kerkut is	8
From Kerkut to Mousul	4
From Mousul to Maidan	8
From Maidan to Orfa	7
From Orfa to Aleppo	5
To which add the distance from Busserah to Bagdad	20
	In all 52

Thus you may perceive there is a considerable difference as to time in travelling the several roads. And with regard to expence, if you have a companion to pay half of the expence of the cajavas and servant, two may pass over the desert almost for the same charge as one. To counterbalance this, you will have the inconveniency of hot sultry weather, and may fall into the hands of people who are not over honest, besides being forced to drink water which in some places is most abominable, and meeting with no fresh provision but hares. If you travel by the way of Bagdad and Kubessa, you shorten your passage over the desert near eight days on a pleasant river, where you will have variety of agreeable prospects, and will be able to procure variety of refreshment throughout the whole passage till you reach Bagdad. Add to this, that after you are two days beyond Cubessa the heat of the desert is not so intolerable. If when you arrive at Bagdad there is no caravan ready to depart, you may proceed to Mousul, in which road you have villages all the way, as well as between Orfa and Aleppo. There is, indeed, a desert of six days' journey between Orfa and Aleppo, but then it lies so far to the northward that there is no scorching winds, and you may ride on horseback all the way. Upon the whole it is my opinion that it will be best for those who are bound from Busserah to Aleppo, to take the first safe conveyance from Bagdad, after procuring a letter of recommendation from the Bashaw; especially as those who come from the East Indies very seldom need to stint themselves in point of expence, though the difference should amount to two hundred rupees. Besides, there being no passing over the great desert but twice a year, you may sometimes be obliged to wait at Busserah for the departure of the caravan; whereas the opportunities of proceeding from Bagdad are frequent; or if you should be tired of waiting at Bagdad, you may proceed to Mousul, and that will afford you a great deal of variety, for there are many remains of antiquity which will yield you an agreeable amusement, especially if you have a taste that way. It must likewise be some pleasure to contemplate the spot where Alexander the Great fought the decisive battle with Darius, near Arbela, now called Harpel or Erbel[1].

[1] The actual battlefield lay to the west of Erbil, on the triangle between the Tigris and the Zab.

With regard to the respondentia, it is sometimes 20 per cent. from Busserah to Aleppo, but I got no more than 15 for 2000 piasters, which I lent on our caravan. But as I committed an error in this respect, it will be proper to explain the nature of this kind of negotiation. At Busserah they have two sorts of piasters, viz. the current piasters and the piasters in specie, named *rumi*. This, as the exchange then stood, was 6 and a half per cent. more than the current piasters. Now the money that I paid was 2000 piasters in specie, and my bill of exchange, which was written in Italian, was for 2000 piasters *rumi* in *moneta correnta del Grand Senhor*. When I came to Aleppo, the merchant to whom I presented my bill, not understanding the word *rumi*, only took notice of *moneta correnta*; and as there is the same difference here as between the current piaster and the piaster in specie at Busserah, he would only pay me in current money, by which I should have lost six and a half per cent. Upon this I chose to refer the difference to the gentleman that drew the bill, having a great opinion of his honesty. I mention this to caution others to take care of the like mistake for the future; and when they pay money of Bassorah which is piasters in specie, to take care that the bill runs for piasters in *moneta bona*, and then the piasters will be paid in specie.

From Aleppo I could only get two shillings and sixpence for a current piaster to England; by which there is a greater loss than what there would be if you can pay it at the rate of two shillings and four-pence for a current rupee. But this will best appear from the following calculation.

At Busserah a current piaster is 6 mamoodies.			
A Surat rupee is 5 mamoodies and 4 tenths.			
At Aleppo a current piaster of 6 mamoodies is ...	00	2	6
By which it appears that an hundred Surat rupees brought into mamoodies make 540, which at 6 mamoodies for half a crown, amount to 90 half crowns, or	11	05	00
But an hundred Surat rupees make 110 current rupees, which at 2*s.* 4*d.* for a current rupee, is	12	16	8
Loss in every 100 Surat rupees	1	11	8

To those who pay their money into the Company's cash at 2*s*. 2*d*., the loss will stand thus:

100 Surat rupees, equal to 540 mamoodies, at six for half a crown	11	5	0
100 Surat rupees, equal to 110 current rupees, at 2*s*. 2*d*. per current rupee, amount to	11	18	4
Loss in every 100 of Surat rupees	00	13	4

This loss in exchange by way of Aleppo is only to be considered by those who reckon their chickens before they are hatched; for it is evident from hence that those who pay their money into the Company's cash, at 2*s*. 2*d*. per current rupee, have almost 6 per cent. And to him that has the advantage of paying it in at 2*s*. 6*d*. per current rupee at 14 per cent., which must be deducted in any estimation of profit any one may propose to himself by bringing money to let out.

From this digression I shall now return back to Aleppo, where I was kindly received and entertained by our Consul during the time of my stay, and I received the compliments of all the British gentlemen, as well as those of the French Consul and most of that nation. My first business was to endeavour to gain satisfaction for the ill treatment of the Sheik; for which reason I represented my case to Mr. Pollard, with its bad consequence to future travellers, if this was made a precedent, because it might probably happen that all Europeans who should hereafter pass this way would be obliged to pay the like sum of money; and therefore I hoped that this man should not only be obliged to restore the extorted money back, but be otherwise punished. Upon this Mr. Pollard, in conjunction with the French Consul, presented a memorial relating to this affair to the Bashaw. The Sheik in his defence asserted he had taken nothing from us by force, but that what he had received was a voluntary present. However, the Bashaw, in hopes of gaining by this cause, ordered him to be seized and clapped into prison. Upon this the Sheik required us to prove, in the Mackama[1]

[1] Arabic *mahkama*.

or Cady's court, that he had made use of force in obtaining the money. This was a very artful step, for he knew that no Christian's oath would be taken there, and as for the Arabs they were too much in his power to dare to appear against him on our behalf. Thus the event appeared to be desperate; when a considerable Turk, who was in the caravan, went before the Cady and swore that the Sheik extorted the money by force. Now as there was another of the same nation along with us at that time, if he comes in and proves the same thing the Sheik will be convicted; and here it must be noted, that though the Turks and Arabs are of the same religion, they have a mortal hatred to each other, which shews the prudence of making them your friends when you travel in this or any other caravan under the direction of the Arabs. It unluckily happened that this affair was brought upon the carpet in the Ramazan or Mahommedan Lent, insomuch that it could not be terminated before that was over, which did not fall out during my stay at Aleppo; which obliged me to leave the prosecution of it in the hands of our Consul. Whether or no I shall be much the better when this suit is ended, at the writing of this I cannot pretend to say; but this I am certain of, that the Sheik will not be able to get rid of this affair without bleeding greatly in the purse; and I am of opinion he will think himself very happy if he comes off only with the loss of his money. Besides, there were others in the caravan who were used much in the same manner, and, when they found the Sheik was in limbo, went directly and made their demands; which renders his case still worse, and he will have enough to do before he obtains his liberty and is in a condition to return back into his own country.

It cannot be expected that during my short stay at Aleppo, I should be able to give a particular description of that noble city, and therefore I shall enlarge the few observations I did make with those which a very worthy physician, Dr. Russel[1],

[1] This would be Alexander Russell, M.D., who wrote *The Natural History of Aleppo*. He went to Aleppo in 1740, as physician to the English Factory, and resigned in 1753.

whom I had the pleasure of knowing when I was at that city, has communicated to the world. The first that strikes us when we come to a strange place is generally the provisions, which made me observe that they have the finest mutton, I think, that I ever tasted, and I have too much reason to remember the plenty and fineness of their fruits, from the bad effect the too free use of them had upon my health. It was then the season for grapes, pears, plumbs, peaches, walnuts and pistachio nuts, which were in perfection.

A description of Aleppo *and the adjacent country.*

Aleppo or Haleb, the metropolis of Syria, is built on eight small hills or eminences, on the highest of which the castle is erected, and is now generally agreed to be the ancient [Greek] Berœa. This mount is of a conic form, and seems in a great measure to be raised with the earth thrown up out of a deep broad ditch which surrounds it. The suburbs to the north-north-east are next in height to this; and those to the west-south-west are much lower than the parts adjacent, and than any other part of the city. It is incompassed by an old wall not a little decayed, and a broad ditch, now in most places turned into gardens. It is about three miles and a half in circumference, but with the suburbs eight.

The houses consist of a ground floor, generally arched, of an upper story which is flat on the top, and either terraced with hard plaister, or paved with stone; the apartments are placed on each side of a stone court. The ceilings are of wood, neatly painted and sometimes gilded, as are also the window-shutters, the pannels of some of their rooms, and the cupboard-doors, of which they have a great number; these taken together have a very agreeable effect; over the doors and windows on the inside are written passages out of the Koran, or verses of their own composition. The court-yard is neatly paved, and has generally a bason with a *jet d'eau* in the middle, on one or both sides of which a small spot of a yard or two square is left unpaved for a garden; the verdure of this, the flowers in pots, and the playing of the fountain produce a very agreeable effect, but they can only be seen by those within, for the passage into the street is closed with double doors, so contrived that there is no looking in when the doors are opened. Besides there are no windows to the street except a very few in the upper rooms, which render the streets very disagreeable to Europeans.

The better sort of houses have an arched alcove in this court open to the north and opposite the fountain. The pavement of this alcove is raised about a foot and a half above the pavement of the court and serves for a divan. Between this and the fountain the pavement is generally of mosaic work made with marble of various colours; as is also the floor of a large hall with a cupola roof, which commonly has a fountain in the middle, and is a cool room in the summer time. The divan is that part of a room, in a Turkish house, raised above the floor, and is covered with a carpet in winter, and in summer with fine mats. Along the sides are thick mattrasses about three feet wide, and commonly covered with scarlet cloth; there are likewise large bolsters of brocade stuffed with cotton set against the walls to lean upon. On these they sit cross legged like taylors, for they have no chairs.

People of fashion have but one or two rooms for themselves in the outer court, the rest are for the servants and stabling. Above stairs is a colonnade, if not round the whole court, at least fronting the west, off from which are their rooms and kiosks. These last are a sort of wooden divans that project a little way from the other part of the building and hang over into the street. They are raised about a foot and a half higher than the floor of the room, to which they are quite open, and by having windows in the front, and on each side, there is a great draught of air which renders them cool in summer. Beyond this court is another, containing the women's apartments, built in the same manner as other houses. Some few have a garden and a tall cypress-tree; there is likewise one of these in the outward yard.

The mosques in Aleppo are numerous, and some few of them magnificent. Before each of them is an area, with a fountain in the middle, designed for ablutions before prayers, and behind some of the larger there are little gardens. There are many large khanes or caravanseras, consisting of a capacious square, on all sides of which are a number of rooms, built on a ground-floor, used occasionally for chambers, warehouses or stables. Above stairs there is a colonade or gallery, on every side in which are the doors of a number of small rooms, wherein the merchants, as well strangers as natives, transact most of their business. The streets are narrow, but well paved and kept very clean.

The bazars or market-places are long, covered, narrow streets, on each side of which are a great many small shops, just sufficient to hold the tradesman and his goods, the buyer being obliged to stand without. Each separate branch of business has a particular bazar, which are locked up as well as the streets an hour and a half after sunset; but the locks are of wood, though the doors are cased with iron. The slaughter-houses are in the suburbs open to the fields. The tanners have a khane to work in near the river. To the southwards in the suburbs they burn lime, and a little beyond that there is a village where they make ropes and cat-gut. On the opposite side of the river to the westward there is a glass-house where they make a coarse white glass in the winter only, for the greatest part of this manufacture is brought from a village thirty-five miles westward.

The city is supplied with good water from springs near the banks of the river Heylen[1], about five miles to the north-east, which is conveyed from thence by an aquæduct, and distributed all over the town by earthen pipes. This is sufficient for drinking, cookery, &c. But the fountains are supplied by wells of brackish water, of which there is one in every house. Their fuel is wood and charcoal in the houses; but they heat their bagnios with the dung of animals, leaves of plants, parings of fruit and the like.

For four or five miles round the city the ground is stony and uneven, there being small eminences; this continues westward near twenty miles, with small fertile plains

[1] The river is the Nahr Quweiq of modern maps, but the aqueduct was diverted from the river at a place called *Ailan* (Thévenot). Teixeira calls the river *Kykan*.

interspersed. Six or seven miles northward and southward the country is level and not stony. To the eastward a vast plain commences, called the desert; however, the soil is good and fertile for a great many miles beyond Aleppo. The rivulet Coic [Quweiq] passes along the western part of the city, within a few yards of the walls, and serves to water a narrow slip of gardens on its banks, which reach from about five miles to three miles south of the town. Here are likewise gardens near a village called Bab Allab [Bab Allah], about two miles to the north-east, which are supplied by the aquæduct. The rising grounds above the gardens are in some places laid out in vineyards, interspersed with olive, fig, and pistachio trees, and in some spots where there are no gardens. The villages are destitute of trees and water, there being no other stream for twenty or thirty miles round; and therefore they save the rain water in cisterns.

The seasons are so regular and the air is so healthy, pure and free from damps, that all the inhabitants sup and sleep in the court-yards or on the house tops, from the end of May to the middle of September. The severity of the winter continues only from the 12th of December to the 20th of January, and then the air is excessively piercing, and yet the ice, even in shady places, is seldom strong enough to bear a man, and the snow very seldom lies above a day. Narcissus's, hyacinths and violets blow during this weather. In February the fields are cloathed with an agreeable verdure to which the springing up of their latter grain greatly contributes. The almond tree blossoms in February, and the trees begin to have leaves at the beginning of March. During this month and April nature assumes a gay and delightful appearance, but before the end of May all the fields appear parched and barren; only some robust plants are capable of withstanding the heat. From this period there is no rain till about the middle of September, at which time a little generally falls which refresheth the air, and bestows a more agreeable aspect to the country. For twenty or thirty days after this the air becomes serene and temperate, tho' the trees retain their leaves till the middle of November. Some begin to make fire at the end of this month, and some have none all the year.

The cold winds in the winter blow from between the north-west and the east, though those nearest the east are more sharp. But from the beginning of May to the end of September the same winds are as hot as if they came out of an oven, and yet the water is much cooler than when there is a westerly wind, which is the coldest in the hot months, and is much more frequent; for the hot winds blow very seldom, but when they do they bring on a faintness attended with difficulty of breathing, which obliges the inhabitants to close their doors and windows. They seem to participate of the nature of the *Samuel*[1], a hot wind in the desert, only they do not kill like that. Near the city the ground is rocky, and the soil is a blackish light mould, which produces the fruits of the earth in great abundance. A great part of the country lies uncultivated because property is not safe under a tyrannical government.

They begin to plough at the latter end of September and sow their earliest wheats about the middle of October, and they continue to plough and sow all sorts of grain till the end of January, and barley sometimes after the middle of February. They plough the land over again to cover the grain, for they have no harrows. The plough is so light it may be carried with one hand, and one little cow, or at most two, or an ass, is sufficient to draw it in ploughing; and it is managed so easily by one man that he generally smokes his pipe at the same time. They sow the fields with wheat, barley, cotton, cicers, lentiles, beans, everlasting peas, small vetches, sesamum, ricinus, a green kidney-bean called mash, hemp, musk-melon, water-melon, a small sort of cucumber, fænu-greek, and Turky millet. They sow few or no oats, the horses being fed with barley. In the gardens they plant tobacco, and ten or fifteen miles off in the fields, and all the hills from Shogle[2] to Latachia, produce such plenty that they trade with it to

[1] See p. 35.

[2] Shogle=Jisr esh Shughur, the bridge over the Nahr el Asi (Orontes) on the direct route between Aleppo and Latakia.

Egypt. The barley and wheat are generally all in by the 20th of May. They generally pluck the corn up by the roots and carry it to a hard spot of ground, where with a machine like a sledge which runs on rollers, and in which are small irons notched like a saw, to [they?] cut the straw and separate the grain. It is drawn by horses, cows or asses. Their granaries are subterranean cavities with narrow mouths like a well, which are commonly left open, which renders riding dangerous near the villages in the night. The cotton is not gathered till October.

They have but few olives near the city, but at Edlib[1], thirty miles to the south-west and the adjacent villages, they have plenty of oil of olives, and make soap of it and the ashes brought out of the desert. The ricinus or greater spurge furnishes the common people with oil for their lamps, and the oil of sesamum is chiefly consumed by the Jews. The vineyards produce good grapes, of which the Christians and Jews are allowed to make wine for their own use, paying a certain tax; but the grapes are brought from some distance. Their white wines are poor, and their red without flavour and heady; but rather makes the drinkers stupid than merry. From raisins mixed with a few aniseeds they draw a spirit which they call arrack, drank liberally by the Jews and Christians. The inspissated juice of the grape, called here dibbs[2], is brought in skins and sold in the publick markets. It looks like honey, is sweet and much used by all sorts.

They have variety of fruits common to Europe, but have very little flavour, and the apples are bad. They have pistachio nuts, and sumach, which is used as a relisher. Their fruit trees are all standards, and are little cultivated, and their other trees are the same as the European; but they have neither goosberries nor currants. The potherbs have nothing peculiar but the seasons in which they are most plenty, which little concerns us. It would take up too much room to describe the vast variety of fine flowers, herbs and plants to be met in these parts, and a catalogue of their names

[1] Idlib.
[2] Arabic *dibs*.

APPROACH TO ANTIOCH FROM ALEPPO

only would be very tedious, for which reason we shall omit them[1].

There being a French vessel bound for Marseilles, which was to sail in a short time, I agreed with the French Consul and the merchant to whom it was consigned for my passage, for which I was to pay two hundred livers. In consequence of this I took my leave of the gentlemen on July the 30th, and hired four horses for myself, my servant and my baggage, at the usual price, which is ten piasters to Scanderoon. I left Aleppo at sunset, and lay that night at a caravansera, called Khantaman[2], seated on a small river about nine miles from Aleppo.

July the 31st, I proceeded on my journey and lay at a village called Mertaban[3], in a house where they are accustomed to receive strangers. The people are Mahomedans, but they have a great respect for Christians, from whom they are originally descended. Our hostess and her daughter made no difficulty in eating and drinking with us, though it was Ramadan, and behaved in other respects with as much familiarity and complaisance as if we had been in an inn nearer home. Their faces were bare and exposed to view, contrary to the women in these parts; which was a great temptation, considering the time which had past since I saw women of their complexion and charms. The daughter in particular was very pretty, and I believe would not have been cruel, if I had been master enough of the language to have told her my mind. For, besides that the women in these parts have a natural turn for gallantry, I knew there were charms in money which few are able to resist.

August the 1st, we set out early in the morning, and reached Antioch that day. They have a tradition that St. Paul was baptized in the water at this place, which made me have a curiosity to taste it. This town is not above a sixth part so large as it formerly was, which appeared from the ruins of the old walls, which run up a steep hill, and when they have reached

[1] Russell, from whom this account of Aleppo is taken, does describe the flora in detail—see *The Natural History of Aleppo*. [2] Khan Tuman.

[3] For *Mertaban* see Drummond's *Travels* (London, 1754), p. 205—'Map of a Part of Syria'; it is the modern Maaret el Ihvan, Martahwan, · miles north of Idlib.

the top, advance along, descending down again on the other side. But there are now few traces of its former grandeur. The river which was formerly called the Orontes [Nahr el Asi] runs close by it, and over it there is a bridge of five arches. One may see, by what remains, that the high roads have been paved in former times.

August the 2d, we got on horseback early this morning, being resolved to reach Scanderoon by night. But we had not proceeded above two miles before we met with two horsemen on full gallop who were going to Antioch; they advised us to turn back, because a village about three miles farther on the road had been plundered by the mountaineers the preceding night. This put us to a stand for some time, but at length, considering the vessels we were going to might be gone if we delayed our journey, I was resolved to proceed. However, we took a by road over some steep hills, and by that means escaped the danger; about three in the afternoon we arrived at Balain, where being informed the vessel was not yet ready to sail, I took up my lodging at our Proconsul's.

The travelling between Aleppo and Balain [Beilân] is much more pleasant than on any road I had hitherto met with. The people in all the villages are extremely civil and obliging, particularly to Europeans. There are some barren and stony places, but generally the country is manured and planted with a great number of fruit trees. The road often lies through gardens full of olive and fig trees, so that all the provision you need to carry with you is a little wine. Between Martaban and Antioch you pass over a steep chain of mountains, as also between Antioch and Scanderoon, which is the worst part of our journey. At the place where you lodge the charge will generally amount to a piaster.

Balain is a village about ten miles from Scanderoon, seated among very high mountains; it is built on the sides of these, which give it a very romantick appearance, because at a distance the houses seem to stand one upon another. When you come into it you will find the foundation of some of the houses as high and upon a level with the tops of those before it. It is very agreeably situated where there is a cool air and fine water, which deserve the highest encomiums. We seemed to be got all of a sudden into another climate, insomuch that I could have wished to have had a thermometer, to have measured the temperature of the air. But according to what I could judge from the sense of feeling, I found myself in a very temperate climate, and as much differing from the heats of Scanderoon as the month of April in England is from the sultry air under the Equator. Therefore it is no wonder that our Proconsuls retire to this charming retreat in the hot season of the year; at which time Scanderoon is a most sickly place, and intolerable on account of the excessive hot weather.

The great quantity of fine water at Balain is certainly a circumstance worth observation; for here we see pure limpid fountains rushing out from the very tops of the mountains, the water of which is as cool as if it had been made so by ice, or by our method at Bengal, which is performed by the help of salt-petre, or rather many degrees beyond them. The streams lie so convenient that the water is conveyed into every house of the town at an easy expence, so that every family has a fountain of their own, unless some few who will not or cannot afford to be at the expence, and even these may take it up in the street, where there are streams as clear as crystal. It is delightful to observe the progress of the water from the fountains heads to the bottom; for in falling from thence it forms above two hundred natural cascades, as it passes between and over the rocks of different figures and shapes. But how vastly might the number be increased if art was brought into the assistance of nature. Besides the water is in such plenty that the streams are sufficient to turn at least five hundred mills. If the streams of Balain were in the neighbourhood of Versailles, the water works at Marly would be quite overlooked, and all the fine engines would be of no farther use.

August the 11th, having waited for the vessel nine days, I at length set out for Scanderoon; but being unwilling to sleep on shore, I embarked as soon as I got there. The next day I dined on board another French ship, which cost me dear, for I had like to have been left behind; and I was forced to give three chekins for a boat to overtake our own vessel.

APPENDIX

DIRECTIONS FOR PASSING OVER THE LITTLE DESERT FROM *BUSSERAH*, BY THE WAY OF *BAGDAD*, *MOUSUL*, *ORFA* AND *ALEPPO*

THE expences on the road in Turkey are nowhere so much in the choice of the traveller in this country. However, there are some things which Europeans are obliged to provide when they pass from one large town to another; for every one must carry their kitchen utensils, and they will find a tent highly necessary. These may be readily met with at Busserah. However, the tent will not be wanted till you come to Mousul, unless you take horse at Ismarck; for there is a passage from Busserah to Mousul up the Tigris by water. As to dress, a turban and an outside coat will be sufficient, for it will be proper to conform a little to the custom of the country, since an hat will in some degree expose you to the insults of children in the towns which you pass through. But with regard to grown persons your being known will the rather command the greater respect, especially as you will have passes from the Bashaws, which are easily obtained by Europeans. Their regard for you will be still greater if you have a servant who can speak the Turkish, Arabick, or Persian languages. But then it will not be proper to let the people of the country know that you are Indian Christians, because this may give some trouble, and expose you to the hazard of losing your servant if a slave.

You will generally find servants at Busserah who speak the country Portuguese or lingua franca of the Mediterranean; but at Bagdad there are few or none who understand any European language. On the road you never stop to bait in less than six hours, and sometimes not in twelve. They generall[y] set out on their journey very early every morning, and seldom travel longer than three in the afternoon.

The proper season for undertaking this journey from

Busserah is from the beginning of January to the end of that month; because then the streams of the rivers Tigris and Euphrates are not so rapid; for the swelling of these rivers depends more on the melting of the snow than the rain. Your having the spring before you will also exempt you from the excessive heat of the weather, and if it is thought dangerous to travel alone, you will then meet with caravans with which you may join company. Besides if you design to travel to England by sea, you will probably meet with the Company's ships, which at that time of the year are generally ready to sail. By this means you will have an agreeable passage through the Mediterranean, and the time of performing quarantine will then be the shorter, as you will in all likelihood have clean patents when you sail from Asia.

It will be proper to have a fusee, a pair of pistols, and a sword upon the road, which you had best provide in India. These will be necessary for your defence against robbers, if you should meet with any such, for those people have a very high opinion of the courage of the Europeans; and I am firmly persuaded that the frequency of robberies is entirely owing to the cowardice of travellers. Besides if you are on horseback and have a mind to go forward, as the camels travel very slow, you will draw all the horsemen after you. Or if it should be otherwise, you and your servant may pass by yourselves along the road we took in great security, except six days' journey from Mousul; and then, if no caravans offer, you may have soldiers to guard you over that part of your way. However, you will always find the dangers greatly exaggerated by the merchants of whom you enquire; and your Christian servants are in general very arrant cowards.

It will not be amiss to provide yourself with a box of medicines; for if you should have no occasion for them yourself, you will have frequent opportunities of doing charitable actions, since they have everywhere an high opinion of the skill of the Europeans in physic. However I would advise every one to travel with as little luggage as possible; for then you will be at less trouble and expence, and may make greater expedition; to say nothing of the aukwardness of your servants.

From Busserah to Aleppo there are several roads, but you cannot avoid some part of the desert, and the quickest passage of all will take up a month. Some Europeans have gone this journey by themselves; and I am apt to think that the risque of robbers, when you are provided with proper passes, is nothing but a mere bugbear. If any will venture to travel in this manner I would advise them to carry nothing of value but what their occasions require, that they may have as little to lose as possible.

The common method of travelling is on the back of a camel, but the motion of this animal is very fatiguing. However, it is somewhat more commodious in a cajava, of which there are two, one on each side of the beast. In one of these you are sheltered from the weather, and if you have a companion in the other, besides the advantage of being balanced, you may have the pleasure of his conversation, provided you understand each other; but if you have no companion you must counterpoise yourself with your baggage. But if you do not like this way of travelling, you may generally hire horses in a caravan.

The want of good water is the greatest inconvenience an European will meet with in most parts of the road over the great desert, for sometimes you will be obliged to travel several days without any but what is brackish; and, as I am informed, in three days you will meet with none at all, except immediately after the rains. For this reason you must take care to carry water with you in skins.

There are generally two caravans in a year that pass over the great desert. The time of the setting out of one is very uncertain; but the other, which consists chiefly of camels designed for sale at Aleppo, generally begins to march in May or June. The Bashaw of Bagdad has prevented the caravan of goods from travelling this way for two or three years past.

If it does not suit your convenience to wait for the desert caravan, the best way will be to proceed to Bagdad, but you must take care to be furnished with a pass from the Bashaw or Mossalem of Busserah; which you may procure by means of the Resident. You must likewise have letters of recommendation to one or more of the Sheiks. You may pass up the

Euphrates and Tigris to Bagdad in a very commodious boat, which they moore to the bank of the river every night; nor will they leave off that custom though they have never so fair a wind. This boat is covered over to defend you from the weather, and the after part is made use of for a kitchen. It will be the best way to lay in all sorts of provisions for the voyage, except fowls and kids, which you may meet with as you pass along. When there is a fair wind, they make use of their sails, but their general method of proceeding forward is by tracking.

You may possibly reach Hella, on the Euphrates, in twelve days; but they are commonly fifteen or twenty in their passage thither. From thence you may travel over the land to Bagdad in two days, and the journeys are but short neither. If you go up the Tigris you will be all the time upon the water; I would therefore advise you, as well on that account, as for the sake of expedition, to take horses at Ismark. When you are arrived at Bagdad, you are again to consider whether you will travel by the way of Kabessa[1], and over the little desert, [or?] by Mousul, which lies farther up the Tigris. The time spent in passing over the little desert is fourteen or fifteen days, and you must make the same kind of provision as for travelling over the great desert. I must confess, I think this road deserves the preference. Europeans have frequently travelled this way singly. Having crossed the Tigris, you must travel by land till you come near Anna[2], where you pass the Euphrates, but it will be necessary to procure a pass; which will be no difficult matter to obtain, if you have a proper recommendation from Busserah.

(As the Captain has given little or no account of the passage from Busserah to Bagdad by the Tigris, we are of opinion the reader will not be displeased to see a relation of a voyage from Bagdad to Busserah, which may in some measure supply that defect.)

On the 15th of April, we took a bark to pass down the Tigris from Bagdad to Busserah. This river below Bagdad has two

[1] Kubaisa, the desert outpost 10 miles to the west of Hit, where the Baghdad caravans joined those from Basra, see pp. 19, 155.

[2] Ana, see p. 156, note 1.

arms[1], one of which runs along the side of the antient Chaldea, and the other towards the point of Mesopotamia, and they both form a large island, which is traversed by several small canals. When we came to the place where the two arms part, we saw what we took to be the ruins of an antient town, near three miles in compass. The walls that remain are so large that six coaches may pass along them abreast at the same time. They are made of bricks burnt in the fire; each of which was ten feet square and three thick. We took that branch of the Tigris which runs along the side of Chaldea, for fear of falling into the hands of the Arabs, who at that time were at war with the Bashaw of Bagdad. We were ten days in passing from Bagdad to Busserah, and lay every night in the bark, and there dressed our victuals. When we came to any village, we sent our people to purchase provisions, which they bought very cheap. The names of the villages by the side of this river are Amurat[2], where there is a fort constructed of burnt bricks; Satarat, with a fort of the same kind; Mansury, a large town; Mazar, Gazar, and Gorno. This stands on the point at the confluence of the Euphrates and Tigris. It hath three small castles, or forts, one of which stands upon the point, and is the strongest of the three; the second is on the side of Chaldea, and the third on that of Arabia. The maps call this city Korna, and Captain Hamilton[3] Cemora; affirming that there are 10,000 Janizaries kept there, and eight or ten river gallies well arm'd, to keep the adjacent countries in awe, who are very apt to rebel. It abounds with all sorts of provisions, both of the animal and vegetable kind. It is 80 miles above Busserah, according to him, but according to Tavernier not much above half that distance; though we believe the medium between both may be the truth[4], for they were seven hours in passing from Comera to Busserah, both with the wind and tide. This last comes up as far as Comera, and, by what we can learn, not

[1] The Shatt Dijla and the Shatt el Hai.

[2] Kut el Imara [Kut=Fort]. *Satarat* and *Mazar* I cannot identify. *Mansury* is probably Mansur; *Gazar* is El Azair, the Tomb of Ezra; and *Gorno* is Qurna.

[3] See Hamilton, *op. cit.* vol. 1, p. 78.

[4] The actual distance is 50 miles.

much farther[1]. Busserah has undergone various revolutions, being alternately in the possession of the Turks and Arabs; but now the former have been master of it many years.

I had intended to have gone over the little desert myself, but the hurry and confusion occasioned by the rebellion of the Arabs gave me reason to believe I should wait a great while for a caravan, though it is usual for them to take this road several times in a year. The caravans which pass by Mousul, which is the road we took, make a shorter cut over the desert of Tagut, to the westward of the Tigris. We had the Bashaw of Bagdad's pass, which we found of very great service, for it procured us a very extraordinary respect, wherever we came. Besides it exempted us from the visits of the customhouse people. Those who have no pass had best gratify the customhouse officers with four or five mamoudies, to prevent the opening of their baggage, though they have no right to demand anything. The Turks are such lovers of money that there is no danger in attempting to corrupt them in their office, for you may make your bargain in as plain terms as you please.

From Bagdad you may get to Thourkat or Karkut[2] in eight days, and from thence to Mousul in four. If your stomach is a little nice, you had best provide yourself with eatables at Bagdad, for the bread and rice which you will meet with on the road may not possibly be so white. However the best bread is to be had at Busserah, and as for butter, you will meet with none after you leave that place till you come to Aleppo. As for our parts, we found the bread upon the road pretty good. As you travel along, you will meet with villages on the road to lodge in from stage to stage. But for the apartments, they will be of little use, except to defend you from the weather; for there is no furniture, and it will be a rarity to find so much as a little stool. As for other conveniences you are not to expect them. However, you may probably travel all along this road, as we did by ourselves, without the least interruption or incivility.

[1] Balbi recorded meeting the tide some way above Qurna.
[2] Kirkuk.

At Karkut, which is a strong city, it is usual to rest a day or two and replenish your panniers; that is, you must lay in provisions for four days at least, which is the time you will spend in going to Mousul, as mentioned above. As for wine you must take care to supply yourself at Busserah, and that for a month or more. At Bagdad you may probably replenish your store as well as at Karkut; and at Mousul you must purchase provisions of all kinds for six days; as also at Cajenisar [Khoja Hissar, see p. 124] or Mardin for Orfa, that is, for six or eight days; and afterwards at that place for Aleppo, which is five days more; and among the Christians you will always meet with wine or brandy.

The place where you are most likely to be detained is Mousul, because you must either wait for a caravan, or hire a convoy; which last you may do at four rupees a man. If you will listen to them, they will tell you that it will be unsafe to travel without twenty or thirty of these people for a guard; but I am persuaded there is no such danger of robbers as they pretend. However, there are caravans which set out from this place once in every ten or fourteen days, unless in the depth of winter, and they take a convoy, the money to pay which is levied by the caravan Bashi upon all the people of the caravan, generally in proportion to the goods which each person carries with him, but sometimes according to the number of beasts, and your share will consequently be but a trifle. But it must be remembered that in these parts of the world they look upon all Europeans to be as rich as Crœsus, and every one will be ready to impose upon you if you will let them.

The usual time of travelling from Mousul to Madan or Mardin is eight days, and from Mardin to Orfa seven days. The first six days of the journey is over a desert almost without inhabitants, and therefore your fare will be good or bad according to the quality of the provisions you brought with you, and three days after you leave the Tigris the water begins to be brackish, and therefore it behoves you to take care to supply yourself with that which is good in time. When we were in those parts our servant either drank or spilt our good water, and filled our leather bottles with the bad, which threw us into violent fluxes; and yet those who are used to such water, as the people of the caravan generally are, can drink it without any bad effect. However, I cannot help taking notice that good careful honest servants contribute greatly to the pleasure of the journey; whereas those that are careless or dishonest may occasion great inconveniences.

The caravan makes a halt at Nisibin, the next town to Mousul, where it is visited by the customhouse officers. But a gentleman that travels only with his baggage is under no necessity of stopping on that account, for he may proceed directly to Cojenissar, or Cojasar[1], which is a day's journey and half farther. Mardin is a large town, about four or five miles out of the road, but it is worth seeing; and, which is a greater inducement, there is good wine to be had there, to serve you on the road to Orfa, which is five or six days' journey more; and there likewise you will meet with people to make up a sufficient caravan for the same road.

The mentioning Cojasar brings to my mind the Carach[2], a sort of capitation tax, imposed by the Grand Signior on all his Christian and Jewish subjects, of five cruize[3] and two thirds per head. This is collected by a set of very impertinent people, who, in hopes of squeezing somewhat out of the Europeans, often molest them, though they have not the least shadow of right to do so. But as this is a little town, there is no appeal to any superior officers, either on account of this tax or the customs. Those sort of molestations can hardly be avoided in these places; but when you come to a town of any note you will meet with nothing but civility and hospitality. Therefore in the lesser towns the best way will be to put on big looks, and to assume the air of a man of consequence; for these people are easily imposed upon, and that will command respect. As we had a pass, they could make no demands upon us, but as our servants were not included, they obliged us to pay for them.

[1] Khoja Hissar, a place of no importance nowadays, but according to Niebuhr (vol. II, *op. cit.* p. 313, French edit., Amsterdam, 1780) the Arabs still called it by its real name *Dunasfir*, a city of note in the 13th century. See Le Strange, *Lands of the Eastern Caliphate*, p. 96.

[2] Arabic *kharāj*. [3] Arabic *ghrūsh*, a piastre.

From Mardin to Orfa the road is sometimes infested with robbers, through the neglect of the Bashaw. However in this passage there are a great many more frightened than hurt. But you must be greatly on your guard against thieves, for the people hereabout are very expert pilferers. Even the robbers can hardly be placed in a higher class, for they ride up to the caravan and snatch whatever they can first lay hands upon, and then retreat in the same manner. If the people of the caravan had but the least courage and conduct, they might easily prevent robberies of this kind. When violent rains swell the river, this road is sometimes impassable for four or five days, till the waters run off.

We must suppose that at Mousul you have hired horses for Orfa; therefore when [you arrive there?] you must make a fresh bargain for Aleppo. At least you ought to take this method, because it is better than hiring them for the whole journey at once; for if you have them from the Catarches[1] of the caravan which you have joined, you will be obliged to travel their pace, and wait their time; nay, though you should make a bargain to the contrary, you will be under a necessity of staying at each stage two or three days at least, to refresh your horses. But remember it will be always best to get an obligation from your Catarche in writing, especially if you hire the horses for the whole journey; and your terms should be particularly specified, reserving to yourself a power of hiring fresh horses, if he loiters by the way, or furnishes you with jades unable to perform the journey, for which he must consent to abate part of the hire.

If these people should happen to be negligent or refractory, or any way deficient in performing their bargain, the principal merchants of the caravan will see justice done you; besides the magistrates of the great towns will quickly redress any grievance of that kind. If you pass for men of consequence, they will expect a fee; which needs be but a trifle, for a small matter will bribe a great Turk. Sometimes threatning alone, when you find it necessary, will keep them in awe. In loading a beast, your bedding is to be laid undermost, then your

[1] Arabic *qitarji*, the leader of a file of camels.

baggage, and your servant mounts on the top. If you carry your clothes and goods in portmanteaus, you will lose package, and therefore it will be best to make use of bags which are to be had for that purpose, and are much more convenient.

From Orfa to Aleppo you will be five days upon the road, and perhaps six; but then you will lie in villages every night, as you did between Bagdad and Mousul. You will seldom want company from any of these places, when your intentions are publicly known.

When you arrive at Aleppo, and are in a hurry to leave that place, you will be under no necessity of being detained; for if there is no vessel ready to sail from Scanderoon[1] to Cyprus, you may pass on to Latikiyah[2], a day's journey farther, where you may cross in small vessels which are continually passing and repassing to and from that island. And at Cyprus there is scarce a week without an opportunity of gaining a passage from thence to Marseilles. In the time of peace the most expeditious way will be to travel through France, for it is not only longer, but more expensive, to travel thro' Italy, Germany, and Holland; though there are a great many more curious things to be seen in that tour, and there are few gentlemen but will be glad to make use of such an opportunity.

Upon the whole, I compute that from Busserah to Aleppo, a passenger, if he meets with no delay, may travel in three or four and thirty days over the Great Desart. From Bagdad, allowing for your stay there by the way of Kabessa, in four or five and forty days, and by Mousul about twenty more. But if a person can undergo the fatigue of the Mansel[3] or riding post, he may reach Aleppo from Bagdad in fourteen or fifteen days. The privilege of travelling in this manner may be obtained by the Resident, if he is a man of interest with the Government, for then he can procure you a Mansel Command, which is an order signed by the Grand Signior, and lodged in the hands of the different Bashaws; by these means you will not only be at your journey's end sooner, but without the least expence. This was offered to us by the

[1] Iskanderun, Alexandretta. [2] Latakia.
[3] One of the meanings of *manzil* is a post-house.

Bashaw of Mousul, and we should have accepted of it if it had not been for our baggage.

With relation to your expences, the quicker you travel they are the less. But you must often submit to necessity: thus an extraordinary severe spring retarded us for several days. Besides, we had more servants than were necessary, and were more extravagant in our clothes than I since have found there was occasion for; insomuch that, including the utensils of the kitchen, it cost us 400 rupees apiece. If you have good gold, you may make ten per cent. of it, but ours was so indifferent that it was reduced almost to par.

I have sent my diary to Mr. Dorril[1], and propose, if I have time, to send him a copy of my expences with remarks. Those who can afford to be free of their money on the road may travel through these countries with the utmost ease and security, and will meet with the highest respect. We might have been introduced to the Bashaws of all the places which we passed through, but we declined it when we found it to be attended with expence. They commonly present you a vest upon these occasions, but then in return you are to give thirty or forty rupees to the servant.

The gentlemen of Aleppo particularly recommended it to me to wipe off the aspersion of inhospitality which has been thrown upon them; which I can do with the greatest justice from my own experience; and they wish for nothing more than to have this road more frequented by gentlemen from India. However, it will not be amiss to bring a line from the Resident at Busserah, as the most ready way to make yourself known, and then you need not fear meeting with the kindest reception.

ELIOT ELIOT.

Aleppo, *April* 2, 1741.

PS. When we were at Busserah there were boats to be hired for Bagdad, which perform the voyage in fifteen days. The

[1] Thomas Dorrill was Agent at Basra from August 1739 to about May 1746, when he returned to Bombay as a member of the Council there, leaving Thomas Grendon in charge at Basra. The latter held office until relieved by Nathaniel Pomfret in May 1748.

boats stop every night, and the passengers lie on shore. But you must furnish yourself with provisions at Busserah for the whole time. However, it will be proper before you leave Busserah to enquire when a caravan will be ready to depart for Aleppo; as it will be more convenient to wait for it at Busserah than Bagdad. There is [are] settled rules for the payment of Customs at Busserah, for which you are to take a sealed receipt, for this will make them easier at Aleppo. The best lodging at Bagdad is with the Padre. And when you set out from thence, it will be necessary to lay in upwards of twenty days' provision to serve you on your passage over the desart, for there is nothing to be had by the way. A camel's load of water will be sufficient for one master and two servants, and you will pay about thirty rupees for each camel. Water must be procured at the charge of the traveller. The charge of horse-hire from Bagdad to Aleppo will be about sixty rupees each horse, but the traveller finds his own furniture. An Armenian or Georgian servant is necessary for a guidelin or gentleman usher; to whom you must pay about sixty rupees. One rupee is five mamoodies, and four mamoodies and a half is one zelot. One Venetian[1] is twenty one mamoodies and a half. Zelotas[2] are the best money to receive at Busserah; as the change for gold is at four and a half per cent. advance. Gold in specie is better than Venetians, and is often to be bought at Busserah. Respondentia are at 20 to 25 per cent. by the caravan from Bagdad to Aleppo. But bills from Aleppo loose by their exchange to England; to Marseilles or Venice they are upon a par. Silk is the best commodity that can be carried from Aleppo for France or Italy.

[1] The Venetian ducat or sequin.
[2] Arabic *zalata*, a Turkish silver coin.

§ IV

NARRATIVE OF A JOURNEY FROM *ALEPPO* TO *BASRA* IN 1751

by

JOHN CARMICHAEL

PREFATORY NOTE

THE following narrative has only previously appeared in print as an appendix to the second edition (London, 1772) of *A Voyage to the East Indies*, by John Henry Grose; and it is from this source that our text is taken, with some alteration in the punctuation and the correction of a few obvious misprints. In his preliminary 'advertisement' Grose explains that he has included the narrative because 'from the many necessary informations and judicious remarks [it] will be both an useful and entertaining companion to those who may have occasion to make that journey, and be the means of procuring further insight into the situation and remains of those antient cities mentioned in sacred history.' He then proceeds to say: 'It may be satisfactory to the reader to know something of Mr. Charmichael [*sic*]. I shall therefore acquaint him that he was in the service of the East India Company at Bombay, where having some disputes with the Governor and Council, he came over to England in order to lay his complaints before the Court of Directors, leaving his affairs in India unsettled. His conduct was so much disapproved that, instead of meeting with redress, he was dismissed the service; and on his application for leave to go back, in order to settle his affairs, was refused a passage on board any of the Company's ships. This occasioned him to take the journey over the desert. On his arrival in India, he entered into the service of one of the country powers; and after meeting with many adventures and experiencing great vicissitudes of fortune, he at last died in distress at Surat.'

To this account of our traveller it has not been found possible to add much from the India Office records, which are very sparse at this date, particularly as regards letters from Bombay. From the Court Minutes, however, we find that on 8 June 1750 there was laid before the Directors a memorial from John Carmichael, late Gunner at Anjengo, complaining of injuries sustained by him at that place and at

Bombay, and praying that he might be compensated and sent out again in the capacity of a covenanted servant. The petition was, as usual, referred to the Committee of Correspondence to examine and report. The result was fatal to Carmichael's hopes. On 12 July the Committee reported that 'finding by the advices from Bombay and Anjengo that his behaviour had been insolent and highly unbecoming at both places, they are of opinion that Mr. Bourchier [the Governor of Bombay] did right in sending him from Anjengo; and as he has the general character of being a very troublesome man, that he be not admitted to serve the Company as a covenanted servant or in any other station in India.' This report was laid before the Directors six days later, and its conclusions were adopted; but as a concession to the petitioner, it was ordered that instructions should be sent to Bombay to provide his family with a passage home at the Company's expense. Far from accepting the decision, Carmichael renewed his application in September and again two months later; but the Directors refused to consider the matter further, and on each occasion his petition was ordered to 'lie on the table.'

Evidently Carmichael thereupon decided to return to India overland, and to this we owe his interesting journal. Of the rest of his career we know nothing but what is told us by Grose, as quoted above. Even the date of his death has not been found, though obviously it had occurred prior to 1772.

It is interesting that anyone dismissed the Company's service, and even refused a passage on board any of their ships, should not only have adhered to his determination to return to India, but should also have made use of his opportunities as Carmichael did.

The outstanding points in his journal are as follows: Carmichael set out from Aleppo and kept a detailed survey, in hours and compass-bearings, all the way to Basra. Over the sections which have been worked out and tested against the most recent maps, his survey does him great credit. He evidently took immense trouble to ascertain the rate of movement of the camel caravan. He measured the average pace of his camel, counted the number of paces per hour, and computed his rate of travel accordingly. Rennell compliments him on his perseverance, and on the result attained. He says: 'Mr Carmichael's whole line of bearing, by compass, about 720 British miles (by road 750 nearly), coincided with the bearing line given by the celestial observations....'

Carmichael also gives a few little panoramic sketches of the principal landmarks. He pays some attention to the ruined sites, and makes several interesting observations. For instance, he records the aqueduct which once supplied the Qusur el Ikhwan from Ain el Qom; and he gives a long account of Ukhaidir, 'the finest example of Sassanian (?) architecture' yet discovered, being the fourth European to see it, and the first to describe it in detail.

Carmichael is indeed, without doubt, Gertrude Bell's 'unknown Englishman,' whom she notes as having preceded M. Massignon and herself, but she was wrong in supposing him to be the first modern traveller to visit the site (see further, p. 161, note 1).

Carmichael's journal was evidently seen by Niebuhr, for in his *Voyage en Arabie*, etc., vol. II, p. 184, 1780 edition (*Reisebeschreibung nach Arabien und andern umliegenden Ländern*, Carsten Niebuhr, Copenhagen, 1778, vol. II, p. 225), he notes having 'found in the Journal of an Englishman' reference to a ruined town which he rightly identifies as 'El Khader' (Ukhaidir). The brief description given by Niebuhr tallies with Carmichael's, but is not given word for word (see pp. 33–5 of Carmichael's text). This passage is quoted by Massignon (see *Mémoires de l'Institut français d'Archéologie orientale du Caire*, p. 7) and also by Miss Gertrude Bell, *Amurath to Amurath*, p. 148.

Rennell refers to Carmichael's journal in such a manner as to make one believe that he saw the actual original, for he makes no mention of Grose or his book, but he records his indebtedness to his friend, Dr Patrick Russell, for 'The Journal of Mr. Carmichael's route across the Great Desert between Aleppo and Basrah, in 1751.' In a paper read before the Royal Society on 17 March 1791, published in the *Philosophical Transactions of the Royal Society of London*, he says 'the manuscript copy of his [Carmichael's] journal was obligingly communicated by my friend Dr Patrick Russell.'

The first instance of Carmichael's itinerary being made use of appears to be on a map attached to Ives' *Journey from Persia to England in* 1755–1759. Here the line of march is described as 'the common route of the caravan from Aleppo to Bassora over the Great Desert of Arabia as described in a Journal kept by Mr Carmichael in the year M.D.CCLI.'

A map showing Carmichael's route was published by Irwin[1] in 1787; this was evidently compiled from the travels of Ives, Niebuhr, Carmichael, and from his own experiences. Rennell also uses Carmichael's material on Sheet IX of his 'Atlas to Accompany his *Treatise*, etc.'[2]

[1] In *A Series of Adventures*, etc. Eyles Irwin, London, 1787, vol. II, p. 153.

[2] See *Treatise on the Comparative Geography of Western Asia*, Major James Rennell (1831, pp. 23, 24). Also *Philosophical Transactions of the Royal Society*, original ed. 1791, vol. LXXXI, p. 39, and map, p. 144.

A JOURNEY FROM *ALEPPO*, OVER THE DESERT, TO *BASSERAH*, OCTOBER 21, 1771[1]

AT two this afternoon took my departure from Aleppo for Basserah, in company with Signior Andrea Johanna; when, directing our course nearly S.S.E. ¾ E., at sun-set arrived at Tilleran[2], a small Turkish village, where we joined the caravan, which was encamped near that place. The wind westerly, with dark cloudy weather; the night cold, with drizzling rain.

22D. This morning at eight mounted my camel, for the first time. His Magnitude seemed highly disgusted with my hat, and twice ran away with me from the caravan, but was soon satisfied with this sport.

From Tilleran, directing our course about S.E. by S., an hour and half brought us to Indahab[3] (i.e. Golden Water), a small village on the south side of the road. The houses are small, and resemble sugar loaves. On the north side of the road is an artificial mount, which seems to have been raised for the defence of the water. The land hereabouts is a fine black soil, mostly arable.

[1] The error of date (1771 for 1751) is proved by his reference to Mr Brabazon Ellis, the English Resident at Basra, whom he was invited to meet at 'Issabier' (Zubair); here he also met 'Mr. Hanmer, surgeon.' In the India Office *Factory Records: 'Persian Gulf'* a despatch from Mr Brabazon Ellis, dated 18 Feb. 1752, reports that 'The Aleppo Caravan arrived here in December with 37 loads of cloths,' etc. This was the caravan with which Carmichael travelled. In the same despatch Francis Hanmer, surgeon, 'a very discreet man,' is mentioned. Mr Brabazon Ellis was appointed in 1751, and at least four other Residents officiated between 1751 and 1771. So there is no doubt as to the real date of Carmichael's journey. Also, on Ives' map (see p. 134) he dates the route as described by 'Mr Carmichael in the year M.D.CCLI.'

[2] Tell Ara or Aran, a considerable village in early days (see Le Strange, *Palestine under the Moslems*, p. 542).

[3] Ain Dhahab, probably the same as Ain Sfira of Sachau's map, and of Kiepert's *Syrien und Mesopotamien*, 1893. Teixeira's Ain Dhahab would appear to be another spring 'rising at a town on its further [northern] side, called Gebul, and the spring itself is called Ahem Dahab, or The Golden Fount, by reason of the value of its waters.' Musil shows two corresponding sources on his map *Northern Arabia*, one entering the Sabkha Jebbul from the north and the other from the west.

Thence continuing a S.E. by S. course, 35 minutes, came to Sphera[1], a small village south of the road. On the north-side are two large fountains of good clear water, near the foot of an artificial mount, on the top of which is a building resembling a tomb.

From this place, travelling S.E. ¼ S., in two hours and a half came to Geboul[2], which lies on the south-side of the road. It appears to have been a more considerable village than any of the former, but is now almost in ruins. At a small distance to the N.E. is seen the Valley of Salt[3], which supplies all the country with that commodity. Continuing our march four[4] hours and a half came to Hagla[5], and encamped. The camel's motion very disagreeable.

23D. The caravan continued here all day, preparing for a regular march. The wind easterly and fresh, with dark cloudy weather. It rained hard all night, which made our lodging but uncomfortable.

24TH. The tents and baggage being made very heavy by the rain which fell in the night, we were forced to defer our departure till they were dry. I took this opportunity to visit a valley at the end of a range of hills to the northward, which terminate at Hagla, where I found several wells about twelve feet deep, built round with stone[6], the water very indifferent; notwithstanding which there seems, by the many remaining foundations, to have been formerly a large town here. There are also many squared stones standing perpendicularly, like those usually erected over graves; but I saw no inscriptions.

The Arabs report that there are many black scorpions among these ruins; for which reason we encamped at a distance. The night dark, cold and rainy, with a fresh easterly gale.

[1] Sfira. Chesney found it 'prosperous'; see *Expedition to the Euphrates*, vol. I, p. 413.

[2] Jebbul, see pp. 6, 9.

[3] Sabkha Jebbul, see footnote, p. 9, n. 3.

[4] From the following table this should be 'two.'

[5] Hiqla.

[6] Plaisted found only 'a pool of standing water.' Capper found it a ruined village; so the author's record of steined wells is important.

CARMICHAEL'S PANORAMIC SKETCHES.

No. 1 JEBEL EL HASS
No. 2 JEBEL BISHRI, from the North West
No. 3 "MOUNT," near AIN EL QOM
No. 4 JEBEL BISHRI, from the South
No. 5—UGLET HAURAN

weather, with a breeze at N.W. The night cold, and inclining to frost. No water.

28TH. This morning, by looking out sharp, got coffee for breakfast, which with a little bread served me the whole day.

Having suffered much last night (which was very cold) from the want of my blanket, I thought of the following stratagem to recover it. I entered into conversation with the Arabs on the subject of my loss, and took occasion to mention how highly they were celebrated by travellers for their honesty; which made me conclude that my blanket had been taken away by some mistake, and would be returned as soon as the error was discovered. This had the desired effect; the Arab who had it, fearful for the national honour, returned it, pretending he had found it on a camel. On the recovery of my property, I complimented the thief on his not deviating from the integrity of his countrymen. We set out early this morning and marched S.E. ½ E. nine hours. At half past three in the afternoon encamped near the Jabian[1] mountains. The weather fair, with a small breeze at east.

From Lahauz to this place the country is perfectly level, and the soil sandy. There are great plenty of hares, whose holes or burrows, of which the ground is as full as a warren, made it very troublesome to the camels. The mountains of Jabia run from the N.E. to S.W.[2] and in a clear morning appear as in the view, No. 2 [opposite p. 136].

29TH. Set forwards at sun-rise. After travelling S.E. ¼ E. thirty minutes, came to some rising ground, which to avoid we kept S.S.E. half an hour, when a steep descent made us decline S. ¼ E. for another half hour; from thence through a valley S.E. one hour and a half, and then shifted our course

initiative probably visited, Isriya, the ancient *Seriana*, a place of considerable interest, previously seen at a distance by Teixeira on 8 February 1615 ('ruins of a great and once Christian city') and visited by Della Valle in 1616 and 1625. Other European visitors were Timothy Lanoy and Aaron Goodyear in 1691.

[1] On the 31st he notes looking back on the Tibian mountains, so I think we may assume Jabian to be Tibian—the hill country of Taiyibe. What he actually saw was the Jebel Bishri of present-day maps, and its outlying ridges the J. Munshar, beneath which Ain el Qom lies.

[2] This is the general trend of the watershed which flanks the Palmyra-Deir ez Zor track on the north.

to S.E. ¼ E. in which direction we marched two hours, and about noon arrived at Ain il Kom, or the Fountain of War[1], where we encamped on a rising ground round a large spring of mineral water, from which issues near four tons an hour. It is blood warm, has a good taste, and is of an excellent quality[2]. At about a hundred yards S.W. of this spring is an artificial mount, near two hundred feet high, raised for its defence. The mount bearing S. by E. at the distance of a quarter of a mile. It appears as in No. 3. *A* is the place of the spring.

We saw a great quantity of cellery about this fountain or spring, and many large bushes on the desart, which were the first we met with since our departure from Hagla. From the mount I could plainly perceive with my glass the ruins of Tibia[3], bearing south, distant about five miles. There still remains a large tower standing, surrounded with many ruins of great buildings. I also observed a hill, which appeared to have been fortified. From these circumstances, as well as its situation, believe Tibia was formerly very strong[4]. I offered an Arab a chequeen to accompany me thither; but he demanding three, I relinquished my intention.

There is a noble subterranean aquaduct cut thro' the rock, which conveys the water from this spring to Gusserah Sawye[5], a large old fort, at the entrance of this pass, ten miles to the southward, on the other side of the mountains. This was a prodigious undertaking, and testifies the former importance of this place[6].

[1] Ain el Qom. If Carmichael is right as to its meaning—the Fountain or Spring of the Enemy. According to Musil, who was there in 1908, it is inhabited again; he hints at its historical interest. See *Palmyrena*, p. 71.

[2] Capper says that 'in colour, taste and also in heat, it greatly resembles that of the Bristol wells.'

[3] Taiyibe, see pp. 85–6.

[4] Compare Plaisted, 18 July.

[5] Qusur el Ikhwan. For identification see pp. 15, 143–44.

[6] Capper, Coote, Irwin, Olivier and Rousseau all mention this aqueduct. Rennell quotes them and adds that it must have been 'at least eleven miles in length, and bespoke an origin anterior to Muhammadan times.' Apparently the aqueduct led onwards to other ruined sites farther south. Rousseau says 'we crossed an aqueduct built of great cut stones, and a quarter of an hour later, another of the same kind, both coming from *Guessour-el-Ekhéwein*, which we saw in the distance to the north.

30TH. There being plenty of proper food for our camels and the water good, we halted here this day, in order to lay in a proper store of that element, as we could not expect to meet with much more on our proposed route, the rainy season being but just commenced.

I fancy Bear[1] is only fifteen miles N.E. from hence, and imagine to be the same place mentioned in Judges ix. 21.

A little to the southward of this place is a large cross road, running from E.N.E. to W.S.W. which seems to pass from Bear [and] Urfa in Mesopotamia to Jerusalem [and] Damascus, Tyre [and] Tripoly, and other places of note on the sea coast and S.W. parts of Syria; and this being likewise the pass from Persia and Chaldea to the north of Syria and Lesser Asia, a constant garrison was kept at this fort; whence the necessity of this grand aquaduct is evident, more particularly as this was probably the way by which those numerous armies, mentioned both in sacred and prophane history, marched from Babylon and other places of the East[2].

About eight miles from Tibia is the ruins of Sachne (i.e. Hot Water), another antient city, so named from a spring of excessive hot water, which issues from a mountain there[3].

Forty miles S.W. of Tibia stands the magnificent ruins of the once great and famous city of Jadmor[4], which with great probability is thought to be the same spoken of in 1 Kings

The first aqueduct led towards the south, and ended at two buildings which I was unable to recognize owing to the inequalities of the ground. The second led to the south-west and disappeared in the hills of *Douetche* [Dhahik] where it is said there used to be splendid gardens.' Musil shows two aqueducts, one coming from Taiyibe and the other from Ain el Qom.

[1] He must mean Deir (Deir ez Zor), which is actually 80 miles north-east of his position at the moment.

[2] Thus Carmichael is the only one of our travellers (for the matter of that, the only early traveller we know of) who notes this great highway of commerce—the Euphrates (Deir) Palmyra-Damascus route. Carmichael also hints at the origin of these desert stations—garrisoned forts—for at one period they marked the Eastern frontier of the Roman Empire. This is a region of considerable interest. We are also near another ancient highway—that which connected Raqqa, Palmyra and Homs. All travellers were struck by the number of ruined sites, the derelict aqueducts, and other signs of a departed prosperity.

[3] Sukhne.

[4] Tadmor (Palmyra).

ix. 18 and 2 Chron. viii. 4. I am the more confirmed in this opinion, as, except this and the two places whose ruins are already mentioned, I could not hear of the least appearance of any other. Besides, there seems nowhere in the desart, unless near these mountains, a sufficiency of water for a large city.

At a small distance from Jadmor is a village of salt[1], thought to be that mentioned 2 Sam. viii. 13; where David defeated the Syrians. If this be admitted, then Tibia and Sackne are probably the ancient cities of Tibhath and Chun, 1 Chron. xviii. 8, from whence David brought that great quantity of brass, with which Solomon made the brazen sea, pillar, and other works of the Temple. My reasons for these opinions are founded on the several passages in the Old Testament, as well as on the similarity in the sound of Tibia and Tibhath.

Places names [in] the carav. route	Courses	Hours	Min.
From Hagla to Lahauz	S.E. by S.	2	30
	S.S.E.	1	—
	E.S.E.	2	—
Lahauz to Auro il Aruneba	S.E. by E.	9	30
Auro il Aruneb to Tellemac	S.E. ¾ E.	8	30
Tillemlack to the Tiebran mountains	S.E. ½ E.	9	—
Tiebran mountains to Ain il Kom	S.E. ¾ E.	2	30
	S.S.E.	—	30
	S. ¼ E.	—	30
	S.E.	1	30
Hagla to Ain il Kom		37	30[2]

By the aforesaid calculation for Ain il Kom, and estimating the distance to Tibia S. by W. five miles, and that Tadmor is

[1] Carmichael was the first to report this saline depression to the south of Palmyra, and its ruined sites. Chesney visited it in 1837, being one of the few travellers who have entered Palmyra from the south-east. Musil, who was there in 1908 and 1912, describes and figures the ruins in *Palmyrena*, pp. 88, 136–43. Gertrude Bell recorded the sites of *Bazuriya* and *Bukharra* in 1914.

[2] This is a fair example of Carmichael's thoroughness as a traveller. At 3 miles per hour he computed his distance from Hiqla to Ain el Qom at 95 miles It is actually 98 miles, as near as one can judge his route on the *Carte Internationale du Monde au* 1,000,000.

S.W. from hence twenty hours of a caravan, I then compute that Tiaba is situated in

		°	′	
Lat. by account and estimate		35	15	N.[1]
Long. a merid. of	Aleppo	1	11	E.
	London	38	45	

Jadmor [Tadmor] is situated in

		°	′	
Lat. by account and estimate		38	52	N.[2]
Long. a merid. of	Aleppo	00	37	E.
	London	38	11	

Having neither books, maps, or tables of latitude and longitude, I am consequently obliged to rely on my memory; from which I think Jerusalem is situate about 32° 30′ N. latitude, nearly 35° 00′ east of London. This being admitted, Jerusalem is only 250 miles S.W. from Tibia, and 200 S.W. from Tadmor.

31ST. Mounted this morning at sun-rise. Marching S.E. ¾ S. one hour, we had a fair view of the ruins of Tibia, which are at present entirely deserted.

Thence moved S.E. ¼ E. two hours and a half, and S.E. ¼ S. one hour, through a fine and large valley between the mountains, and came to Gusserah Swaye (i.e. the palace of Swaye[3]),

[1] Carmichael's computations for latitude and longitude cannot be expected to be very accurate, for they only depend on his distance and bearing, but it is to his credit that he got as near as he did to the true positions of places so far removed from known points. Taiyibe, for instance, is actually 35° 3′ N., as against Carmichael's 35° 15′, and the longitude is 1° 35′ east of Aleppo as against Carmichael's 1° 11′.

[2] 38° 52′ must be a misprint, for Carmichael describes Tadmor as being 20 hours S.W. from Taiyibe. It was probably 34° 52′ in the original, the true latitude being 34° 35′.

[3] Beawes had already noted *Gussorah Seveyge* in the same locality, and since Carmichael quotes part of an inscription which Rousseau records in full 57 years later, I think there is no doubt as to its identity, namely Qusur el Ikhwan, *i.e.* 'The Castles of the Two Brothers,' situated 13 to 14 miles to the south-east of Ain el Qom. Rennell thinks it was actually one of the guard stations on the caravan track, and it certainly was a place of strategic importance, for it guarded both the Aleppo-Basra and the Deir ez Zor-Palmyra routes.

Capper followed Carmichael and described it quite well, under the name *Keffer el Ackwien* or *Gussur el Bain*; Evers notes *Kassar Luckween*; and Irwin conjectured *Kasr Akhein* to be 'a summer palace of Zenobia, or of some of the Palmyrene monarchs...though after all, it may be of the

a large old fortress on the south side of the mountains and at the entrance of the pass, which is here only about a mile wide, with steep hills on either side.

age of the Caliphs of Damascus and Baghdad, and no more than a patched edifice, reared from the ruins of Palmyra'; his account is worth reading. The building probably dates from the Umayyad period. Taylor calls it 'a small castle in the Gothic style.'

It remained for Rousseau to give us a detailed description of the two castles, with their measurements; he also procured the inscribed stone, and carried it away to Aleppo. In Rousseau's original manuscript there was a copy of the inscription, which Clermont-Ganneau has reproduced and translated (*Une Inscription de Calife Hicham*, C. Clermont-Ganneau in *Recueil d'Archéologie Orientale*, Tome III, 1900).

Rousseau made two sketches of the Castles, one of which is reproduced in his *Voyage de Bagdad à Alep*, and the other by Clermont-Ganneau in the publication noted above.

Della Valle mentions this ruin on both his journeys. In 1614 he came to 'a town with a strong castle with walls of great stones, very well built, but entirely ruined and abandoned. The Arabs call it *el Her*.' On his return journey he records 'the ruinous castle called Hheir,' which he 'found to be a great Building, all of good and large white Marble stones; the form of it is a long square, the walls round about, here and there distinguished with small round Turrets; within are many contrivances of Rooms, all likewise of white stone, but so ruinous that it cannot be known what they were.'

The two sites are obviously identical, for Rousseau's description of Ikhwan is the same as Ostrup's of *Kasr el Hêr* (see plan of same, Ostrup, *op. cit.* p. 67), and the twin castles were further described and figured under the name *Kasr al-Hêr*, by Musil, who visited them in 1908 (see *Palmyrena*, pp. 72–80).

Eyre Coote described a nameless ruin, about two hours east of Taiyibe, which was obviously Qusur el Ikhwan. 'It consisted of two square buildings, one of 200 paces, the other of 100; the walls are of fine hewn stones of a reddish colour, and about 12 feet thick and 40 feet high all round, excepting some portion which had fallen down. The largest building had 24 towers, the smallest 12; the entrances were not very large, but elegantly finished, in Grecian style within. We saw a number of arches supported by pillars of white marble finely polished;...the capitals had double flowers, exceedingly well finished. There was the ruin of an aqueduct that came from the mountains on the right of this palace, and from thence across the plain into the other building.' Coote's description is in no way improved upon by Ostrup, except that his description is illustrated by a plan (*op. cit.* p. 67). Ostrup observes, 'The only power which could have had any interest in making this sort of fortification in the region was the Roman, as the purpose of such a fort must have been against sudden attacks by Bedouin. It might possibly have been one of a chain of forts which extended from Raqqa [or Circesium] to Palmyra to protect the Eastern frontier' (see also *Syria as a Roman Province*, Bouchier, p. 153).

The castles may equally well have been used *against* Rome by the Palmyrene independents of the latter half of the 3rd century, who reverted again to allegiance with Byzantium when they lay within the sphere of the Christian Beni Ghassan.

QUSUR EL IKHWAN

This valley is about fifteen miles long, and at Tibia eight or ten broad. The soil is good, and was formerly well watered by the aquaduct which I before mentioned, and which I had now an opportunity of examining. It is arched over, and at proper distances had receivers with wells over them to draw water, many of which still are to be seen, but all defaced and ruined. At these places I observed great quantities of jepsing [gypsum], a kind of sparry matter, resembling the chrystals of nitre. It only appeared about the aquaduct where the water was stopped, or on the desart where mineral water had been spilt on the hot sand. The Arabs say there is an inscription in Gusserah Swayeagee to this purport: 'we filled this Gusserah (or palace) with figs.'

About an hour S.W. are the ruins of Sackne, on the south side the mountains. I had not time to visit the old fortress, being situated on the west side of the pass, and my cameler keeping on the east.

The rocks on this side the pass are very white, and seem to be a kind of alabaster.

Thence directing our course S.E. by E. ¼ E. two hours and a half, over a dry sandy soil quite level, encamped at two on the plain at Geboul Busheir[1], from whence the south-side of the Tibean[2] mountains appear [on?] a clear evening as in No. [4 on Plate opposite p. 136]. No water.

November 1. Decamped this morning; travelling between S.E. and E.S.E. (I allow the medium S.E. by E.) nine hours; and about three in the afternoon encamped. We met with no water here, the country sandy, and quite level. A small breeze from N.W. all day, with cloudy weather. The night cold. The point of the black mountains at Sackne N.W. by W. ½ W., distance about nine leagues.

2ND. Marched at sun-rise, proceeding E.S.E. seven hours over a hard soil, full of small stones, and quite level; came then to a small descent, from whence kept E. by S. ¾ E. three hours, till near sun-set, when we encamped. A small breeze from east all day, with pleasant weather. Night cool. No water.

[1] Jebel Bishri, the author's *Jabian Mountains*, the hills which border the Palmyra-Deir ez Zor track on the N., see Musil's map *Northern Arabia*. See also Plaisted's journal, 16 July. [2] See p. 139.

3D. Decamped at sun-rise, course E. by S. four hours and ten minutes; at eleven encamped at Jeul il Ganam[1] (i.e. the Sheeps Pool), a low sandy bottom, where there are several wells, or rather holes in the sand, about ten feet deep, from whence they draw a kind of mineral water, but much inferior to that of Ain il Kom. Near these wells, where water had been spilt, is abundance of jepsing, which looks very pretty, glittering in the sun like glass. It has a rough pungent taste, and might probably produce allum, if the proper means were made use of.

Here we found a wounded man. He said he had remained eight days in that condition, without nourishment of any kind. Indeed he appeared almost spent. There were also several dead bodies thrown into the wells. After taking some refreshment, he gave us the following relation.

Two parties of Arabs who were enemies, chancing to meet eight days ago at Jeub il Ganam, they had an obstinate

[1] Jubb el Ghanam, the Sheep's Well, is a watering of some importance, on which nearly all caravans converged, it being the only certain supply over a long waterless stage. Jubb (a deep well) appears in many forms, *Jupp*, *Djerb*, *Juab*, *Juba*, *Jeul*, *Geubil*, *Jubil*, *Jabil*. Carmichael himself spells it three different ways—*Jeul*, *Jeub* and *Jubil*. Ghanam (sheep) becomes *Canam*, *Chanum*, *Kunnun*, *Guenem*, *Rhanum*, *Gannem*, *Gannon* and *Ganam*. The alternate word *Harrof* (Kharuf) is also used. The wells are situated approximately 25 miles south-south-west of Rahba, the ruined Qasr overlooking the Euphrates, and forty-five miles north-west of Abu Kemal. They number two to ten, according to the different authorities, who also contradict each other by saying the water is 'fresh,' 'sweet,' 'muddy,' and 'brackish'; indeed, it is difficult to apply some of the descriptions of this watering to the same place. Coote's *Gibbut* well 'narrow as a chimney, built with free-stone, about 15 fathoms deep,' with a horizontal shaft at the bottom, tallies with Taylor's 'wells extremely deep, cut out of rock with a border of masonry around the inside.' But Carmichael's 'several wells, or rather holes in the sand, about 10 feet deep' must refer to another watering-place in the same locality, such as, for instance, Fowle's 'five wells, 5 feet below surface, water brackish but drinkable.' Taylor comments upon the name Sheep's Well, suggesting that 'although the country round is extremely barren, in former days it might have afforded pastures to numerous flocks' (see also Irwin, *op. cit.* pp. 305, 306). In Teixeira's day, however, the district was full of nomads with their flocks and herds (*op. cit.* pp. 88, 94–6). All the way from Ana to Sukhne he found encampments of 'Turkyman' with great flocks of sheep and many camels. Rennell notes the region as a 'Great Sheep Walk' on his map; and it is a fact that until quite recently Damascene drovers still brought sheep from Mesopotamia by this very route. It is an uncertain undertaking in these days, and sometimes meets with disaster (see also *Geog. Journ.* January 1910, p. 14).

engagement, in which many were killed and wounded on both sides; at length they parted, as it were by consent, the one party standing to the northward, the other towards the south. They left this man, supposing him dead.

We had reason to suspect they both came with the intent of plundering the caravan, which we escaped by this unexpected meeting, when they vented their rage and disappointment on each other. On account of this lucky escape, the Arabs killed a camel for a festival of joy. There are a few bushes here, but no appearance of any antient or other buildings. I was told that the city of Rackba is about nine hours E.N.E. from this place[1]; wherefore shall calculate the situation of Jubil Ganam to guess at Rackba.

Names of Places in the Carav. route	Courses	H.	Min.
From Ain il Kom to Gusserah Swaygee	S.E. ¾ E.	1	—
	S.E. ½ E.	2	30
	S.E. ¼ S.	1	—
Gusserah Swaygee to Geboul Bussheir	S.E. by E. ¾ E.	2	30
	S.E. by E.	9	—
Geboul Bussheir to Jabil Ganam	E.S.E.	7	—
	E. ¼ S.	3	—
	E. by S.	4	10
Ain il Kom to Jabil Ganam is		30	10
Aleppo to Ain il Kom was		48	35
Aleppo to Jabil Ganam is		78	45

Racba is situate in					
	Lat. by acct. and estimat.		34°	34′	N.[1]
	Long. a merid. of	Aleppo	2	29	E.[2]
		London	40	03	

Rackba is still a large place, but much inferior to its ancient condition[3]. Indeed this country affords a melancholy proof of the instability of human affairs, when it is remembered that, of [in] the part adjacent to the river Euphrates and within the compass of thirty miles, there were formerly not less than three hundred and fifty cities, towns, and villages, of whose ruins scarce a single trace at this time remains.

1 Rahba, actually 30 miles distant.

2 Rahba is on the 35th parallel and stands 3° 13′ east of Aleppo.

3 Olivier, in 1797, our nearest contemporary authority, makes no mention of any inhabitants. Rousseau in 1808 says: 'a few Arab families inhabit it to-day.'

10-2

4TH. Mounted this morning at forty minutes past seven. E.E. ¼ E.[1] three hours and a half. Came then to Batton Swab[2], i.e. Gathering of Water, which seems in the rainy season to be a large river, but it is now dry. From thence kept S.E. ¾ E. four hours. At ten minutes after three encamped on a fine soil, where we found plenty of food for our camels.

Our march was delayed till the return of some spies sent to Jabil Ganam, the next water, in order to reconnoitre.

A fresh breeze in the morning. The night cool and agreeable. The country in this day's march not so level as in some of our former, as we met with several risings and descents, but no more difficult of passage. The soil is hard and good, but no water; tho', from the size and verdure of the shrubs, it is probable that on digging plenty would be found.

5TH. Decamped this morning at sun-rising. Marched S.E. by E. one hour and three quarters; thence S.E. three hours, E. by S. forty five minutes, and E. ¼ S. half an hour, when we came again to the track or course of Battan Swab[3], which was also dry here. Encamped about half an hour after noon. The spies being returned said they found some people at the river, but that they were friends; and reporting that they saw abundance of rain water much nearer and directly in our route, it was determined to go thither. A small northerly breeze all day, and pretty warm; but the night cool and pleasant. The soil hard and good. Land uneven, but no hills in sight, except one running from N.E. to S.W. about a league in length, bearing north from hence, and distant about [a] mile; on the other side of which is, in the rainy season, a river; but it is at present dry.

This evening the camp was alarmed by the appearance of nine strangers; who on their first approach we suspected to

[1] Obviously an error for S.E. ¼ E.

[2] Batn Suab, *i.e.* the valley or depression of Suab.

[3] More usually Wadi Suab, one of the most important drainages of the north Syrian Hamad. See Musil's map *Northern Arabia*. Jubb el Ghanam, which the caravan had left 3½ hours earlier, is situated on a northern branch of this wadi. The Suab, which Carmichael thought he met again the following day, must be the Wadi Rathqa, if we accept Musil's map of the region as correct, but Cernik's map is worth considering in conjunction with this section of the route.

be thieves, coming with an intention to steal our camels. Our horsemen, on seeing the smallness of their number, rode out toward them with much affected bravery, and firing their pieces all the way. It proved, however, that they were friends, and come from Jurfa[1], a small village on the river, to compliment the Sheik, and to invite the caravan thither to fill water. The merchants presented each of them with a vest of cloth.

By this evening's amplitude found the variation to be about three quarters of a point west.

6TH. Mounted this morning at a quarter past seven. Travelling E.S.E. five hours over hard, stony and uneven ground, till a quarter past twelve; came then to Battan Forda[2], i.e. the Brook Farda, and encamped. There is now much rain water here; and in the rainy season I believe it forms a pretty rivulet. A fine westerly breeze all day, and the weather very warm; but the night agreeably cool.

About four miles E.S.E. from hence is Irfa[3], a small Arab village, on the other side the river Euphrates; and about thirty miles thence N.E. is the city of Urfa[4], from which I calculate the situation of this place.

Places names in our route	Courses	Hrs.	Min.
	S.E. ¼ S.	3	30
	S.E. ¾ E.	4	—
	S.E. by S.	1	45
	S.E.	3	—
	E. by S.	—	45
	E. ¼ S.	—	30
	E.S.E.	5	—
From Jubil Ganam to Battan Farda is		18	30
Aleppo to Jubil Ganam was		78	45
Aleppo to Battan Farda was		97	15

[1] This may be Beawes' *Jorsa*.

[2] Batn Farda—probably identical with an ancient site Al Furdah or Furdah Nun, see Le Strange, *Lands of the Eastern Caliphate*, pp. 107, 125.

[3] Irzi. For an early record of Irzi, and the great extent of its ruins, see Gasparo Balbi's *Viaggio dell' Indie Orientali*; also Purchas, MacLehose edit., vol. x, p. 144.

[4] His information was, of course, quite inaccurate. Urfa is more than 200 miles to the N.N.W., north of the 37th parallel, and west of the 39th meridian (or 1° 45′ east of Aleppo). He gives two positions. I think the first refers to Irzi and the second to Urfa. Irzi is actually 34° 27′ N. latitude and 4° east of Aleppo.

By the calculation for Battan Farda, and estimating the distance from hence to Irfa (four miles E.N.E.) and that the city of Urfa is thence N.E. thirty miles, I conclude that Urfa

			°	′	
is situated in	lat. by acct. and estimation		34	26	N.
	long. from the meridian	Aleppo	2	43	E.
		London	40	17	
is situated in	lat. by acct. and estimation		34	47	N.[1]
	long. from the meridian	Aleppo	3	08	E.
		London	40	42	

N.B. This calculation for Urfa is not to be relied on, as the Arabs do not seem to be clear in either their course or distance from Urfa hither.

The city of Urfa is the capital of the province of Dierback [Diarbekr], and is with good reason thought to be the Ur of the Chaldeans, mentioned Gen. xi. 31, and is perhaps one of the most ancient cities in the world[2].

The Mahometans, who highly venerate it, on account of its being the birth-place of Abraham, tell a great many marvellous stories about it, one of which is as follows: 'They say Abraham's father was a gross idolater, and being a statuary by trade, used to carve idols for Nimrod. His son had frequently, in vain, expostulated with him on the absurdity of worshipping gods he had himself made. One day he took the opportunity of the old man's absence, and broke and defaced his whole stock in trade. The father, on his return, finding his deities in this mutilated state, enquired into the cause; when Abraham answered him he supposed they had quarreled and treated each other in that rough manner. The father, enraged at this sarcasm, and rightly guessing at the author of the sacrilege, complained to Nimrod, who ordered Abraham to be seized and thrown from a place raised on two high pillars into a great fire; which was accordingly executed. When God immediately changed the fire into a pond of water, and the billets of wood into fishes; so that Abraham fell into the pond without receiving the least injury.' The pond is large and full

[1] See p. 149, note 4.

[2] Like nearly all his generalizations, very inaccurate.

of fish, which are very tame; no one daring to take them, they being held sacred to the memory of Abraham.

I asked some Jews of the caravan whether they believed this story? They answered they had tradition to the same import.

At noon many people came from Urfa. As the camp was too far for any supply of provision, their numbers made us keep a good look out, as on all occasions power and right are with them synonymous terms.

Here a great fat fellow, a Sheik (i.e. squire or gent.), came to our tent in search of a doctor. I felt his pulse, and finding it feverish, prescribed bleeding; but having no lancet amongst us, our barber, with a rusty razor, made a large orifice, or rather a hole, which with great difficulty was afterwards closed. After the operation he slept for about three hours, got up, broke wind, eat a large dish of pillaw, and found himself perfectly recovered. Had my friend Dr. Russel seen him eat, I am persuaded he would admit my knowledge in therapeuticks.

7TH. Proceeded this morning at eight, and directed our course S.E. two hours and a quarter. Thence S.E. by S. half an hour to avoid some rising ground; then E.S.E. two hours, and E. by S. one hour, when we passed a valley between some hills. E.N.E. ½ one hour; then turning in the direction of the valley two hours, encamped, about three quarters after four in the afternoon, in a low valley, not quite a mile broad, between the Hills Manelyal[1] (i.e. Hills of Defence). A fine westerly breeze all day, with serene pleasant weather. The night agreeably cool. The country hilly. The soil hard and barren, and no water.

8TH. Mounted this morning at ten minutes after six; travelling E. by S. one hour and a quarter; then E.S.E. three hours and three quarters; E. ½ S. two hours, and E. ½ N.

[1] Newberry, in 1580, recorded 'a village called *Manalle* to the west of the river' in this neighbourhood (Purchas, MacLehose edit., vol. VIII, p. 453). We have no modern equivalent for the name, which appears in many itineraries, viz. *Manahyat* (Teixeira), *Manceyal*, *Manie*, *Manget*, etc. It also applies to the hill country south of El Qaim. Rousseau calls it *Gour-el-Astaf*. Taylor records *Gour Alaflaf*. Plaisted notes its rugged nature, p. 82.

three hours. At ten minutes past four encamped in a bottom, called Jacabjamus, or Buffaloe's Hole[1].

A small breeze at west all day, with cool cloudy weather, Soil, &c. as before. No water.

9TH. Decamped this morning at seven. Our course was E.S.E. three hours; E.S.E. ½ one hour and a quarter; then E.S.E. three hours and three quarters; then went down a deep descent into a plain; from whence we kept E.S.E. two hours; S.E. by E. one hour; and E.S. by S. another hour. At four this afternoon encamped.

A small fresh breeze, southerly all day, with dark cloudy weather. The soil hard. The country level. No water.

10TH. Mounted this morning at seven. Our course E. by S. ¼ one hour and a half; then, going round some rising grounds, kept S.E. ¾ E. two hours and a quarter; when we arrived at Oglet Haran[2], i.e. K[n]ot of Haran. Encamped in a low bottom surrounded by hills.

This valley is about one mile broad, and two long[3]; in the middle of it are several large bushes, and many wells of indifferent Spaw water. There are a number of graves with cut stones on the hill, on the south-east side, which make it probable it was formerly inhabited. There are also several others of later date on the hill on the north side of the valley, which I imagine were made for passengers belonging to the caravans, who died in their passage. Haran is the antient name of this place, and Oglet[4], a knot or knowl, was probably derived from a hillock resembling a knot on the high land on

[1] Tagab Jamus, or Taq abu Jamus—the arch of Abu Jamus; this is obviously the nameless ruin seen by Plaisted on the 9th of July—'old ruined building, there being nothing left but a door.' The name occurs as *Shackabujamus* (Taylor), *El Djamouz* (Rousseau), and probably marks the tomb of a Sheikh of the Abu Jamus Bedawin tribe, see Blunt's *Bedawin Tribes*, vol. II, p. 193. Capper also records a ruined site somewhere in this vicinity.

[2] Aqulat or Uglet Hauran, see p. 19.

[3] This wadi is in fact the most important affluent of the Euphrates from the Syrian Desert; it has a length of at least 230 miles.

[4] *Oglet* appears in various forms in the narratives of other travellers, viz. *Agelat, Haglet, Auglat.* It may be Aqulat=fortress, confirming Carmichael's suspicions, or possibly Doughty's Âkilla, 'desert site where ground water is near.' Gertrude Bell applies *'Uglet Hauran* to the wadi itself, where she crossed it at its junction with the Euphrates.

the south side, which appears as in No. 5. On the top are great heaps of stone, but no signs of any building.

The name of this valley reminds me of the Haran of Abraham and Laban; and there is reason from different parts of scripture (which I shall mention after I have found the situation of this place) to believe their dwelling was somewhere hereabout.

Names of places in the rout[e] of the caravan.

	Course	Hrs.	Min.
From Battan Forda to Mancayal	S.E.	2	15
	S.E. by S.	—	30
	E.S.E.	2	—
	E. by S.	3	—
	E.N.E. ¼ N.	1	—
Mancayal to Jacabjamus	E. by S.	1	15
	E.S.E.	3	45
	E. ¼ S.	2	—
	E. ¼ N.	3	—
	E.S.E.	5	—
Jacabjamus to Oglet Haran	E.S.E. ½ E.	1	—
	E. by S.	1	—
	S.E. by E.	1	—
	S.E. by S.	1	—
	E. ¼ S.	1	30
	S.E. ¾ E.	2	15
From Battan Forda to Oglet Haran is		34 [31]	30[1]
Aleppo to Battan Forda was		97	15
Aleppo to Oglet Haran		124	45

According to the estimation I made at Battan Forda, the city of Urfa should be only fifty-six miles N.N.W. from hence; and I imagine Abraham and his family came thence hither; which seems agreeable to the Mosaick account in Gen. xi. 31.

I formerly thought Haran was in Mesapotamia; but on farther enquiry believe the contrary; for in Acts. vii. 3–4. St. Stephen says, 'then came he out of the land of the

[1] This total is incorrect. If we assume the total distance in the table of the 6th (Aleppo to *Battan Forda*) to be correct, viz., 97 15, and the same in the table of the 12th (Aleppo to *Oglet Haran*) 124 45, then the time-total for the stage *Battan Forda* to *Oglet Haran* should be 27 30, that is to say 4 hrs. less than the corrected total. The error is in the stage *Mancayal* to *Jacabjamus*—15 hrs., which is too long for the distance covered; also in the text there is no mention of the last 5 hrs. E.S.E.

Chaldeans, and dwelt in Charan or Haran.' By which it is evident Charan was not in Chaldea. But Hosea xii. 12, is more particular, 'and Jacob fled into the country of Syria; and Israel served for a wife, and for a wife he kept sheep.' Hence it is plain Haran was in Syria; and Father Laban, who was born at Haran, is often called a Syrian; Gen. xxviii. 5, xxxi. 20. Now when Jacob fled from Laban, he was only ten days in reaching Mount Gilead, and could hardly march more than twenty five miles a day, for the reason given his brother Esau, Gen. xxxi. 13. At which rate the distance from where Jacob passed the river to Mount Gilead cannot be supposed more than two hundred and fifty miles; and Laban came up with him in seven days. This agrees with the distance, at about the rate of thirty-five miles a day. This was a long march with camels. But I am at a loss to determine the situation of Mount Gilead, tho' by Deut. iii. 17, and Numb. xxxii. 40, it should be on the east side of the river Jordan, and about sixty miles E.N.E. from Jerusalem. And if Jerusalem be in lat. 32: 30 N. and long. 35: 00 E. from London, then say

Mount Gilead is situated in		° ′	
Lat. by account and estimation		32:07	N.
Long. from the meridian	Aleppo	1:28	E.
	London	36:06	E.

By which calculation Mount Gilead bears from Haran S.W. by W. ¾ W., distance two hundred and fifty miles, which is near the distance [it is] supposed Jacob marched in ten days; and as any place farther to the S.E. or N.W. upon this river would much increase the distance. If I am right in my conjecture as to Mount Gilead and Oglet Haran being on the way from Urfa to Canaan, near the river, and about the distance of Jacob's march from Mount Gilead, I am inclined to think Oglet Haran is the Haran of that patriarch. Mahomet pretended to affirm by inspiration that the Haran where Abraham dwelt was that very spot where the temple of Mecca now stands, and which the Mahometans still call Haran. If this had been true, Jacob would have had no river to pass till he came to Jordan, and must then have marched near six hundred miles with his sheep, &c. in ten days, which is impossible. Besides, we read, Gen. xii. 9, after Abraham came from Haran to the land of Canaan, 'and Abraham journeyed, going on *still* towards the *south*'; by which it appears he came from the northward; and it must be remembered Mecca lies six hundred miles south from Canaan. Therefore I may safely conclude Mahomet very boldly asserted a falsehood, and was influenced by a different spirit from Moses; but as this impostor generally enforced his assertions by club eloquence, few cared to oppose such forcible arguments.

11TH. Mounted this morning at half past six. Course S. ¾ E. one hour and twenty minutes; then S.S.E. ¾ E. one hour; afterwards S.E. one hour; and S.E. by E. three hours; then changing to E. by S. another hour, and E. one hour, through a narrow pass between high white rockey clifts, at the farther end of which lies Ain il Arnab[1] (i.e. Hares Pool), where we encamped at four. I allow ten minutes for stoppages and interruption the camels met with in going thro' this defile.

The country from Oglet Haran is hard and rugged. In many parts of the road are heaps of stones, about seven feet in length, and four in breadth, which I imagine are to cover graves. The water here is of the mineral kind, having a sulphureous and disagreeable taste. A small westerly breeze all day, with pleasant weather. The night cold.

12TH. Decamped this morning at fifty past six. Course S.E. by E. ¾ E. one hour; then east, over hard stony ground, two hours and a half. At twenty minutes after ten arrived at Cabassee[2], where we encamped on a rising ground, the town bearing N. by E. about one mile distance, and a large mosque on the top of the hill on the N.E. at the distance of about three hundred yards.

Here is a deep aquaduct, cut in the rock thro' the hill, from which there is a run of water sufficient to work a mill, of a disagreeable sulphureous taste; but before it reaches the town, it is much meliorated by the earth and air.

[1] This is Beawes' *Ain il Ernul* of 19 Aug. It is in the bed of Wadi Turaif.

[2] Kubaisa. Gertrude Bell calls it a mud-walled village of 50,000 palm-trees, but notes that even in Yaqut's day, early in the 13th century, its inhabitants lived 'in the extreme of poverty and misery by reason of the aridity of the surrounding waste.'

The Arabs esteem Cabassee a very ancient town; and by its many ruins it appears to have been once considerable. Its present inhabitants consist of only four hundred Arab families.

Here one third of our caravan left us, being bound for Bagdat, and went about three hours journey to the N.E. to Hit, where there is a bridge[1] over the Euphrates, from which place Bagdat is about four days journey.

There are many date trees[2] to the northward of this town, whose verdure formed a very agreeable prospect to us, who were just come from the desart, and reminded me of that beautiful simile in Psalm I, verse 3.

Tho' here is great plenty of mutton, fowls, eggs and onions, yet they are not to be had without paying an exhorbitant price; for if you employ the Arabs of the caravan to purchase them, they constantly impose on you, and it is not safe to go one's self, strangers here being very liable to insults. A small westerly breeze all day, with fair weather. The night cold, inclining to frost.

Places names in the caravan route	Courses	Hrs.	Min.
From Oglet Haran to Ain Il Arnab	S. ¾ E.	1	20
	S.S.E.	1	—
	S.E. ¼ S.	1	—
	S.E.	1	—
	S.E. by E.	3	—
	E. by S.	1	—
Ain il Arnab to Cabassee	East	1	—
	S.E. by E. ¾ E.	1	—
	East	2	30
From Oglet Haran to Cabassee		12	50
Aleppo to Oglet Haran		124	45
Aleppo to Cabassee		141	35[3]

[1] There is no record of the Euphrates ever having been bridged at Hit. Caravans usually crossed at Falluja (there is a bridge of boats there now), or by the camel-ford, practicable at certain seasons, by the island of Jubba. More often they crossed at Ana, by ferry-boats; but there are traces there of the island of Lubbad being connected with both banks by a bridge.

[2] Estimated nowadays at 50,000 palms.

[3] The table does not tally with the text, and if we are to assume the total, which is carried forward, to be correct, the time from *Oglet Haran* to *Cabassee* should read 16 hrs. 50 mins.

By this calculation, and estimating the bridge [at Hit][1] to be N.E. three hours hence, then,

		°	′	
Lat. by account and estimation		33	49	N.
Long. from the merid.	Aleppo	4	07	E.
	London	41	41	

13TH. Decamped this morning at seven. Course S. ¾ E. one hour and a half, to avoid some high land to the S.E. which runs east and west; then S.S.E. one hour and a half, which brought us on a plain; kept S.E. by S. two hours. Encamped at Ardel Mahumedy[2] at half after one. The country rough and stony, till we got round the hills, and then a fine smooth soil, but no water. A small breeze at N.E. all day, with dark cloudy weather. At two a squall of rain, with thunder and lightning.

14TH. Proceeded this morning at seven. Course S.E. by S. one hour and a half; then S.E. ¼ S. seven hours, when arrived at Tammel[3], and encamped, at half an hour after three, near a large spring of mineral water, strongly impregnated with sulphur, defended by an artificial mount, forty feet high. Within some walls, on the summit, are several graves. At some distance the ground seemed ploughed, or dug up for the purpose of sowing grain, but no houses or people were to be seen. The shrubs appeared more flourishing than we had before met with. There was much rain-water in several places. In this day's march the soil was generally good, and the country level, excepting some gullies, or broken channels, formed by the rain-water, where the stones were very trouble-some to the camels. At noon saw, at about a league to the N.E. of our rout[e], Ain il Gar (or the Fountain of Pitch)[4], a bituminous spring, many large clots of which lay near the road. A fresh breeze from the S.E., with dark cloudy weather, and some showers of rain.

[1] Hit is 33° 37′ N. latitude and 5° 33′ east of Aleppo.

[2] Ardh el Muhammadi, or the Land of Muhammadi; it is on the latest maps.

[3] Thumail. Compare p. 78, also *Amurath to Amurath*, pp. 129–30.

[4] Ain el Qir or Abu Qir, 'The father of pitch'; see *Amurath to Amurath*, pp. 125–27.

15TH. This morning mounted at half an hour past six. Course from S.E. to S.E. by S., chiefly S.E. ½ S., ten hours and a half; encamped at five in the afternoon at Ermach[1] (i.e. Launces) near and to the N.E. of five hillocks. The country mostly level, and the soil rich, but no water. A small northerly breeze all day, with cloudy weather.

16TH. Mounted at half an hour past six, course S.E. by E. one hour and a half, and E.S.E. two hours. Saw about a mile to the eastward the ruins of Gusserah Muken[2] (i.e. Palace of Muken) which, like most of the towns and buildings of this country, has little more than its foundations remaining. Thence we proceeded S.E. by E. one hour. Came then to Ain il Bassalin[3], or Fountain of the Eyes, a large spring of indifferent water. The soil hereabouts is hard and stoney. From thence S.E. by S. three hours, over a loose black spoil [soil?] thick set with high shrubs. At two in the afternoon encamped at Miniaphen[4], where are several wells of pretty good water. About two miles N.N.E. of the camp is Rachelle[5], a mean Arab village; and E.N.E. another called Stata[6], inhabited by professed robbers. From the latter they brought dates to sell to the caravan, of which I bought sixty pounds. A strong bleek northerly wind all day, with dark cloudy weather. The night cold.

17TH. Decamped this morning at seven. Course S.E. by S. four hours, S.E. one hour and S.E. by E. three hours. Encamped at three.

At the distance of about four miles, bearing N. ¼ E. of our camp, stands Alcander[7], a large and antient fort, said by the Arabs to be built by a Christian queen[8], who on account of

[1] This might be Urma, a ruined site to the west of Rahhaliya, noted by Massignon as *Qaṣrōūmīyeh*.

[2] For this Qasr we have no identification.

[3] Ras el Ain, see p. 78.

[4] *Miniaphen*, no identification, but the position is the same as Bell's 'low-lying marshy ground, rich in springs,' about an hour to the south of Rahhaliya.

[5] Rahhaliya, reputed to be an oasis of 16,000 palm-trees (G. Bell).

[6] Shithatha, see pp. 21, 78.

[7] Ukhaidir.

[8] If the date of Ukhaidir is pre-Muhammadan, as generally supposed, it would belong to either the Sassanian or Lakhmid periods; and if Lakhmid, as Massignon conjectures, the Arab tradition would be justifiable.

the scarcity of stones had recourse to the following stratagem to procure them. She caused publick proclamation to be made throughout the country that she would give a load of gold for the like quantity of stone. On this publication a multitude of people flocked thither with their beasts of different kinds heavily laden. The first to arrive was a man with an ass, who, depositing his load, received the stipulated reward. Then the queen informed the others that her promise extended to one load, and that no more than that quantity was wanted. They, rather than return with their burdens, threw them down, by which she became possessed of more than sufficient for the completion of this fortress. They likewise add, that this place, which held out for many years, was at length taken by the following contrivance. The Arabs, having first privately lodged a number of men near the fort, ordered a small caravan slightly guarded to pass by, consisting of a number of camels, each carrying two armed men enclosed in baskets, disguised like bales of goods. The Christians sallied out and, seizing the supposed booty, carried it into the fort. At this instant the Arab party, discovering themselves, seemed to prepare for an assault, when all the garrison running to the walls, gave the men hid in the baskets time to disengage themselves; which they instantly did, and seizing one of the gates, let in their comrades. Could it be supposed that the Arabs had ever read Virgil, I should have imagined they had formed the plan of this stratagem from that of the Trojan horse.

I am confidently told that a caravan may march from Alkander to the E[u]phrates in three hours, and after crossing that river, may reach Bagdat in five. So that, estimating the march of a caravan at its usual rate of two miles per hour, the distance from Alkander to Badgat is about sixteen miles[1].

Probably somewhere hereabouts stood the antient city of Babylon[2]. History informs us Cyrus took it by turning the course of the Euphrates, and making himself an entrance into the city through the deserted bed of that river. It was likewise

[1] This is a fair example of the inaccurate information given to Carmichael. The Euphrates at Musaiyib, on the direct road to Baghdad, is 45 miles from Ukhaidir, while it is another 40 miles on to Baghdad.

[2] Babil, site of Babylon, is 47 miles east of Ukhaidir.

said to be near Bagdat, which city still stands on its original foundations. If therefore Babylon was, as Doctor Prideaux describes it, 'a square each side fifteen miles in length,' it could not have fallen very far from Alcander.

The name and situation of Alcander gave me a desire to view it, but could not prevail on my cameller to go with me for less than a chequin, but my finances not being in the best of order, night approaching, and being fearful of losing the caravan, I did not gratify my inclination.

The country here was quite level soil, sandy, and full of high shrubs. Plenty of water.

A fresh gale from the N.W. with dark hazy weather. At two it began to rain, and continued drizzling all night. The many gusserahs or palaces we met with in our march persuades me there were formerly several petty princes in this country; some of whom might possibly be those who were informed of the birth of Christ by the appearance of the star, as mentioned in the Gospel of St. Matthew.

Names of Places in the Carav. route	Courses	Hrs.	Min.
From Cabassee to Air il Mahumedy	S. ¾ E.	1	30
	S.S.E.	1	30
	S.E. by S.	2	—
Ardil Mahumedy to Tammel	S.E. by S.	1	30
	S.E. ¼ S.	7	—
Tammel to Ermat	S.E. ½ S.	10	30
Ermat to Ain il Basalem	S.E. by E.	1	30
	E.S.E.	2	—
	S.E. by E.	1	—
Ain il Basalem to Maineaphen	S.E. by S.	3	—
Maineaphen to Al Kander	S.E. by S.	4	—
	S.E.	1	—
	S.E. by E.	3	—
		39	30
Aleppo to Cabassee		141	35
		181	5

		°	"	
Lat. by account and estimat.		32	42	N.
Long. from the merid.	Aleppo	4	6	E.
	London	42	20	E.

By this account it is 360 miles to Jerusalem.

18TH. The caravan being obliged to halt here, in order to dry their tents, &c. furnished me with the wished-for opportunity of visiting Al Kander[1]. Accordingly, by the persuasive argument of a dollar, I prevailed on a cameller to accompany me thither; when, arming myself with a brace of pistols, I set out at eight o'clock, and arrived at the castle about thirty after nine.

The magnificent appearance of these ruins almost persuaded me they were part of the antient Babylon.

The Arab, my companion, declined entering for fear of serpents or wild beasts. So taking a pistol in each hand I ventured alone, creeping thro' a hole in the gate-way, which was nearly filled up with rubbish.

I crossed the building over heaps of stones, and went out at the north gate. After which, going round it as close as the ruins would permit, I counted my paces, in order to form some guess at its dimensions.

This fortress consists of a square castle, surrounded by an envelope, or exterior wall, of the same shape, casmated and fortified with towers and turrets. The envelope, or surrounding wall, is an exact square, whose sides face the cardinal points of the compass; each measuring seven hundred feet, being two hundred and fifty of my paces[2].

On each angle is a round tower of about twenty feet in

[1] Although Roberts probably saw Ukhaidir, and Beawes certainly did, it remained for Plaisted to record its name. But to Carmichael belongs the credit of being the first Englishman to appreciate its wonders, to have the initiative both to explore it, and to attempt a detailed description of the ruins. Two other travellers had visited Ukhaidir long before this. Tavernier, in 1638, saw it, and described it shortly, but Della Valle, in August 1625, was actually the first European to record its existence, and was probably its rediscoverer. He called it 'the ruins of an ancient Fabrick, perfectly square with thirteen Pillasters, or round Columns on each side without....The Arabs call this Fabric *Cafr Chaider*.' For details of this imposing ruin see *Mémoires de l'Institut français d'Archéologie orientale du Caire*, vol. XXVII, 1910, M. Massignon; also *Amurath to Amurath*, pp. 140–58.

[2] The outside walls of Ukhaidir would appear practically a square; actually they measure 508 feet by 531 feet. From whichever side it is viewed, thirteen bastions can be counted, the central doorway on each side making up the odd one. See *Amurath to Amurath*, Fig. 77 and plan, Fig. 79.

diameter, and in the center of each side is another of the same size and figure; thro' these last are gates, on each side of which are disposed at equal distances five small turrets, of about ten feet diameter, and between every tower or turret are two arches, making in all twenty-four on each side of the square; these are filled up to within one foot of the surface of the wall, and give it a magnificent appearance.

Most of the walls are near fifty feet high and thirty thick, with loop holes for four thousand men, exclusive of those on the top of the works. Having thus surveyed the outer part of the envelope, I entered at the south-gate to examine its internal construction.

This and the other gates are only ten feet wide at the entrance, but enlarge to fifteen, and are about twenty feet high. Here I saw a door which seemed the entrance into the casmates. It was six feet high, and arched over; but being very dark, I could not observe the way which mounted to the loop holes, but imagine it was by stairs in the towers at the angles.

The arches over the gates are well turned, being segments of circles. At present the gates are almost entirely filled up with rubbish and loose stones. The walls on the inside are plain. Next adjoining to the south-side is a parade of six hundred and twenty feet long, and two hundred and sixty broad, affording sufficient room to draw up ten thousand men.

On the south-side of the parade stands the castle, which is likewise a regular square, whose interior side is three hundred feet; fortified like the envelope with round towers at the angles, and on the center of the curtains. The interior diameters of these towers are only eight feet.

The only entrance into this building was from the north-gate, except at the north-west angle, where there has been a little door.

The inside is divided into four divisions or squares, the lower parts of which seems a cluster of arches. These were, I suppose, the magazines, and over them the rooms for the officers, but they are all now ruined; and by the great quantity of rubbish which has fallen down, it appears these buildings were formerly very high. In the N.W. square are three large arches, the middle one about twenty feet high; under is a large hall, about seventy-two feet in length, and thirty-six broad. Over the entrance from the north-gate on the inside are three niches in the wall, and one on each side, where there have been images. But for its situation, which is to the north, I should have thought it a Christian altar. Perhaps the primitive Christians might be wiser than to think that directing their prayers to any particular point of the compass added to their efficacy. But be this as it may, it is either the work of Christians or Pagans, for the Mahometans admit of no images in their buildings; and as they conquered this country in the sixth century, this building must consequently be very antient, and was erected above eleven hundred years ago[1].

On the east and west sides of this castle are two oblong spaces or parades, each two hundred and seventy feet long and one hundred broad; and the north wall is prolonged from the N.E. and N.W. angles till it joins the walls of the envelope.

Between the castle and the north side of the envelope is an intermural space, six hundred and twenty feet long and seventy-two broad. This may have been barracks for the troops.

At about twenty yards distant from this fortress stood a building 360 feet long and one hundred and eighty broad, also divided into four squares; one of which is fortified with towers, the other three are vaulted stables for horses[2]. The walls of the fortified part are of the same height as those of the fortress; the others are only twelve feet high. By the ruins I observed a communication from the stables to the other building.

The whole of these buildings are composed of hard brown squared stones, laid like bricks, and strongly cemented with black earth mortar, excepting the arches, which are white, and seem to have been laid with lime.

Before the use of artillery, this must have been a very strong fortification, and was capable of containing a garrison of

[1] For the part these niches play in the architecture of Ukhaidir see *Amurath to Amurath*, pp. 154–55; and for its date—probably pre-Muhammadan—see Massignon.

[2] See ground plan of Ukhaidir, *Amurath to Amurath*, Fig. 79.

thirty thousand men. I was told by some of the caravan that there were inscriptions in this castle, but I met with none.

About two hundred yards from the N.E. angle of the great gate are the ruins of a strong house built with stone and lime; and at about the distance of a mile and a half to the N.E. are other remains. But noon approaching, and the weather being clear, I was fearful the caravan might proceed, so would not venture to be absent any longer; otherwise should have remained here till evening.

I should have been glad, with agreeable company, to have made a progress along the river, being persuaded we should have met with many magnificent remains.

The tomb of Ezekiel is said to be only twenty miles east from hence[1], and, as he died in captivity, it is probable he was buried somewhere near Babylon. This is another reason justifying my opinion of this city being situated hereabouts. Not that I imagine Alcander to be any part of it, as I think it of much later date; perhaps the work of the Greek or Palmyrian states; for, after the destruction of Babylon, there still remained several large cities in this part of the country. The fort then might be erected for the protection of the commerce carried on between them and Palmyra. Though the soil is good, and plenty of water, it is at present totally deserted of every living creature, except serpents and wild beasts; so thoroughly is accomplished the prophecies of Isaiah xiii. 19, 20, 21, 22, and Jeremiah li. 29, 53.

Indeed, when I consider the once magnificent state of Babylon, its stupendous walls and hanging gardens, so pompously described in antient history, it seems little less than miraculous that it should be so totally eradicated as not to leave sufficient traces to determine, with any exactness, its former situation. If I was to interpret literally the prediction of Jeremiah li. 63, 64, where he says, 'And it shall be, when thou hast made an end of reading this book, that thou shalt bind a stone to it, and cast it into the middle of Euphrates, and thou shalt say, thus shall Babylon sink, and shall not rise

[1] The reputed Tomb of Ezekiel is at Kifl, 17 miles to the north of Najaf.

from the evil I will bring upon her,' I should be tempted to suppose it swallowed up by the river, which is the most possible, as the country hereabouts is a perfect bed of dry sand, and the river appears to have shifted greatly to the north-east of its antient channel.

About a mile to the south of the fort are two hillocks, seemingly artificial, and a ridge running strait to the N.E. These I take to be the foundations of buildings now covered with sand; but not having sufficient time to examine them, or tools to move the sand, I could not verify my conjectures.

At noon set out for the caravan, which I joined by half an hour after one. I found them still encamped, and determined to remain there till next morning. On this information I repented my returning so soon.

A fresh bleak N.W. wind all day; the night very cold.

19TH. Mounted this morning at seven. Our course S. by E. one hour, S.S.E. one hour, S.E. by S. two hours, S. ¼ W. one hour, S.E. ¼ S. three hours, and E.S.E. one hour. Encamped at four in the afternoon on a dry barren plain, no water near us, but found enough on the road. A small S.E. breeze, with dark cloudy weather. The country a barren level. Our course this day has, in my opinion, been more southerly than was necessary, as no impediments appeared to the eastward, and a south-east course would have been much more direct.

20TH. Decamped this morning at seven. Directing our course S.E. by E. two hours, came to deep descent, where are some hills at a distance resembling buildings, on one of which, to the right, called Tick de Gana[1], is said to be water. Proceeded thro' a valley between sandy hills E.S.E. five hours, and at two in the afternoon encamped on the plain, from which it is only six hours S.E. by E. to Machadali[2]. A strong bleak north westerly wind all the morning, with

[1] Tuqtuqana, an ancient site, recorded by Ibn Khurdadbeh as the first stage on the desert route from Kufa to Damascus, see de Goeje's translation, p. 71; more recently explored by Massignon, and in 1912 visited by Musil, who found the district in process of being reoccupied.

[2] Meshed Ali.

dark hazy weather, and drizzling rain; the afternoon fair; the night cold and frosty. No water here. The country barren and the soil sandy. We met with several elevations on the road.

Some of our caravan told me they had seen the ruins of Babylon about eight hours journey east of hence; but I imagine they mistook the ruins of Cuffa[1] for those of that city. Cuffa is below Bagdat, and Babylon is generally supposed above it[2]. A Persian merchant of our caravan informed me some remains of the tower of Babel were still to be seen about twenty miles above Bagdat; and that it was called Nimrod, from its founder; and on this occasion he amused me with the following traditional story: "That Nimrod, in defiance o : the Almighty, gathered together all the people for the purpose of erecting this tower, and under the direction of seventy-two Armenian architects, the most famous builders of their time; when having advanced the fabrick to a great height, God was pleased to make each of the builders speak a different tongue. This caused great confusion, and ever since there has been seventy-two different languages." Finding him so very particular, I asked which were the languages then formed, but this exceeded his knowledge. However, it is not improbable that Babel was hard by Bagdat, or Bagsdeth, which, as well as Babel, signifies confusion.

21ST. This morning the water and sand being frozen, was obliged to wait till the sun had thawed them. However, mounted at nine, our course S.W. ¾ S. one hour and a quarter, then S. ½ W. one hour and a half, over a hard, stony, and hilly country; thence S.E. by E. three hours, over a plain, and came to Rackma[3], a rockey cliff, where were several pools of rain water. Stopped here to let our camels drink, and afterwards proceeded round the cliff E. ¾ N. three quarters of an hour, and came to another rockey craig, which joins the former, and in the rainy season makes a large rivulet of water.

[1] Kufa.

[2] Kufa and Najaf lay within sight, 25–30 miles due east. The site of ancient Babylon is of course below Baghdad.

[3] Ruhaima.

About forty minutes after three in the afternoon encamped in sight of Meched Ali, bearing E. by N. distant about eight miles.

Fair clear weather all day, with a bleak cold breeze from the N.W. The night frosty.

The country hard, hilly, and very barren; only in the valleys or clifts where the water runs are many large bushes, bearing a berry the size of a haw, called Zarour, having an agreeable acid taste.

At sun-set the cupels of Mechad Ali (i.e. a full view of Ali)[1] appeared like a globe of fire on the side of the hill. That dome is said to contain the corpse of Ali, the Persian Prophet, and one of the four Caliphs who succeeded Mahomet; on which account this place is held in high veneration by all the Musselmen of that sect bearing his name.

This mosque has been lately repaired and adorned, at a vast expence, by Nader Shaw[2], the Sophy of Persia, so well knówn in Europe by the name of Thamas Kouli Kahn[3].

The whole dome is covered with gilt copper, and the doors, windows, and galleries profusely decorated with gilding, azure borders, freeze work, and every other ornament suited to the taste of the country.

But it is in the tomb of Ali that the eastern magnificence is more particularly manifested; which, according to an account I have seen written by a gentleman who visited it, is of exquisite workmanship, and set with jewels of immense value, altogether making a most dazzling appearance. I would fain have gone for the sake of personally examining the truth of his description, but was dissuaded on account of the great risque I should have run of being murdered, or at least ill-treated, by the guardians of the prophet's tomb, who are reported to be the most abandoned miscreants on earth, and, like their master, declared inveterate enemies to the Christians, from whom this country was conquered, under the conduct of Ali and his sons.

[1] Meshed, of course, means Mosque or praying place.
[2] Nadir Shah, who started life as Nadir Kuli. [3] See p. 22.

Place-names in carav. route	Course	Hrs.	Min.
Alcander to Tack de Gana	S. by E.	1	—
	S.S.E.	1	—
	S.E. by S.	2	—
	S. ¼ W.	1	—
	S.E. ¾ E.	3	—
	E.S.E.	1	—
	S.E. by E.	2	—
	E.S.E.	5	—
	S.W. ¾ S.	1	15
Tack de Gana to Rackma	S. ¼ W.	1	30
	S.E. by E.	3	—
Rackma to Gerseme[1]	E. ¾ N.	—	45
Aleppo to Alkander is		22	30
Aleppo to Gerseme is		182	35
		205	5

		°	'
Lat. by account		32	08 N.
Mechad Ali is situate in Long. a merid.	Aleppo	5	21 E.
	London	42	55 E.

22D. Our bedding and other equipage being frozen, and the ground very slippery and dangerous for the camels, we were obliged to wait till the sun had thawed them; were forced to remain here till half an hour after nine, when we set out, our course being S. by E. ¾ E. five hours. At half an hour past two came to Battan il Hash[2], and encamped near a pool of rain water. The country uneven and stoney. A small breeze from the S.W. with fair pleasant weather. The night moderate.

23D. This morning about four it rained hard for half an hour, but soon after clearing up, we set out at seven, directing our course S.S.E. one hour, S.E. three hours, and S.S.E. three more. Came to Mugaroon (i.e. the Square), an old ruined fort on the S.W. side of the road. I was a mile to the eastward when I first saw it; I immediately dismounted and

[1] Not mentioned in the itinerary; but apparently his camp on the evening of the 21st may be Huber's Shaib el Khats'amy (*Voyage dans l'Arabie Centrale*, Charles Huber, see *Bull. Soc. de Géog.*, VIIme série, vol. VI, p. 122). There is a district and site *al Girṭmi* [el Jirtsmi] on Musil's map *Northern Arabia*, to the west of Wadi Hisb.

[2] Batn, or Wadi Hisb, or Husub.

went up to it, but the caravan being on their march, and night approaching, I had not time to make many remarks. This fort is a square, each side about sixty yards in length, and fortified with five round towers at equal distances. On the S.E. side is a large tank or reservior for water, near five hundred yards in circumference, and about ten deep; the sides faced with stone, and at two or three places there are steps to descend into it. On each side are two mounts thrown up for its defence[1].

I also saw a tower with many other ruins about half a mile to the westward, from which I imagine here formerly stood a considerable town[2]. The Arabs say the Caliphs of Bagdat used to maintain a large garrison at this place for the protection of pilgrims going to Mecca; also magazines of provision, in order to supply them for their journey. They likewise added that there is hereabouts a well of a prodigious depth, covered with a stone, on which is an inscription in the Chaldean characters, and that there were others in the same language on the tower abovementioned. I could not examine them for reasons being assigned. Besides, the Arabs are so extremely jealous of any strangers who appear inquisitive in their researches into the antient buildings and ruins of this country that it would be running a great risk to give a loose [rein] to one's curiosity. I therefore returned to the caravan. Marching S.E. by E. two hours, at six encamped with them on a plain, where we found plenty of food for our camels but no water.

The night proved extremely cold; most of our bedding was frozen, so that our lodging was very disagreeable.

[1] Carmichael can thus claim to be the discoverer of the famous line of reservoirs built by Zobeida, the wife of the Caliph Haroun er Rashid, for the use of Mecca-bound pilgrims, along the route which bears her name. The reservoir of Umm el Qurun is the second of the series going south from Najaf. The late Col. Leachman visited it in 1918 and described it to me as 'a reservoir 50 yards square, overlooked by an ancient castle. A mile away is a fallen tower of great thickness and probably 100 ft. high.'

[2] Here Carmichael confirms Ibn Jubayr's account of *Minārat al-qurūn*, Minaret of the Horns, a tower decorated with gazelle horns, and near by it a castle and reservoir, not far from *'Udayb* (see Schiaparelli's translation, pp. 197–98). Huber recorded no feature of this description in 1881.

Place-names in carav. route	Courses	Hrs.	Min.
From Gersume [to Battan] il Hash	S. by E. ¾ E.	5	—
Battan il Hash to Mugaroon	S.S.E.	4	—
	S.E.	3	—
Gersume to Mugaroon		12	—
Aleppo to Gersume		205	[5]
Aleppo to Mugaroon		217	5

		°	′	
Latitude by account		31	45	N.
Mugaroon is situate in long. from	Aleppo	5	19	E.
	London	42	53	E.

24TH. Decamped this morning at seven. Course variable; I judged it nearest S.S.E. ½ E. eight hours and [an] half. At half an hour after three in the afternoon came to Um il Hasshem[1], and there encamped on the plain. A small breeze from the S.E. The day clear and pleasant, the night cool. The country for the first five hours was mostly level, the soil good, full of small loose stones, but afterwards barren, with hard gravel. No water.

25TH. Mounted this morning at seven. Course variable from south to south east, nearly S.S.E. five hours. Came to some rain water; when, after letting the camels drink, proceeded E.S.E. three hours farther, and encamped at Abilmuris[2], on the plain. The country in general level; soil barren, hard and stony. The weather cold and raw. A fresh breeze from the S.S.E. with drizzling rain, which, being directly in our faces, made the march very disagreeable.

26TH. A hard frost this morning, which detained us till the sun had dried and thawed our bedding, &c. At eleven mounted. Our course S.E. by E. ½ E. five hours. At four in the afternoon encamped on the plain, near a pool of rain water. The country and soil mostly as yesterday, the weather dark and cloudy, with hard rain from sunset to eight at night.

[1] I cannot identify this site. Chesney records a Well Haban in the same district, and hereabouts is Khaffan, the rendezvous of the Arab hosts before the battle of Buweib, 634 A.D.

[2] We know of the *Wadi abul m'ris* from Huber's *Journal d'un Voyage en Arabie*, p. 20, as rising at the wells of *Gill* (El Jil) and entering the Euphrates near Shinafiya. Modern maps (1927) have Shaib Abu Maris rising in the same locality but flowing towards the Euphrates at Samawa.

Our conductor being informed that Sheik Gasme, with his tribe of Arabs, four thousand in number, lay encamped in the road near the rivers, we shifted our course more towards the desart, in order to avoid them.

27TH. Decamped this morning at seven. Course S.E. by E. two hours, E.S.E. four hours, and E. by S. four more; some southerly turnings make me allow the compound course E.S.E. The country plain; soil hard and stony. A small S.W. breeze, and pleasant weather. No water.

28TH. Decamped fifty minutes after six. Course chiefly E.S.E. ¾ E. seven hours. At two encamped on the plain, where was plenty of food for our camels. A great dew this morning, with a fog, which lasted till noon. A cold north west wind, weather fair, and the country as before. No water.

29TH. Proceeded at seven. Course S.E. by E. and E.S.E. till eleven. Then rounded a hill S.W. ¾ S. half an hour, and came to Gurna[1] (i.e. Corner), where we stopped near ten minutes, to water the cattle at a large pool: then re-assumed our march. Course nearest E.S.E. three hours and a half. Came to Batten Gusserah[2] (i.e. the Palace Rivulet), where we encamped near a large pool. A cold wind from the N.W., but the weather fine and clear. Country hilly, the soil hard and stony.

The Arabs say Gusserah, an antient palace with many ruins, is to be seen about four miles N.E. from hence, but I had no time to visit them. The many Gusserahs, or palaces, whose ruins we meet with on our tour[e], shows the number of petty princes who formerly possessed this country, and who were mostly of Abraham's family; namely, the Dukes of Edom, Gen. xxxvi. and Ishmaelites, Gen. xxv. 12, 13, 14, 15, 16, with the Moabites and Ammonites, descendants from Lot, who drove out the Emmims and Zamzummims, Deut. ii. 18 and 20. I take the Emmims to be the present inhabitants of the southern parts of Arabia[3], the king of Muscat still retaining the title of Immim, or as they pronounce it Imaum.

[1] I cannot identify this.
[2] Batn Quseir, doubtless the wadi bed above El Quseir.
[3] This is nonsense. 'Imaum' is not a tribal name.

Place-names in carav. route	Courses	M.	H.
Mugaroon to Unil Hashem	S.S.E. ½	8	30
Unil Hashem to Belmuris	S.S.E.	5	—
	E.S.E.	3	—
Abelmuris to Gurna	S.E. by E. ¼ E.	5	—
	E.S.E.	10	—
	E.S.E. ¾ E.	7	—
Gurna to Gusserah	S.W. ¾ S.	—	30
	E.S.E.	3	30
Mugaroon to Battan Gusserah		42	30
Aleppo to Mugaroon		217	5
Aleppo to Battan Gusserah		259	35

		°	′
Lat. by account		30	49 N.
Gusserah is situate in long. a merid.	Aleppo	6	35 E.
	London	44	9 E.

30TH. Decamped this morning at seven. Course E.S.E.¼E. six hours. Came to Battan Amaba[1], where, finding plenty of water, we halted to let our camels drink; then proceeded S.E. one hour, and S.S.E. another, which brought us to Battan Arah[2] (i.e. Rivulet of water), and encamped near a rocky cliff, where are many pools of rain water. The soil barren, hard, and stony; the country mostly level, excepting these cliffs near the Battans. A small pleasant breeze N.W., with fine clear weather.

This being the Jewish sabbath, those belonging to our caravan remained behind, in obedience to the Mossaic law, which prohibits their travelling more than a stated distance on that day. This they had always observed, ever since we left Aleppo, commonly re-joining us in the night. They therefore, on their [our?] setting out, requested the Sheik to allow them a guard, to stay with them till the expiration of the sabbath, and to escort them to the caravan, not without hopes he would have denied their request; on which occasion the sin would, as they believed, have been charged to his account. They were, however, disappointed, as it furnished him with

[1] For this region see *Carte Internationale du Monde au* 1,000,000, Basra, Jan. 1927. *Battan Amaba* is doubtless a *batn*—low ground or hollow, named from the local landmark Arnaba.

[2] Corresponds with the Wadi Abu Adhr of the above map.

a pretence for levying sixty or seventy dollars, every week, for guard money and camel hire; and he was too clear-sighted and attentive to his own interest to let slip so favourable an opportunity.

December 1. Mounted at seven. Course E.S.E. four hours. Came to Battan Naum[1], where were several good pools. Thence E. by S. two hours, and reached Battan Canagan[2], which appears as if it was a large rivulet in the rainy season; there was at this time plenty of water. Hence proceeded E.S.E. two hours, over a loose dry land, covered with shrubs. At three encamped on the plain. The country level, with a hard barren gravely soil, with fine warm weather.

2D. Decamped at seven. Course S.E. ¾ E. two hours, and E.S.E. ¾ E. four hours. Came to Battan Shagare[3], where we encamped on the plain. Country and soil as yesterday. Pleasant weather, with a gentle S.E. breeze. N.B. Several wells near the camp.

3D. Marched off at seven. Course E.S.E. ¾ E. three hours; then S.E. by E. two hours. It began to rain at ten, which encreasing, obliged us to encamp at noon on a plain, where we were met by an express, with letters from Busserah.

Cloudy weather with rain till two.

4TH. Mounted at seven. Course S.E. by E. six hours and a half, which brought us to Chapda[4], where we encamped on the plain. The soil sandy, and country level, excepting some eminences which we met with the last hour's march. A light N.W. breeze, with pleasant weather. No water.

5TH. Decamped at seven. Course E. ¾ N. seven hours, came to Abuan[5], and encamped on the plain. Our people seem not to know exactly where they are, and to suspect we are to the southward of Busserah. A hard barren gravely soil, the country level. A fresh easterly gale. The weather dark and cloudy, with hard rain from sunset to nine o'clock.

6TH. Moved at seven. Course variable, allowed E.N.E. ¾ E.

[1] We have no identification for this.

[2] This is doubtless Plaisted's Khunigha, see p. 70.

[3] The wadi named after the local Qasr Shagra.

[4] Shabda.

[5] Abuan of modern maps.

six hours. Encamped at Indhollibee[1] on a plain. Country level and soil sandy. Squally weather, the wind various.

7TH. Remained here till the Sheik had seen the Mussulman[2] of Busserah, who he was informed lay at Issabar. He (for private reasons) being afraid of him, was determined to adjust matters here before he proceeded to Busserah, and discharged the caravan. A raw cold N.W. wind with clear weather; the night frosty. No water.

8TH. Mounted this morning at eight. Course E.N.E. ½ E. six hours. Came to Quibda[3] at two, and at three encamped on the plain about a mile south of the town, in which there appears some ruins. I was told it is an antient place, but contained nothing worthy of notice; therefore, not having much leisure, did not visit it.

At three Mr. Brabazon Ellis, the English Resident at Busserah, accompanied by Mr. F. Hanmer, surgeon, visited the caravan, and gave me an invitation to go with them to Issabier[4]. Therefore, leaving my things in charge of a friend, mounted on horseback at four. Course N.E. ½ E. two hours; which I compute equal to three hours march of a camel. Came to Issabier about six, where I met Mr. Hanger, another English gentleman.

9TH. This morning the caravan arrived, and encamped about a mile S.S.E. of the town.

Issabier is a mean Arab town, consisting of many houses or rather huts, containing about six or seven hundred inhabitants, and appears a most dirty and wretched place.

10TH. Sent my things this morning on an ass to Busserah, and after dinner, at about two o'clock, set out for that place, in company with the before-mentioned English gentlemen. Arrived at the English factory at five, our course being N.E. ¾ N. three hours march of a caravan. The way was belly deep in water, the roads being overflowed. Here I had the pleasure of meeting Captain John Dick, who gave me the

[1] *Indhollibee* I cannot identify.
[2] See note on p. 178.
[3] Kuwaibda, the ruins being those of Barjisiya.
[4] Zubair.

news of Bombay, and a prospect of procuring a passage with him to India.

Place-names in carav. route	Courses	Hrs.	M.
Battan Gusserah to Battan Amaba	E.S.E. ¾ E.	6	—
	S.E.	1	—
Battan Amaba to Battan Arah	S.S.E.	1	—
Battan Arah to Battan Naum	E.S.E.	4	—
Battan Naum to Battan Canagah	E. by S.	2	—
	E.S.E.	2	—
Battan Canagal to Battan Shagerah	S.E. ¾ E.	2	—
	S.E. ¾ E.	4	—
Battan Shagera to Chapda	E.S.E. ¾ E.	3	—
Chapda to Abuan	S.E. by E.	8	30
	E. ½ N.	7	—
Abuan to Indholibie	E.N.E. ¼ E.	6	—
Indholibie to Quibda	E.N.E. ¼ E.	6	—
Quibda to Issabier	E.N.E. ¼ E.	3	—
Issabier to Busserah	N.E. ¾ N.	3	—
Battan Gusserah to Busserah		58	30
Aleppo to Battan Gusserah		259	35
Aleppo to Busserah		318	5

		°	′
Lat. by observation		30	22 N.
Busserah is situated in long. a merid.	Aleppo	8	6 E.
	London	46	1 E.

I find by the Coasting Pilot for Oriental Navigation, with which Captain Dick favoured me, that Busserah is there laid down more to the east than I made it; but am persuaded it is not more from the meridian of Aleppo. And if the table of longitude in Patoun's Navigation is right in the situation of Alexandria, then this account of the longitude of Busserah is perhaps nearer the truth than those draughts, which I presume were formed from journals to India by the Cape of Good Hope. The situation of Scandaroon, as laid down in the general draught of the Coasting Pilot, differs from that assigned in Patoun; but as my whole journal was calculated from that table, the situation of Jerusalem should be computed by the same.

The motion of my camel would not admit of that exactness

I could have wished, in estimating our course by the compass; I therefore used the more attention to correct it by different methods. Neither am I certain that my allowance of seventy miles to a degree is right; as adjusting the log line to that length has never yet answered at sea.

It is a pity the gentlemen residing at Aleppo or Busserah have not endeavoured to come at this truth. No people on earth have a better opportunity, for near either of those places may be found several hundred miles almost as level as the sea, where, by means of a theodolite and chain, proper observations might be made for ascertaining this very essential proposition.

Though this passage proved long, it did not fatigue me so much as I expected, and was I to undertake it again in the winter, which I must here observe is the properest time, I would bring both horses and camels, particularly from Aleppo, where the former may be bought at such price as to be sold to advantage at Busserah. By which convenience one may occasionally either ride before or stay behind the caravan, to view the ruins or antient buildings (which cannot be done on a camel); and half freight for the latter would carry water, provisions, and corn for the horses. It is not amiss to caution travellers that locks and keys are extremely necessary against the Arab camellers, who have not the greatest regard for the eighth article of the Decalogue.

On a returning passage from Busserah, you may there buy camels at about forty rupees per head, and they commonly sell at Aleppo for as many dollars; which yields a profit of near cent. per cent. The hire of a cameller to look after and drive eight or ten of them is only eight or ten dollars for the journey.

The freight of a camel loaded with five hundred pounds weight of goods is seven pounds sterling, and the hire of one to ride upon about half that sum. I paid 3*l.* 5*s.*, or twenty-six piasters, and had about two hundredweight of provisions and effects.

This journey greatly resembles a voyage at sea, where good salt and dried provisions are very convenient, as well as some hampers of European liquors. Firing is to be met with in great plenty; and with a little management one need not want water. If there were a few Europeans together, with good dogs and guns, they might meet with plenty of hares, which would afford them excellent food, and make the journey very agreeable.

I found the weather not to be complained of, and water in plenty, for which reason, as I before observed, winter seems to me the best time for crossing the desart. It certainly must be much worse in summer, both on account of the scarcity of water and the excessive heats, which at that time, and on those dry barren sands, must be intolerable.

But any person, having money and leisure, may perform this journey much more agreeably by the way of Mossol and Bagdat, where they will meet with refreshments at every stage, and if curious in the survey of antient buildings, they may hire a (bursie) boat, about three days journey from Aleppo, and come down the Euphrates to Busserah, in which track they must undoubtedly find many noble ruins of antient cities on both sides of the rivers.

The Arabs value themselves highly on being a free and unconquered people; a circumstance to be solely attributed to their poverty and the sterril state of their country—a better security against the rage of conquerors than the greatest virtue or the most consummate valour.

They are certainly a bad people, though better than the commonality of Egypt and Turkey. There is no danger of being ill treated by them in the caravan, farther than a few insolent freedoms they think themselves justified in taking, on the strength of being Mahomet's countrymen, on which account they conclude themselves superior to the rest of mankind.

Busserah is situated on the south side of a creek running W.S.W. from the Euphrates; the body of the city being about two miles from that river. It is a place of great trade, and the only seaport for Assyria and great part of Arabia; it carries on besides a considerable commerce with Syria, by means of caravans from Aleppo and Damascus.

The tide flowed here about N.E. by E. and S.W. by W., being high water at three quarters after three, and rises near five feet perpendicular in the creek, which is fresh water[1] and, if in the hands of industrious people, might be made to convey goods to every house, by means of canals. This would render it both a commodious and agreeable place.

The country near the river is extremely fertile, capable of producing every necessary in great abundance, were the natives inclined to tillage and improvements. But their scandalous indolence render[s] these advantages useless; their whole husbandry being confined to the planting of dates, which, requiring but little trouble, they raise in great plenty. So that provisions in general are very dear; their wheat and rice being brought from India and Persia at a vast expence.

This city was formerly surrounded by a wall, which, being only clay, is mostly broken down and ruined. The houses are very mean, being generally built of the same materials, as they have neither wood or stone but what is transported from India.

It is at present governed by a Mussulman[2], appointed by the Bashaw of Bagdat, who is subordinate to the Grand Seignior, but has now made himself almost independant[3]. There is also a Captain Bashaw who commands the marine, consisting of galleys, kept here for the defence of the place. I saw one of them which was very large, in a dock at the Captain Bashaw's house, about two miles below the town, where the creek joins the Euphrates, which is there about a mile broad.

Since I have seen Busserah, I am not so much surprised that the ruins of Babylon and some other antient cities are nowhere discovered; because it is highly probable they never

1 'For the tide is felt here, though the water is ever fresh' (Teixeira).

2 Mutasallim.

3 The Mutasallim (Deputy Governor), or the Qaptan, attempted to proclaim the independence of Basra, in 1751. Sulaiman Abu Leilah, the 'Bashaw of Bagdat,' was preoccupied with the Kurds, but crushed the rising on the return of his forces. See Longrigg, *op. cit.* pp. 170, 171.

had a sufficiency of wood fit for building, or burning bricks, and in many places a scarcity of stone; therefore I imagine the antients did as the moderns now do, that is, generally build with clay. Should any vicissitude of fortune at this time depopulate Busserah, its situation in a few ages would nowhere be traced; as its ruins would soon be levelled by the rain, and covered with sand from the desart, which possibly was the fate of those ancient cities before mentioned.

Busserah I take to be the Buxrath mentioned in Isaiah xxxiv. verse 6, Jeremiah xlviii. verse 24, Isaiah lxiii. verse 1, Genesis xxxvi. verse 33, Jeremiah xlix. verse 22, Amos i. 12. I do not mean the present city, which is of later date, or the old one whose ruins are to be seen on an island S.E. thirty miles hence, from whence the people removed for fear of the Portuguese, who were then formidable; but the province of Busserah and cities already mentioned, which I apprehend stood hereabouts, whose total demolition accomplished the prediction of the Prophets.

TITLES OF WORKS AND MAPS

AFONSO, Mestre. Viagem por terra da India a Portugal em 1565. (Reprint of original documents published in Annaes Maritimos e Coloniaes. Lisbon, 1840–6. 6 vols. *See* 4th Series, No. 5, pp. 214, 255, 315, 344 and 408.)

AINSWORTH, W. F. A Personal Narrative of the Euphrates Expedition. London, 1888. 2 vols.

ANDREW, Sir W. P. Memoir on the Euphrates Valley Route to India. London, 1857.

ARVIEUX, Laurence. The Chevalier d'Arvieux's travels in Arabia the Desart.... 2nd ed. London, 1723.

—— Mémoires d'Arvieux. Paris, 1735. 6 vols.

BALBI, Gasparo. Viaggio dell' Indie Orientali. Venice, 1590. Also Purchas (MacLehose ed.), vol. x, pp. 143 et seq.

BARKER, E. B. B. Syria and Egypt under the Last Five Sultans of Turkey. London, 1876. 2 vols.

BARROS, João de, and DE COUTO, Diogo. Decadas da Asia. Nova ed. Lisbon, 1778–88. 24 vols.

BELL, Gertrude Lowthian. Amurath to Amurath. London, 1911. Map.

BELL, Richard, The travels of — (and John Campbell) in the East Indies, Persia, and Palestine, 1654–1670, by Sir Richard C. Temple. [This is a copy of the original MS. in the British Museum and appeared in the Indian Antiquary, vols. 35–37, 1906–8, *passim*.]

BENGAL PAST AND PRESENT. Calcutta Historical Society, vol. XVII.

BERJEW, John P. *See* Parsons, A., Travels in Asia and Africa.

BERNARD, Dr Edw. Phil. Trans. Roy. Soc. vol. XIX, pp. 83–110, original ed. Edinburgh, 1695. Abridged ed. 1694–1702. *See also* under Phil. Trans. Roy. Soc.

BERNARDINO, Fr. Gaspar de São. Itinerario da India. 1611. Reprint, Lisbon, 1854. *See also* Hakl. Soc. Publ., ser. ii, No. IX, pp. xxi, 84, 104; and Hugh Murray, Hist. account...Asia, vol. I, chapter VIII.

BIRDWOOD, Sir George. Report on the Old Records of the India Office. London, 1891. 2nd reprint.

BIRDWOOD, Sir G., and FOSTER, W. The Register of Letters, etc., of the Governour and Company of Merchants of London trading into the East Indies, 1600–19. London, 1893.

BISCHOFF, Dr Theodor. Reise von Palmyra durch die Wüste nach Aleppo. Globus, 1881, vol. XL, No. 23, pp. 363–6.

BLUNT, Lady Anne. Bedouin Tribes of the Euphrates. London, 1879. 2 vols. Maps.

BLUNT, Lady Anne. Pilgrimage to Nejd. London, 1881. 2 vols. Map.

BOUCHIER, E. S. Syria as a Roman Province. Oxford, 1916.

BURCKHARDT, John Lewis. Travels in Syria and the Holy Land. London, 1822.

BUTLER, H. C. Publications of an American Archaeological Expedition to Syria. Part II. New York, 1903. *See also* Garrett, Robert.

CAMPBELL, John. *See* Bell, Richard.

CAPPER, James. Observations on the Passage to India, etc. 3rd ed. London, 1785.

CARMICHAEL, John. A Journey from Aleppo over the Desert to Basserah, Oct. 21, 1771 [1751]. Appendix to Vol. I of 2nd ed. of John Henry Grose's Voyage to the East Indies. *See also* Phil. Trans. Roy. Soc. vol. XVII, pp. 38 et seq., abridged ed. 1791–6; Maj. J. Rennell's Geogr. Western Asia, vol. I, pp. 23, 24; Geogr. Journal, vol. LII, 1918, p. 163.

CARRUTHERS, D. The Arabian Ostrich. The Ibis, July, 1922, pp. 471–4.

CARTWRIGHT, John. The Preacher's travels through Syria, Persia, etc. London, 1611. *See also* Purchas (MacLehose ed.), vol. VIII, pp. 482–523; Hunter's Hist. of British India, vol. I, p. 268.

ČERNIKS STUDIEN-EXPEDITION durch die Gebiete des Euphrat und Tigris. (Petermanns Mitt., Ergänz. Nos. 44 and 45. 1875.) Map.

CHEESMAN, Capt. R. E. Recent Notes on the Arabian Ostrich. The Ibis, April, 1923, pp. 208–11.

CHESNEY, Gen. F. R. Expeditions for the Survey of the Rivers Euphrates and Tigris in 1835–37. London, 1850. 4 vols. Maps in separate folio.

—— Narrative of the Euphrates expedition. London, 1868.

CLERMONT-GANNEAU, Charles. Recueil d'Archéologie Orientale. Vol. III. Paris, 1900. (Une Inscription de Calife Hicham.)

COOTE, Gen. Sir Eyre. Diary of a journey from Bussora to Aleppo in 1780 (?). J.R.G.S. vol. XXX (1860), pp. 198–211. [The date was really 1771.]

CORDIER, Henri. *See* Yule, Sir Henry.

COUTO, Diogo de. Continuation of Decadas da Asia. *See* Barros, João de.

DALLAM, Master Thomas. The Diary of —, 1599–1600. Early Voyages in the Levant. Hakl. Soc. Publ., ser. i, No. LXXXVII.

DELLA VALLE, Pietro. Viaggi di Pietro della Valle, etc. (Bologna, 1677.)

—— Fameux Voyages de Pietro della Valle, Gentilhomme Romain, etc. Paris, 1664–70. 4 vols.

—— The Travels of Sig. Pietro della Valle into East India and Arabia Deserta. London, 1665. *See also* Hakl. Soc. Publ., ser. i, Nos. LXXXIV, Map, LXXXV.

DOUGHTY, Charles Montagu. Travels in Arabia Deserta. Cambridge, 1888. 2 vols.

DOWNTON, Capt. Nicholas. *See* Purchas (MacLehose ed.), vol. IV, p. 217.

DRUMMOND, Alexander. Travels through different Cities...and several parts of Asia, as far as the Banks of the Euphrates. London, 1754. Map.

ELDRED, John. *See* Hakluyt (MacLehose ed.), vol. VI, pp. 1–9.

[EVERS, Lieut. Samuel.] A journal kept on a journey from Bassora to Bagdad...in the year 1779 by a Gentleman...etc. Horsham, 1784.

FINCH, Allan George. Historical Manuscripts Commission Report on the Manuscripts of. London, 1913, 1922. 2 vols.

FITCH, Ralph. *See* Hakluyt (MacLehose ed.), vol. V, pp. 450, 465–505; Purchas (MacLehose ed.), vol. X, pp. 165–204; *also* J. H. Ryley, and Foster.

FOSTER, Sir William. Early Travels in India, 1583–1619. Oxford, 1921.

FOWLE, Capt. T. C. Travels in the Middle East. London, 1916. Map.

FREDERICK, Caesar. *See* Hakluyt (MacLehose ed.), vol. V, pp. 365–449; Purchas (MacLehose ed.), vol. X, pp. 88–143.

GARRETT, Robert. Publications of an American Archaeological Expedition to Syria, 1899–1900. Part I. Topography and Itinerary. New York, 1904. Part II. Architecture and other Arts. By H. C. Butler. New York, 1903.

GODINHO, Manuel. Relaçao do novo caminho...vindo da India para Portugal. Lisbon, 1665. 2nd ed. Lisbon, 1842. *See also* Murray's Asia, vol. I, chap. VIII; Birdwood, Report on the Old Records of the India Office, p. 182.

GOEJE, M. J. de. Bibliotheca Geographorum Arabicorum. Leyden, 1885–1892. Vol. VI has Translation, in French, of Ibn Khurdadbeh.

GOLLANCZ, Sir Hermann. Chronicle of Events between the years 1623 and 1733 relating to the Settlement of the Order of Carmelites in Mesopotamia (Bussora).

GOODYEAR, Aaron. *See* Phil. Trans. Roy. Soc. vol. XIX, pp. 129 et seq. Original ed. Edinburgh, 1695. *See also* Halifax, Dr Wm.

GREEN, John. A Journey from Aleppo to Damascus. London, 1736. Map.

GRIFFITHS, J. Travels in Europe, Asia Minor, and Arabia. London, 1805.

GROSE, John Henry. Voyage to the East Indies, etc. 2nd ed. London, 1772. 2 vols. Vol. I has Appendix: A Journey from Aleppo, over the Desert, to Basserah, by Mr Carmichael.

HAKLUYT, Richard. The Principal Navigations, Voyages, etc. London, 1809. 5 vols. *Also* MacLehose ed. Glasgow, 1903–7. 20 vols.

HALIFAX, Dr William. A Relation of a voyage from Aleppo to Palmyra in Syria. Also An Extract of the Journals of two several voyages of the English Merchants of the Factory of Aleppo to Tadmor, anciently call'd Palmyra. (Both papers appear in Miscellanea Curiosa, London, 1708, vol. III, pp. 84–159.)

—— Relation of a Voyage to Tadmor in 1691. This is an exact reprint of the original MS. published in the Palestine Exploration Fund. Quart. Statement, 1890, p. 273. *See also* Phil. Trans. Roy. Soc. vol. XIX, pp. 83–110, 129–60, original ed. Edinburgh, 1695.

HAMILTON, Capt. Alexander. A New Account of the East Indies. Edinburgh, 1727. 2 vols.

HELFER, J. W. Travels of Dr and Madame Helfer. London, 1878. 2 vols. Map.

HENEAGE, Charles. Journey in the Caucasus, Persia, etc. *See* Thielmann, Max von.

HOLFORD, —. *See* Phil. Trans. Roy. Soc. abridged ed. 1791–96, vol. XVII, p. 40.

HOWEL, Thomas. Voyage en retour de l'Inde par une route en partie inconnue jusqu'ici, etc. Paris, 1797.

HUBER, Charles. Journal d'un Voyage en Arabie (1883–4). Paris, 1891. Maps.

—— Voyage dans l'Arabie Centrale. In Bull. Soc. de Géog. VIIme série, vol. VI, pp. 92–148. Map.

HUNTER, Sir W. W. A History of British India. London, 1899. 2 vols.

IBN JUBAYR. *See* Schiaparelli, C.

IBN KHURDADBEH. *See* Goeje, M. J. de.

IRWIN, Eyles. A Series of Adventures in the course of A Voyage up the Red Sea, etc. With a Supplement of A Voyage from Venice to Latichea, and of a Route Through the Desarts of Arabia, by Aleppo, Bagdad, and the Tygris to Busrah in 1780 and 1781. In letters to a Lady. London, 1787. 2 vols. Map.

IVES, Dr E. A Voyage from England to India, in the year 1754, also a Journey from Persia to England by an unusual Route, in 1758 and 1759. London, 1773. Map.

JAMES, William. The Naval History of Great Britain. London, 1824. 5 vols.

LANOY, Benjamin. *See* Finch MSS., pp. 95 et seq. (First mention of, Feb. 1660, last letter dated Aug. 1668.)

LANOY, Timothy. Phil. Trans. Roy. Soc. vol. XIX, pp. 129 et seq. original ed. Edinburgh, 1695. *See also under* Halifax.

LE STRANGE, Guy. Palestine under the Moslems. London, 1890.

—— Lands of the Eastern Caliphate. Cambridge, 1905.

LINSCHOTEN, John Huyghen van. Voyage of — to the East Indies. Hakl. Soc. Publ., ser. i, Nos. LXX, LXXI. *Also* Purchas (MacLehose ed.), vol. X.

LONGRIGG, S. H. Four Centuries of Modern Iraq. Oxford, 1925.

LOVE, Col. H. D. Vestiges of Old Madras. Indian Records Series. London, 1913. 4 vols.

MANESTY, —. Bombay Factory Records at the India Office. Persia and Persian Gulf. No. 20. 1799–1811.

MANWARING, G. E. *See* Teonge, Henry.

MARCO POLO. *See* Yule, Sir Henry.

MASSIGNON, Louis. Mission à Mésopotamie (1907–8). 1910–12. 2 tom.

—— Mémoires de l'Institut français d'Archéologie orientale du Caire, vol. XXVIII, Cairo, 1910. Map.

MAUNDRELL, Henry. A Journey from Aleppo to Jerusalem, 1697. Oxford, 1703. 4th ed. 1749.

MILDENHALL, John. *See* Purchas (MacLehose ed.), vol. VIII, p. 482, and Foster.

MILES, Col. S. B. Countries and Tribes of the Persian Gulf. London, 1919. 2 vols.

MISCELLANEA CURIOSA. Vol. III. Containing a Collection of Curious Travels, Voyages, etc. London, 1708.

MORITZ, Dr. Reise in Syrien. In Verhandl. Gesell. für Erdkunde, Berlin, Bd. XIII, 1886, p. 163.

MUIR, Sir William. The Caliphate, its Rise, Decline and Fall. Revised ed. by T. H. Weir. Edinburgh, 1924.

MURRAY, Hugh. Historical Account of Discoveries and Travels in Asia. Edinburgh, 1820. *See* vol. I, chap. VIII, for accounts of Tenreiro, Bernardino, Godinho, etc.

MUSIL, Alois. American Geographical Society Publication. Oriental Exploration and Studies, No. 2, Arabia Deserta. New York, 1927. No. 4. Palmyrena. New York, 1928. Maps in separate case, entitled Northern Arabia.

NEWBERRY, John. *See* Hakluyt's Voyages (MacLehose ed.), vol. V; Purchas (MacLehose ed.), vol. VIII.

NIEBUHR, Carsten. Voyage en Arabie et en d'autres pays circonvoisins, traduit de l'allemand. Amsterdam, 1774–80. 3 vols. Maps.

—— Reisebeschreibung nach Arabien und andern umliegenden Ländern. Copenhagen, 1778.

OLIVIER, G. A. Voyage dans l'Empire Ottoman, l'Égypte et la Perse. Paris, 1801. 3 vols. and Atlas.

ORMSBY, Lieut. *See* Bombay Factory Records at the India Office, Persia, No. 46, 1831; *also* Trans. Bombay Geographical Soc. vol. II, part III, 1838–40, p. 18.

OSTRUP, J. Historisk-topografiske Bidrag til Kendskabet til den Syriske Ørken. København, 1895. Map.

PARSONS, Abraham. Travels in Asia and Africa, etc. Edited by John Paine Berjew. London, 1808.

PEARSON, J. B. A Biographical Sketch of the Chaplains of the Levant (Aleppo) Co. Cambridge, 1883.

PHILOSOPHICAL TRANSACTIONS OF THE ROYAL SOCIETY. Original ed. Edinburgh, 1695–7. Vol. XIX, pp. 83–110, 129–60: Relation of a Voyage from Aleppo to Palmyra in Syria; sent by the Rev. Wm Halifax to Dr Edw. Bernard (late) and by him communicated to Dr Thomas Smith.

Abridged ed. vol. IV, pp. 49–59: An Extract from the Journals of two several Journies of the English Merchants of the Factory of Aleppo, to Tadmor, or Palmyra.

Abridged ed. vol. XVII, pp. 38–43: On the rate of travelling, as performed by Camels; and its application, as a scale, to the purposes of geography, by James Rennell. Original ed. vol. LXXXI. Map, Tab. III, p. 144.

PINTO, Fernão Mendez. Peregrinaçiones. Lisbon, 1725. Reprint, Lisbon, 1829. 4 vols.

PLAISTED, Bartholomew. A Journey from Calcutta in Bengal, by Sea, to Busserah: From thence across the Great Desart to Aleppo: etc. London, 1st ed. 1757, 2nd ed. 1758. *See also under* Ritchie.

PRATER, S. H. The Arabian Ostrich. Journal of the Bombay Natural History Society, March, 1921, pp. 602–605.

PURCHAS, Samuel, His Pilgrimes. MacLehose ed. Glasgow, 1905–7. 20 vols.

RAUWOLFF, Dr Leonhart. Journey into the Eastern Countries. *See* John Ray, Travels, London, 1693, vol. II, pp. 61 and 88.

RAY, John. Travels. London, 1693. 2 vols.

RENNELL, Major James. A Treatise on the Comparative Geography of Western Asia. London, 1831. Atlas.

—— Rate of travelling by Camels. Phil. Trans. Roy. Soc. vol. XVII, pp. 38–43, abridged ed. 1791–6. Map.

RITCHIE, Capt. John. Bartholomew PLAISTED, and Benjamin LACAM. Directions for Sailing in the Northern Part of the Bay of Bengal. London, 1785.

ROUSSEAU, Louis Jacques. Voyage de Bagdad à Alep. Edited by Louis Poinssot. Paris, 1899.

RUSSELL, Alexander. The Natural History of Aleppo and Parts Adjacent. London, 1756. 2nd ed. Revised and enlarged by Patrick Russell. London, 1794. 2 vols.

RYLEY, J. Horton. Ralph Fitch, England's Pioneer to India and Burma. London, 1899.

SACHAU, Dr Eduard. Reise in Syrien und Mesopotamien. Leipzig, 1883. Maps.

SCHIAPARELLI, C. Ibn Gubayr. Rome, 1906. (Translated from the original Arabic.)

SHIRLEY, Sir Anthony. The Three Brothers. Travels of Sir Anthony, Sir Robert, and Sir Th. Shirley. Anon. London, 1825.

STEELE, Richard. Purchas (MacLehose ed.), vol. IV, p. 279; Wilson's Persian Gulf, p. 136 footnote; Birdwood and Foster's The Register of Letters, etc., 1893, pp. 457, 460; Sykes' Hist. of Persia, vol. II, p. 274.

SYKES, Lieut.-Col. Sir P. M. A History of Persia. London, 1915. 2 vols. Second ed. 1922.

TAVERNIER, Jean-Baptiste. Les six voyages de Jean-Baptiste Tavernier. Paris, 1682. Ditto, made English by J. P. London. 1678.

TAYLOR, Major John. Travels from England to India in 1789, etc. London, 1799. 2 vols. Map.

—— Considerations on the Practicability and Advantages of a more speedy communication between Great Britain and her Eastern Dependencies. 1795. 2 vols. Map.

TAYLOR, J. E. Notes on Abu Shahrein and Tel el Lahm. Journal of the Royal Asiatic Society, vol. XV, 1855, p. 404.

TEIXEIRA, Pedro. Hakluyt Soc. Publ., ser. ii, No. IX. *See also* B. Tellez, Travels of the Jesuits in Ethiopia, etc. 1710.

TELLEZ, B. The Travels of the Jesuits in Ethiopia, etc. London. 1710. Maps.

TENREIRO, Antonio. Itinerario. Lisbon, 1560. 2nd ed. 1565.

TEONGE, Henry. The Diary of —. 1675–79. Ed. by G. E. Manwaring in the Broadway Travellers Series. London, 1928.

THÉVENOT, Jean de. Relation d'un Voyage fait au Levant 1665. The Travels of Monsieur de Thévenot into the Levant. London, 1687.

THIELMANN, Baron Max von. Journey in the Caucasus, Persia, and Turkey in Asia. Translated by Charles Heneage. London, 1875. 2 vols. Map.

VALLE. *See* Della Valle, Pietro.

WEIR, T. H. The Caliphate, etc. *See* Muir, Sir William.

WHITEWAY, R. S. The Rise of Portuguese Power in India, 1497–1550. London, 1899.

WILSON, Lt.-Col. Sir A. T. The Persian Gulf. Oxford, 1928.

WILSON, C. R. Old Fort William in Bengal. Indian Records Series. London, 1906. 2 vols.

YULE, Sir Henry. The Book of Ser Marco Polo. 3rd ed. Revised by Henri Cordier. London, 1903. 2 vols.

MAPS *consulted in addition to those noted in the foregoing list of works under the names:* Bell, Blunt, Černik, Chesney, Della Valle, Drummond, Fowle, Green, Helfer, Huber, Irwin, Ives, Massignon, Musil, Niebuhr, Olivier, Ostrup, Phil. Trans. Roy. Soc., Rennell, Sachau, Taylor, Tellez, Thielmann.

ARROWSMITH, A. Outlines of the Countries between Delhi and Constantinople. 1814. Additions to 1816. (Shows the Desert Route.)

BUTLER, H. C. Map of Syria in the IV, V, and VI Centuries. *See* Geographical Review, vol. IX, No. 2, 1920, Pl. 1, published by the American Geographical Society of New York.

CARTE INTERNATIONALE DU MONDE AU 1,000,000. Sheets—ERZERUM, ESH SHAM, BAGHDAD, BASRA.

D'ANVILLE. L'Euphrate et Le Tigre. Paris, 1779.

GARRETT, Robert. Northern Syria. III. New York, 1903.

—— Corrected version of Kiepert's Syria to accompany The Desert and The Sown by G. L. Bell, London, 1907.

HOLT, Major A. L. Syrian and Arabian Deserts, Survey of, 1920–22. Ordnance Survey, 1925.

KIEPERT. Syrien und Mesopotamien. 1893.

—— Zeitsch. Gesell. für Erdkunde zu Berlin, 1881, Taf. 1; also 1883, Taf. 1.

OPPENHEIM, Dr Max F. von. Von Mittelmeer zum Persischen Golf, durch den Hauran, die Syrische Wüste und Mesopotamien. Berlin, 1899–1900. 2 vols. Maps.

—— Bericht über seine Reise durch die Syrische Wüste nach Mosul. In Verhandl. Gesell. für Erdkunde, Berlin, 1894, No. 4. Map.

POCOCK, Richard. Map of the Holy Land and Syria. In Descriptions of the East, etc. London, 1743–45, 2 vols.

WALKER, John. Sketch Map of Routes, Constantinople–India. 1867.

INDEX